Just Growth

NO LONGER
SEATTLE PUᴅᴸᴵᴄ ᴸᴵᴮᴿᴀ...

In recent years, analysts have pointed to rising inequality in the U.S. as an under-lying factor in both our social fragmentation and economic underperformance. This book argues for the possibility of "just growth" – a framework in which the imperatives of equity have been coupled with strategies to shore up the economy – and suggests that much can be learned from efforts to couple prosperity and inclusion at a metropolitan or regional level in the United States.

The authors use a nested approach that combines quantitative analysis of the largest 192 metropolitan regions in the U.S. with a set of seven in-depth case stud-ies to help uncover the subtle and detailed processes, policies, and institutional arrangements that might help explain more equitable growth (or its absence) in metropolitan settings. In both their regressions and their narrative, the authors point to the stabilizing effect of the public sector, the impact of deconcentrating poverty, the growth-enhancing but equity-reducing impacts of having a large immigrant population, the influential role of a minority middle class, and the importance of leadership efforts to develop a shared understanding of regional problems and futures amongst diverse constituencies.

Breaking new ground in its innovative blend of quantitative and qualita-tive methods, the book essentially argues that another sort of growth is indeed possible. While offering specific insights for regional leaders and analysts of metropolitan areas, the authors also draw a broader – and quite timely – set of conclusions about how to scale up these efforts to address a U.S. economy still seeking to recover from economic crisis and ameliorate distributional divisions.

Chris Benner is Associate Professor in Human and Community Development at the University of California Davis, USA.

Manuel Pastor is Professor of Geography and American Studies and Ethnicity at the University of Southern California and Director of the USC Program for Environmental and Regional Equity, as well as co-Director of the Center for the Study of Immigrant Integration.

Regional Studies Association

THE INTERNATIONAL FORUM
FOR REGIONAL DEVELOPMENT
POLICY AND RESEARCH

*The Association welcomes as
members all individuals and
organisations who are interested
in the study and understanding
of regions and regionalism*

Regions and Cities

Series editors:
Ron Martin *University of Cambridge, UK;*
Gernot Grabher *University of Bonn, Germany;*
Maryann Feldman *University of Georgia, USA;*
Gillian Bristow *University of Cardiff, UK.*

Regions and Cities is an international, interdisciplinary series that provides authoritative analyses of the new significance of regions and cities for economic, social and cultural development, and public policy experimentation. The series seeks to combine theoretical and empirical insights with constructive policy debate and critically engages with formative processes and policies in regional and urban studies.

Just Growth

Inclusion and prosperity in
America's metropolitan regions

**Chris Benner and
Manuel Pastor**

Routledge
Taylor & Francis Group

LONDON AND NEW YORK

First published 2012
by Routledge
2 Park Square, Milton Park, Abingdon, Oxon OX14 4RN

Simultaneously published in the USA and Canada
by Routledge
711 Third Avenue, New York, NY 10017

Routledge is an imprint of the Taylor & Francis Group, an informa business

© 2012 Chris Benner and Manuel Pastor

The right of Chris Benner and Manuel Pastor to be identified as authors of this work has been asserted by them in accordance with the Copyright, Designs and Patent Act 1988.

All rights reserved. No part of this book may be reprinted or reproduced or utilised in any form or by any electronic, mechanical, or other means, now known or hereafter invented, including photocopying and recording, or in any information storage or retrieval system, without permission in writing from the publishers.

Trademark notice: Product or corporate names may be trademarks or registered trademarks, and are used only for identification and explanation without intent to infringe.

British Library Cataloguing in Publication Data
A catalogue record for this book is available from the British Library

Library of Congress Cataloging in Publication Data
Benner, Chris.
Just growth: inclusion and prosperity in America's metropolitan regions / by Chris Benner and Manuel Pastor.
p. cm.
Includes bibliographical references and index.
1. Income distribution—United States. 2. Equality—United States. 3. Cities and towns—United States—Growth. 4. Metropolitan areas—United States. I. Pastor, Manuel II. Title.
HC110.I5B46 2011
339.20973'091732–dc23
2011021917

ISBN: 978–0–415–68194–0 (hbk)
ISBN: 978–0–415–51781–2 (pbk)
ISBN: 978–0–203–15558–5 (ebk)

Typeset in Times New Roman by Prepress Projects Ltd, Perth, UK

Contents

Figures

Tables

Acknowledgments

For more than a decade, we have been blessed to be working with a series of social movement organizations seeking to craft a new approach to economic development. Frustrated with economic models that cast fairness as either a secondary concern or one that actually hurts the economy, we and they have sought to see what econometric evidence, case studies, and policy experiments might suggest about the possibilities for a new sort of "just growth."

For inspiring us in that long journey, we thank a whole series of key thinkers and doers, including Carl Anthony, Angela Glover Blackwell, Amy Dean, John Powell, David Rusk, and many others. For forcing us to think more critically about our own approach, we thank Peter Dreier, Ned Hill, Todd Swanstrom, Margaret Weir, Hal Wolman, and so many other friends in and out of the academy. And for funding our intellectual explorations in this field – and particularly the research we report on here – we thank Rick McGahey and Don Chen of the Ford Foundation; we acknowledge also the support of the Building Resilient Regions network by the John D. and Catherine T. MacArthur Foundation for the construction of the dataset used in this project.

Although two names are attached to this volume, this was like many other research projects – it took a village. Our particular village included both quantitative and qualitative residents. On the numbers side, we had Justin Scoggins and Jennifer Tran of the University of Southern California (USC), and Mateusz Filipski of the University of California-Davis, with Justin doing the heavy lifting of designing the underlying database and conducting regressions and Jennifer and Mateusz designing an innovative case selection process and just growth indices (as well as some pretty cool maps and charts). Hitting the field with us (and sometimes without us) were Rhonda Ortiz from USC and Rosa Ramirez from UC Davis; Jennifer Tran lifted her attention from the numbers long enough to conduct interviews in Denver and Nate Sessoms from USC helped out in both Cleveland (where he grew up) and Columbus. Bringing up the rear with able editing support on the final draft was Vanessa Carter of USC, while Mirabai Auer developed our final metro maps. And making sure we were moderately organized along the way – particularly as we criss-crossed the country in search of inclusive prosperity – was Jacqueline Agnello, office manager for USC's Program for Environmental and Regional Equity.

Our village was actually bigger in another way: we were blessed by the willingness of so many people in the regions we visited to share their perspectives and experiences. We thank the interviewees for responding to our queries, providing us with their insights, and gently noting when we seemed to be heading in the wrong direction. We hope that some of their collective wisdom is captured in our conclusions and recommendations.

We are finishing this manuscript as the U.S. economy is slowly emerging from the worst recession since the Great Depression. It is worth remembering that one of the factors that drove us into that ditch was rising inequality, a situation in which those becoming richer and richer found themselves increasingly drawn to speculation, while those whose incomes were stagnating were borrowing just to stay solvent. If unjust growth played a role in this crisis, it is critically important that the principles of just growth be part of our guide to the future. What is at stake right now is not just the design of metropolitan policies but more broadly what kind of economy we want and what kind of America we will be.

Chris Benner and Manuel Pastor,
Davis and Los Angeles, California

1 Inequality and its discontents

Introduction

The financial crisis of 2008–2009 and the lingering Great Recession that resulted have raised some profound questions about the nature of our economic system. Some have suggested that the meltdown was an inevitable consequence of deregulation and have called for firmer control over the creation and implementation of new financial instruments (Crotty 2009). Others have pinned the blame on an unsustainable run-up in housing prices and argued that the Federal Reserve should slow future bubbles in asset prices (Demyanyk and Van Hemert 2009; Fligstein and Goldstein 2009). Still others have pointed to excess consumer demand, particularly in the United States, and argued that we need to lift our savings rate to a higher and healthier level (Dynan 2009).

We concur on the need for regulation, protection against asset run-ups, and even a more future-oriented approach to savings and investment. However, we would suggest that another element at play in the crisis also deserves attention: income inequality. After all, what emerged in the years before the crisis was a nearly unprecedented – well, except before that other Great Depression – rise in the gap between the rich and the poor (Atkinson et al. 2011). With some so wealthy that they shifted to increasingly speculative investments to place their excess funds and others so strapped that they borrowed to prop up their falling household incomes, the financial trap was set. It could have been better regulated, to be sure, but the fundamental problem was not the market but the distribution that the market confronted.[1]

If inequality was among the factors that got us into the crisis, dealing with inequality may be one of the steps to getting out of it. Yet this is not a simple matter of legislating fairness in taxes, social policy, or government spending; renewed economic growth is critical because the poor rarely do well in an economy that is stagnating. At the same time, recovery alone is not sufficient; the recent decades have been full of examples of national and metropolitan economies in which rapid expansion in employment and/or income has been accompanied by sharper social differentiation.

We need, in short, more than just growth (or growth alone); we need instead "just growth," a framework in which the imperatives of equity have been coupled with strategies to shore up the macro-economy, spur new industrial development, and re-regulate the financial system. Such a new framework will require a stretch on the part of business leaders, many of whom have long been concerned about economic expansion but not worried much about equity – and it will also require a commitment and an analytical stretch by those who have long fought for "economic justice" but have not always thought about how best to promote the economic part of that couplet.

This book seeks to help point the way to a new model by looking at the ways in which prosperity and inclusion have been occasionally coupled at a metropolitan or regional level. To some, the metro focus may seem odd, particularly given that we have been more recently confronting a national and international crisis. But long before the national meltdown helped to make this point, the notion that inequality might actually damage economic growth was gaining ground with key metropolitan actors – including collaboratives of business, labor, civic and community leaders – who were increasingly clear that a more inclusive economic approach could actually strengthen the social consensus and human capital needed to compete in a global economy. Backing up that perspective was a range of empirical studies, including from the Federal Reserve, showing that strategies that reduce social, geographic, and other disparities are actually correlated with broad economic success.

Is there really a possibility of "just growth"? What are the circumstances under which the imperatives of fairness and the need for economic drivers really do come together at the metropolitan level? What are the social and political arrangements, particularly given the lack of specifically *regional* government institutions, that allow this to happen in some regions? And what are the potential lessons for a U.S. economy seeking to stop the economic bleeding and the distributional divisions?

Prosperity, inclusion and the new economics

Linking regional prosperity and regional equity has great appeal – after all, who would not like it if all good things came together? But the interesting thing is that this is not simply a question of wishing for the best: statistical research is suggesting that doing good and doing well can go hand in hand.[2]

We acknowledge that this is a somewhat controversial conclusion – after all, one of the first things taught in undergraduate economics is that there is a trade-off between equity and efficiency, between fairness and robust economic growth. Kaldor (1977), for example, argued that a high level of savings among the rich, in order to invest in industries with large sunk costs, was a prerequisite for rapid growth, and so the imperative of growth implied that income must be concentrated amongst the wealthy. More benignly but no less forcefully, Kuznets (1955) argued that, as labor shifts from sectors with low productivity to those with high productivity, inequality must increase initially with the new growth, and will decrease only later as the economy matures. The Kuznets curve, which justified initial inequality as part of the growth process, quickly "acquired the force of economic law" (Robinson 1976: 437).

However, a rush of new research in the 1990s and early 2000s challenged conventional views on the relationship between inequality and growth at the national level, particularly for developing countries. Alesina and Perotti (1996), for example, argued that inequality leads to social tension and political instability, higher uncertainty and lower investment, and thus lower economic growth. Dani Rodrik (1999) noted that the ability of countries to handle external shocks in large part depends on the strength of conflict-management institutions, such as the quality of governmental institutions, rule of law, and social safety nets. Both Alesina and Rodrik (1994) and Persson and Tabellini (1994) suggested that, the more inequitable a society's access to productive resources, the more likely that society will seek redistributive policies that can reduce growth by introducing economic distortions, partly because the median voter may see less interest in protecting property rights.

Birdsall et al. (1995) and Deninger and Squire (1996) build on these insights to argue that policies that target poverty and increase the productive nature of the poor, such as investments in education, can increase growth. In one of the most recent (and most convincing efforts), Lopez and Serven (2009) argue that poverty deters investment, which in turn lowers growth – and show that this relationship holds across broad samples of countries (depending on data availability) that range from the developing to the developed world, that it holds across numerous time periods, and that it holds across a wide range of econometric specifications, including attempts to control for the impacts of inequality on growth. They conclude that "the biggest growth pay-off is likely to result from policies that not only promote growth, but also exert an independent, direct impact on poverty – hence reducing the drag of poverty on growth" (Lopez and Serven 2009: 21). More recently, Berg and Ostry (2011) provide econometric evidence linking equality to longer spells of growth and hence a more sustainable development path.

Drilling down to the region

Little of this emerging view of a positive relationship between equity and long-term growth has made its way to the American political and policy context. The argument for redistribution remains largely confined to issues of fairness or perhaps a Keynesian-style notion that placing money in the hands of less well-off consumers will yield a bigger economic bang for any stimulus dollar (Reich 2010; Stiglitz 2010). But this is surely not the same thing as the argument now being made in the developing country context that the old narrative that economic inclusion hurts economic output is fundamentally wrong – and that we need to adjust strategies for long-term growth accordingly.

One strand of work that sought to investigate whether positive equity–growth relationships held in the U.S. context looked at growth and equity at the state level (Partridge 1997). In that research, more initial income equality, as measured by a Gini coefficient, was negatively correlated with growth; on the other hand, a larger share of income held by the middle quintile (another sort of measure of distribution and one perhaps more consistent with the median voter notion

of Persson and Tabellini 1994) was positively correlated with economic performance. This mixed finding may be an anomaly: using slightly different data,
a longer time period, and more sophisticated econometric techniques, Panizza
finds that there is *not* a positive relationship between inequality and growth at
a state level and does find some evidence, as in the developing country literature, of the expected negative relationship (depending on specification) between
inequality and growth (Panizza 2002).

Economists and others are accustomed to looking at economic performance
for states, a geographic level where there are actual jurisdictions and policy tools.
But we think that the reason why the connection between growth and equity at
a state level is not as robust as it might be is partly because it is the wrong unit
of analysis – there is a gap between political jurisdiction and economic activity.
Recent research suggests that metropolitan regions are an increasingly important
economic unit in a globalized world, partly because this is the level where the
intangibles of industrial clusters and innovation occur (Storper 1997; Scott 1998;
Maskell and Malmberg 1999; Morgan 2007).[3] Our own econometric work suggests increasing heterogeneity in the long-term performance of America's metro
areas, including growing differences in the ways in which poverty and growth
interact at the regional level (Pastor et al. 2009a). And it is at the metropolitan
level where the argument for coupling equity and growth has gained substantial
analytic and policy ground in the U.S.

The emergence of the region is striking because, unlike states, there are generally no government structures that can seemingly make a policy difference. In
terms of making the connection between growth and equity at the metro level,
some of the initial impetus may have been political; after all, one of the first
studies came from National League of Cities researchers Larry Ledebur and Bill
Barnes and showed, in a sample of seventy-eight metropolitan areas in the United
States, that those regions with the widest gap between central city and suburban
income in 1980 had the most sluggish job growth during the following decade
(Ledebur and Barnes 1993). While this was a finding conveniently amenable to
those promoting more attention to cities, it was not just policy proponents beginning to make a new set of linkages; a study by Savitch and colleagues in the same
era examined fifty-nine different metropolitan areas and found that those with
wider city–suburb disparities – one measure of the lack of social cohesion across
metropolitan geography – were associated with a higher likelihood of regional
stagnation (Savitch, Collins et al. 1993).[4]

Of course, early research can sometimes be too enthusiastic and Paul Gottlieb
(2000) rightly argued in a review of the early work that the results were too
optimistic: testing for the correlation of two variables is not the same as a multivariate analysis that considers other factors, and growth itself can impact equity,
raising questions of simultaneity. Both Voith (1998) and Pastor et al. (2000) did
address these issues, incorporating other explanatory factors *and* considering
the feedback effects. The findings remained supportive: even in a simultaneous
setting, Voith found a positive association of suburban growth with city growth
while Pastor et al. found that various measures of inequality (i.e. the city–suburb

poverty ratio, the geographic concentration of the poor, the change in central city poverty, and more direct measures of income disparity) had a negative impact on per capita income growth over the 1980s in seventy-four regions.

Do these basic results hold in the more recent past? Utilizing data from the 1990 and 2000 census on 341 metropolitan statistical regions in the United States, Pastor (2006) found that real per capita income growth was negatively affected, controlling for other variables that should promote growth, by such distributional measures as the ratio of city to suburban poverty, the percent of poor residents in high poverty neighborhoods, the ratio of income at the sixtieth percentile to household income at the twentieth percentile, and the index of dissimilarity between Blacks and whites at the metro level. In more recent work, Pastor and Benner (2008) found that such a dragging effect of inequality on growth held even in what might be termed "weak market" metros – places where some would say that anemic growth is an excuse for making attention to equity a sort of luxury concern.

And it is not just us. Federal Reserve economists conducted a similar analysis for nearly 120 metropolitan areas throughout the United States as part of a report for the Fund for Our Economic Future based in Northeast Ohio (Eberts et al. 2006). Using factor analysis, the researchers identified eight key clusters of variables that influence economic growth at the regional level: a region's skilled workforce, active small businesses, ethnic diversity and minority business ownership, level of racial inclusion, costs associated with a declining industrial base, income inequality (measured by income disparity and number of children living in poverty), quality of life variables (including universities, recreation, and transportation), and concentrated poverty in core cities. The results: a skilled workforce, high levels of racial inclusion and progress on income equality correlate strongly and positively with economic growth.

Understanding the connection

Why is there a positive correlation between equity and growth, particularly given the long-standing views that these two goals stand in conflict?

First, it is quite possible that this is a relationship that may have changed over time. In an earlier Fordist era of simple mass production, reducing wages and costs – as long as one could also find a way to make up for the aggregate demand gaps triggered by wage drops and under-consumption – may have been both profitable and growth-inducing. This was, in fact, when the economic world was truly flat à la Thomas Friedman (2007) – lowering costs could attract investment across an otherwise identical economic landscape. The challenge is that such a "low road" strategy may make less sense in a world of regionally rooted clustered industries – in this world of "spiked" industrial activity, skills matter, the quality of life is key to retaining talent, and the social tensions that are either exacerbated or ameliorated by economic inclusion are an important part of such quality of life (Persky and Wiewel 1994; Storper 1997; Christopherson et al. 2008). In other words, the new regionalization prompted by globalization may be what is calling for a new attention to equity and inclusion as part of the prosperity agenda.[5]

Second, it could also be that too much inequality violates a sense of social norms and social cohesion – and that this might be more sharply felt on a geographic level where relationships are often face to face. Again, this may seem against the usual grain of economics in which my welfare is not affected by yours – and so inequality is both benign and none of my business unless I choose to work it into my utility function. But this is a pretty thin version of human nature and new work by Akerlof and Kranton (2010) suggests that individuals also seek to construct identities and adhere to norms consistent with those identities. Akerlof and Kranton specifically suggest that organizations in which identity counts can utilize a flatter wage structure because some of the motivation is internal rather than extrinsic; we suggest below that metropolitan regions with leadership efforts that create a sense of a shared regional destiny may be creating new norms and new identities that facilitate the search for strategies that can generate more prosperity and more inclusion.

But as often happens in the real world, the reasons for the relationship remain a bit murky in both theory and practice. In our view, the impact of equity on growth may have something to do with the ways in which less equal areas underinvest in basic education, the impact of social tensions on economic decision making, the erosion of the "social capital" that can tie a region together, and perhaps the effects on health problems and hence worker efficiency (Bernasek 2006).[6] We argue specifically in our most recent effort on this topic that inequality tends to:

> erode social capital that ties regions together, leading to underinvestment in basic capital (think families fleeing the public school system and then rebelling against taxes to support public education), significant conflict over the direction of economic development (think battles over subsidies and the location of new investments), and a general desire to jump the regional ship in favor of less problematic circumstances (think younger workers flocking to more diverse settings).
>
> (Pastor and Benner 2008: 93)

But the reality is that the studies we cite (and have conducted) have suggested the pattern but have not firmly established causality.

There is, of course, a similar problem in the comparative national literature. Researchers in that arena have made some progress offering econometric evidence of causality (particularly regarding the feedback of poverty on investment and the role of income distribution in creating a sense of fairness that leads to a higher level of property rights protection – and, in turn, innovation and investment). Still, for the most part, the comparative work has tried to fill in the "black box" of explanation through political economy comparisons of various countries – looking at the land reform policies of Asia versus Latin America, comparing the adjustment strategies of Turkey and Korea, and so on.

In our view, a similar political economy approach could be useful in the domestic context; to explain *why* we see growth and equity coming together, we may need more statistical work but we definitely also need the sort of qualitative case study approach that can uncover the political and economic dynamics that produce the circumstances for generating shared prosperity. Such an explanatory exercise should be accompanied by few prior convictions, particularly those associated with our own ideological beliefs – we should seek to determine what the cases tell us and not what we would like them to tell us. And it should have an eye on what factors are structural – not quite the luck of the draw but at least predetermined – and which are amenable to human agency – that is, the capacity to make our own luck.

Achieving growth with equity

This book represents an attempt to get at these issues with a combination of quantitative and qualitative analysis. Utilizing a sample of the largest 192 metropolitan regions in the country, we first use a quantitative approach to identify those regions with above median performance in terms of both economic growth and social equity indicators, and conduct regression-style analysis to explore the demographic, political, and economic determinants behind these growth and equity patterns. We then identify a set of seven regions for more in-depth case study research in order to help identify the more subtle and detailed processes, policies, and institutional arrangements that might help explain more equitable growth (or its absence) in our metropolitan settings.

The research provides insight into both the *why* and the *how* of achieving growth with equity. On the why side – what factors explain superior performance on both growth and equity – some of our findings square with previous work in the field while others represent both a challenge to current thinking and a reason for further research. For example, the case study work suggests that jurisdictional fragmentation is bad for a region's economic and social health, a point previously made by David Rusk (1993). But there are a series of other factors that emerge in both our statistical and qualitative work: the dragging effect of unionization on growth and the uneven impact of unions on equity (to our surprise), the stabilizing effect of the public sector (less to our surprise), the generally positive impact of deconcentrating poverty, the growth-enhancing but equity-reducing impacts of having a large immigrant population, and the important role of an influential minority middle class (which we argue contributes to both a political economy interest in prosperity and a continuing attention to fairness).

But the case studies also suggest a factor that is a bit harder to quantify precisely (although our quantitative analysis did suggest this indirectly as well): the importance of efforts to create a diverse *epistemic community*. It is hardly a bumper sticker slogan – "no justice, no peace" has a more fighting ring and romantic tone than "let's share the same facts" – but conscious efforts to develop a shared understanding of the region amongst diverse constituencies seems to make a difference for blending the imperatives of equity and growth. Formally, epistemic communities are defined as like-minded networks of professionals whose authoritative claim to consensual knowledge provides them with a unique source of power in decision-making processes (Haas 1992, 1997). The members of an epistemic community have similar normative values, and draw similar interpretations and make similar policy conclusions when presented with given situations (Thomas 1997).

In full academic garb, the words sound fancy but the concept is clear: epistemic refers to *what* you know (what facts, figures, and perspectives) and community refers to *who* you know it with (whether alone or in collaboration with others). When such collective knowledge includes not just the "usual suspects" of urban growth coalitions (Logan and Molotch 1987) but a broader constellation of community interests and perspectives, it seems to make a difference in regional trajectories. In the various cases studies, we find that creating a regional consciousness about the problems of poverty and their impacts on growth potential tends to focus attention; jurisdictional ties can help (because suburbs that are annexed, for example, realize more quickly that they cannot escape the drag on regional growth from high levels of poverty) but this can be pushed along by intentional leadership programs and other strategies for collaborative governance. In short, inclusion in knowledge generation and related decision-making processes is important for inclusive sharing of a growing economic pie.

The second level we consider in the work is just *how* regions are achieving growth with equity. Regions may find themselves with exactly the right structural elements to generate fairer growth, including stabilizing public employment, limited jurisdictional fragmentation, and, as the case studies suggest, industrial or sectoral diversity. But one can easily imagine a region blessed with all the right attributes but unable to fully exploit them to capture the potential for prosperity and inclusion. This requires not just the diverse epistemic community – the shared values and vision across diverse constituencies – but also policy practices that link distressed neighborhoods to economic development opportunities, that insure that workforce development includes everyone, and that join up the driving sectors of the economic with previously disadvantaged employees.

In each of the cases we consider, we try to lift up what sort of policy strategies make a difference. We complement this toward the end of the book with a consideration of some of the policies that have become the standard litany for those promoting regional equity, including community benefits agreements, workforce development, and community college promotion. We argue, however, that the usual tools of progressives have focused primarily on ensuring that poor people are getting more of their fair share of the "economic pie." Equity advocates have had little success, and in many cases little interest, in contributing to job creation or economic growth *per se*, or even to paying attention to selecting among equity strategies those that have the highest pay-off in terms of increased economic performance.

But this is the other half of just growth – you need a compelling economic growth agenda as well as a commitment to fairness. You cannot assume that the proper balance of policy is struck in the balance of politics – that the business sector will worry about economic growth, that community advocates will worry about "the people," and that politicians will sort out the differences. You cannot press for equality in a stagnant economy – as we have seen in dramatic fashion recently, when the economy does not work, people do not work. Moreover, poor people are most dependent on economic growth and most in need of the jobs created by a region's economic drivers. Equity proponents, we would suggest, need a clear economic growth model and agenda and this is often missing in (in) action.

As we complete this book, it is clear that the national opening that may have existed for progressive economy policy has been closing. Although the election of Barack Obama as president in 2008 led some to think that a new New Deal was coming, the constraints of domestic policies and the power of Wall Street insured that we had a stimulus too small to make a real dent, an approach to regulating the financial system that was insufficient to the task, and a brief burst of attention to equity that was quickly eclipsed by efforts to resuscitate the macro-economy. Meanwhile, the rise of a right-wing response in the form of the so-called Tea Party is partly (and maybe largely) due to monied interests but also to its coherent and consistent message: that the best government is limited government, that the best economy is a market economy, and that the best anti-poverty strategy is no strategy at all. Left on its own, conservatives contend, growth will eventually lift all boats.

Counting just on growth is not likely to lead to "just growth" – a set of outcomes that include economic expansion and social equity but also an inclusive conversation about how best to achieve economic inclusion. This book seeks to contribute to that conversation – for unless there is an alternative that makes sense at both regional and national levels and a way to get all residents into a shared understanding of their common fate, the unique opportunities for policy change in this era will continue to be squandered. Thus, we hope this work informs the regionalist debate for which it was originally intended – but that the lessons will also inform national strategy, particularly the ways in which federal policy could encourage the expansion of equitable development in America's metropolitan regions.

A roadmap to the book

These are grand ambitions – and we try to get there one analytical step at a time. We begin the analysis in the next chapter with a discussion of data and case selection. We note that simply asking our colleagues which regions best exemplified "just growth" could lead to a range of answers based more on feelings than on data; the Bay Area, for example, is the site of numerous exciting and high-profile initiatives to be more inclusive (and it is also a very fun place to do field visits), but the income gap there has been widening steadily in past decades (Pastor et al. 2009b). As in a related effort (Pastor et al. 2000), we chose instead to focus on what the numbers would tell us – and devised a method to determine which metropolitan areas were doing better on generating new employment, improving earnings per worker, reducing poverty, and reducing income inequality (benchmarking their performance against their respective census regions of the country to control for factors such as an unlucky presence in the older and battered industrial areas of the American Midwest)

We use data from the 1980s and 1990s in this process, because these were the best data available when we started our research and because we were interested in long-term trends; at the end of the book, we discuss what the most recent data from 2009 and 2010 suggest and find it comforting that our general characterization of our case study regions remains broadly consistent. In order to identify regions of interest, we specifically start with a simple quadrant analysis in which we try to see which regions showed up as high growth and high equity (or rather high improvements in equity) in the periods under consideration, again taking care to benchmark the metros against their broader census region (e.g. West, Northeast, etc.). We note that cases can vary over the two decades and so develop a more sophisticated approach based on whether patterns of growth and equity were consistent (or not) over the two decades.

This offers a broad range of regions of which we selected twenty-five cases for further investigation, including mostly metropolitan regions that were strong performers but also a few that either bounced back from mediocre performance or slipped back from strong to less strong patterns. Even if we had been eager to collect all the frequent flyer miles available from site visits, twenty-five cases were too much for a research team to manage so we first conducted a series of short regional profiles based on written materials, web resources, and some interviews. Blending all this quantitative and qualitative material, we then selected a balance of cases that might stretch across geography and, based upon our pre-existing knowledge and the brief profiles, across some potential lessons. We also placed some weight on demographic diversity; because we are convinced that one of the impediments to building regional alliances for growth and equity is racial tension, we wanted to be sure to explore cases in which minorities were present in significant numbers and hence crossing racial boundaries was likely to be an important dimension of the regional work.

Our final case study regions included four that were consistently above median performers on both growth and equity (at least for the time period considered): Kansas City, Jacksonville, Nashville, and Columbus. We also identify three other cases – Sacramento, Denver, and Cleveland – that we explore because they slipped back, bounced back, or were stuck back over the twenty-year period, and we wanted to investigate these trajectories by way of comparison. We say more about the listing below but it is probably clear to those in this area of research that few of these regions would have surfaced in a less quantitatively driven process. It is also clear that these are not the usual suspects – indeed, we were explicit about avoiding regionalist favorites, such as Portland and Minneapolis–St. Paul, because we wanted to explore cases that were surprising, not the ones about which volumes had already been written.[7] As it turns out, some of the lessons from the usual cases apply – especially the desirability of linking jurisdictions together through formal and informal mechanisms – but the beauty is that we found them in unexpected places.[8]

Before departing to the field – and before leaving Chapter 2 for the next – we then decided to use the data to create more continuous measures of growth *and* equity, rather than just a bifurcated classification scheme. To do this, we created a set of z-scores – in which the values are judged against the mean and expressed in terms of standard deviations of the sample, all normed or "de-trended" by the census region of which the metro is a part. This allows us to do several sorts of analysis. The first is a set of correlational and regression analyses in which we looked for those factors associated with either growth or equity, including employment composition, union membership, the presence of a state capital, spatial residential patterns by poverty and race, educational characteristics of the population, the size of the minority middle class, and the percent immigrant; we even included participation in PolicyLink's Regional Equity summits and national conferences of the more business-oriented Alliance for Regional Stewardship (on the grounds that this signaled some degree of leadership intentionality on either equity or prosperity – or possibly both).

The results are somewhat complex – and readers who find z-scores, odds ratios, and multinomial specifications a bit off-putting may want to leapfrog from the close of the case selection discussion in the middle of that chapter directly to the start of the cases themselves in Chapter 3. But for those willing to slog through the data, analytical treats are waiting: it turns out that having construction employment is associated with both growth and equity while high-tech seems more tied to growth than equity; that economic diversity (at least as we were able to measure it) is not helpful to growth or equity; that small firms tend to contribute to growth but not to equity; that hosting a state capital makes a difference for both growth and equity; that unionization hurts growth and does not facilitate equity; that a high share of immigrants helps growth but hurts equity; that a less educated population hurts both; and that a minority middle class may help with making a region be truly high performing in terms of both equity and growth.

We realize that some of these results are controversial and we nuance them in the discussion. First, industrial diversity may be poorly measured – although we are using a standard specification, it only measures how evenly employment is spread across broad categories of employment, and does not capture more complex dimensions such as whether manufacturing employment itself is diversified or highly concentrated in a few subsectors or among a few firms. Unionization is also complex – it may well be that what we are picking up is the age of the industrial sector (with older sectors being more unionized) and it is also the case that many of the exciting innovations in the labor movement, including new organizing of immigrants and service sector workers and the development of labor-affiliated think-and-do tanks working with community partners, emerged in the period after 2000. Still, we found a remarkable resonance between many of the basic results from this quantitative work and what we found in the field.

Chapter 3 begins that exploration in the field. As noted there we visited seven regions, four of which are reviewed in Chapter 3 and three in Chapter 4. In each region we conducted interviews with key actors in four broad constituencies: the private sector, including chambers of commerce and other major business associations; the public sector, especially regional planning bodies and public–private partnerships; labor unions, especially the regional Central Labor Councils and Building Trades Councils; and community-based and non-profit organizations, particularly social movement and base-building organizations.

These are not complete histories of these places – nor are they meant to be. In each case study we were instead focused on uncovering what might have made for more equitable growth in that particular context. For each case we therefore developed and used a detailed interview protocol, asking questions about perspectives on factors shaping economic growth and engagement with economic growth policies in the region, as well as thoughts on factors shaping shared prosperity in the region, and engagement with efforts designed to promote equity.

In Chapter 3, we look at the regions that were getting it (more or less) right – they all tended to have above median performance on growth and equity over the period we examined. The basic lessons from each:

- *Kansas City* boasts a diversified economy and strongly locally rooted business leadership as well as a strong influence of local philanthropy. A resilient African-American community has a deep community development tradition and the region hosts a comprehensive and effective metropolitan planning organization (MPO) that integrates many social and economic issues along with typical transportation planning. There are also elements of municipal annexation and consolidation in this metro although the story is a bit complex as the region is split over two states.
- *Nashville* had an early history of city–county consolidation and regional collaboration as well as a strong Black middle class rooted in regional educational and health institutions. The metro has a comprehensive private sector leadership with demonstrated interest in issues of social equity and there are efforts to develop cross-constituency civic leadership. Nashville is also a state capital, giving it a base of public sector employment that can help with equitable growth.
- *Jacksonville* also has an early history of city–county consolidation and hence some degree of regional governance. The region has a long history of private/public collaboration and significant public sector (military) employment that provides an economic buffer to hard times. What is most impressive about Jacksonville is a highly effective and long-lasting community council that has built a shared sense of regional destiny and created collaborative processes to determine public policy responses to the region's social and economic challenges.
- *Columbus* is a state capital and has a high level of public sector employment that provides a buffer in economic downturns. There does seem to be an element of luck in the story: Columbus was less dependent on manufacturing, and apparently de-industrialized earlier than other areas in Ohio and so went through restructuring and diversification early as well. It is also one of the cases in which municipal annexation and an effective Council of Governments has helped reduce regional fragmentation. Finally, we note

that Columbus is reported to be a good place for members of the Black middle class; although it is by no means a nirvana for race relations, it lacks the profound history of racial segregation that characterizes, say, Cleveland and this may lead to more collaboration as well.

Chapter 4 turns to those cases that fared less well – and also tries to uncover the reasons why. Those cases run as follows:

- *Sacramento* is what we call a "slip-back" case. The region experienced above median growth and improvements in equity in the 1980s, but then slipped below median in the 1990s. The slowdown seems to have been driven by several processes in the latter decade – military base closures that led to lower overall growth and disproportionately hurt African Americans in the region, and the migration of high-tech employment from the Bay Area to Sacramento, which drove up inequality in the region, as more highly educated professionals saw their incomes soar at the same time as the declining employment opportunities for less skilled workers as a result of the base closures. Interestingly, Sacramento has seen the rise of some very creative regional planning efforts – including land use and transportation planning that became part of the template for California's effort to reduce greenhouse gas emissions – but it has remained an underperformer in the recession and recovery in terms of both growth and equity.
- *Denver* is labeled a "bounce-back" case. The region experienced tepid performance in the 1980s, and then turned around to show outcomes on both growth and equity (compared with the Western census region) in the 1990s. This "comeback" may seem typical of boom–bust Western economies that are dependent on natural resources but the turnaround can also be explained by major infrastructure investments in the 1990s in an airport, a convention center, and other regional attractions and a growing sense of collaboration amongst business and private sector leadership in the region as well as between the central city and the suburbs (including suburban support for a new light rail system). Unfortunately, this did not eliminate the boom–bust cycle: between 2000 and 2007, Denver's employment growth was slightly worse than the census region median and its performance on poverty reduction and income inequality was among the worst in its census region. As for the Great Recession, it actually weathered the economic storm much better than other metros in the Western United States. Apparently, it continues to just bounce back and forth, not finding a sustainable path.
- *Cleveland* was what we called "stuck back." The story here is quite similar to that of other parts of the industrial Midwest: a heavy reliance on manufacturing led to vulnerability in the 1980s and 1990s; suburban sprawl and jurisdictional fragmentation fueled a lack of regional collaboration to recover; and all this was sprinkled with a big dose of racial segregation and political conflict. Cleveland itself was actually host to a new wave of equity and advocacy planning in this period but there was little spill-over to the

region and the central city continued to decline. The 2000s brought a new regional approach, most prominently in the form of a philanthropic effort, the Fund for Our Economic Future, but also through an effort of inner-ring suburban mayors. This is a region making a conscious effort to reverse its past trajectory and strive for higher ground; it has recently picked itself up (albeit just barely) from the bottom but it still has a long way to go to overcome a deep history of regional division.

In Chapter 5, we step back from both the statistical work and the cases themselves to examine the broader lessons for efforts to promote growth with equity. We argue that there are a series of structural characteristics that seem to create more favorable conditions for equitable growth and a series of deliberate strategic interventions that might be helpful. The structural factors include:

- *Political consolidation*: Whether through specific city–county mergers as in the case of Nashville and Jacksonville and annexation in the case of Columbus, or through effective regional political and planning bodies, as in the case of Kansas City and in more recent years in Denver and Sacramento, having some degree of strategic interdependence seems to facilitate growth and equity.
- *Economic diversity*: Although industrial diversity does not show up as a factor in our statistical analysis, regional leaders argue that this helps make them less vulnerable to boom–bust cycles as well as to longer-term pressures from de-industrialization. As noted earlier, we think that the diversity measure in our statistical work is imperfect and this "on the ground" sense of what makes for resilience should be taken seriously.[9]
- *The public sector*: Public sector employment can be a valuable stabilizing factor for both growth and equity. State capitals are important in this regard, given the higher percentage of public employment they bring, but military employment can also be important, evident in the case of Jacksonville and also in Sacramento, where the decline in military employment undermined previous patterns of more equitable growth. Universities and community colleges are an important component of the public sector story in terms of both immediate employment and the spill-over impacts on innovation and workforce development.
- *A Black and Latino middle class*: The presence of a minority middle class was mentioned by respondents as a direct measure of increased opportunity. But something else seems to be at play: a strong minority middle class can elect more minority political leaders throughout the region, with these candidates likely to be concerned about equity as well as growth, partly because of the history legacy of Black politics in particular and partly because of current concerns about community members "left behind."

Of course, structural factors change slowly over time – if they change at all. Regional leaders can try to promote industrial diversity, support anchor universities and community colleges, and encourage the creation and attraction of a minority middle class; they will find it much harder to simply declare their central city the state capital, and the jurisdictional consolidations of the type we study have become increasingly rare. So what is a concerned regional leadership to do?

Perhaps the most significant element we found in the case studies was the role of some process or organization that helped bring together people from widely different constituencies in a way that helped overcome widely differing perspectives and knowledge bases. This does not necessarily mean resolving conflict – our case study regions still exhibited many examples of conflicting priorities, viewpoints, and strategies. But regional leaders in the higher-performing areas seemed to have an appreciation for, and acceptance of, a wide range of diverse perspectives, and a sense that, although they may not necessarily agree with those other viewpoints, those viewpoints are based on valid knowledge, and the future of the region in some way involves accommodating the diversity of priorities and perspectives. We call this a diverse "epistemic community" and argue that leadership development efforts to promote this "soft" factor – hinted at somewhat imperfectly in our econometric work albeit less clearly than the public sector, and middle-class factors – can be very important.

We take up other issues in this chapter, including the role of labor, the impacts of transportation systems, and some emerging new approaches that were out of the time period of our initial research concerns. We specifically suggest that the failure to find unions behind the growth with equity patterns in our case studies does not mean that they do not have a role for the future; there has been a big shift in the labor movement in the 2000s, including the emergence of regional think-and-do tanks that promote community collaborations and regional equity (Dean and Reynolds 2009). We suggest, however, that some of the current fascination with how transit-oriented development could promote equitable growth does not really show up with any degree of evidence in our case studies. We then highlight a few emerging efforts, including community benefits agreements, workforce development collaboratives, and community college investments, that do offer promise at blending equity and growth.

The last chapter turns to "just growth" itself. We first draw a very simple set of three conclusions:

- First, to achieve equity, you need ties that bind – through inclusive political boundaries, solidarity across the lines of class and race, or a constructed sense of regional destiny.
- Second, to achieve sustained growth, you need a responsive and stable employment base – one that has the capacity to adjust to broader market change but which may be cushioned by a public sector that can act as an automatic stabilizer.
- Third, to achieve both, you need leadership – and although it can come from virtually any sector, it must be sustained through efforts to develop a shared understanding of a region's problems and possibilities.

This, in turn, suggests that "just growth" means more than a set of outcomes, more than simply getting above the median on employment expansion and poverty reduction. Just growth is also a process – a sustained conversation about the future of the region in which the twin objectives of growth and equity become embedded in the region's norms and practices.

What is happening in America's regions should not just stay in America's regions and so this final chapter takes on the issue of scaling up as well. We consider how all this learning at a regional level can be transferred to other regions, especially by sharing best practices in terms of both policy and process. We stress the need for civic infrastructure, because ultimately investments in "just growth" development strategies will be sustainable only if there is a broad enough and strong enough political constituency advocating for such an approach – that is, if numerous actors are both thinking regionally and thinking equitably

But we also discuss a different sort of scaling: how the lessons learned at a regional level could translate into supportive federal policy. Our central message here is simple: if we are learning that equity can help support growth at a regional level, we need to make sure that federal policy stops promoting sprawl and inequality and instead makes equity and opportunity a key feature of both regional and national economic policy making.

This is most definitely not a one-way message. It is not just that those who have traditionally focused on growth should also pay attention to equity – it is also that those who have made equity their central concern need to have an economic strategy that goes beyond redistribution. We thus criticize some of the favorite strategies of progressives that pay too little attention to expansion, take too little time to heed the concerns of business, and offer too few reasons why supporting their efforts would generate rather than throttle recovery.

After all, the central task of the current era is not reallocating the fruits of growth but rather figuring out how to reboot the entire economic model. Equally in need of a reboot: economic theory itself. The financial crash has ripped asunder not just retirement savings but also the basic assumption that an unregulated market would always deliver equilibrium. And the role of inequality in triggering the crisis should equally strip away any notion that equity should be an afterthought, an altruistic luxury made available only when times are good.

Such transformative moments are rare; in the twentieth century we perhaps had two: the dramatic changes of the Roosevelt presidency and the less dramatic but equally long-lasting changes of the Reagan presidency. In each case, the entire structure governing investment and growth was overturned: the relationship between the market and the state was altered, the balance of power between corporations, workers, and communities was reconfigured, and our very ideology – the story we tell ourselves about who we are and how the economy operates – was refashioned.

We are in just such a moment once again. What is at stake is not just a recovery but the very rules of the game for years to come and, just as important, the story about what works and what should be valued in our economic thinking.

An emerging body of evidence has suggested that "growth with equity" is not a contradiction but a necessity; this volume seeks to explain why some regions get that mix exactly right, what others can do to follow their path, and why this can and should be a model for the national economy as a whole.

2 Measuring what we mean

Introduction

If you ask regional experts about where prosperity and inclusion are coming together in America, you are likely to hear stories about the pioneering work on community benefits agreements in Los Angeles, the innovative organizing to generate regionwide affordable housing in New Jersey, or the exciting efforts to link city and suburb residents around public transit issues in metro Chicago. We know the drill; we have taken exactly that approach of following the "buzz" in our own survey of social movement organizing for regional equity in metropolitan America (Pastor et al. 2009b).

But often the flash of change and the long grind of transformation occur in different places and at different times. Wolman et al. (1994) made this point effectively in a project in which they took a set of cities that scored high on an index of "urban distress" based on unemployment rates, poverty levels, household income, and growth in output and population, and asked over 150 "experts" which of these low performers had experienced the strongest "economic turnaround or urban revitalization" during the 1980s. They compared the results from this sort of crowd view of "cool cities" with an objective index based on income growth, poverty reduction, and other factors. The mismatch was startling, with many of the cities deemed revitalized by the experts having performed no better and often worse than other cities that did not make the expert grade.

The implication we derive from this work – one already used to good effect in our volume *Regions That Work* (Pastor et al. 2000) – is that it makes sense to rely initially on a quantitative approach that can be unaffected by the previous beliefs of the researchers (or their desire to schedule site visits in places with higher restaurant rankings on Zagat). And so that is the approach we took in this project: we utilized a "quadrant analysis" that placed metro regions in categories depending on how well they did on growth, how well they did on equity, and how well they did on both. We then identified twenty-five regions for more detailed profiling and used those profiles, along with some other criteria (such as demographic and geographic diversity), to narrow our attention down to a select group of metros that would be visited with full interview teams.

That we were driven more by the data than by restaurant rankings can be seen in the list of regions we eventually visited: Cleveland, Columbus, and Kansas

City in the Midwest, Denver and Sacramento in the West, and Jacksonville and Nashville in the South (Nashville and Kansas City at least had musical appeal, with country twangs in the one case and jazz and blues harmonics in the other). As we will see, these were not all cases chosen for excelling in growth and equity; although Columbus, Kansas City, Jacksonville, and Nashville were ranked as consistently good performers in terms of prosperity and inclusion over the period considered, we included Denver, Sacramento, and Cleveland as examples of places that had either bounced back, slipped back or seemed stuck back over the time period we examined.

Understanding the reasons for those outcomes is fundamentally a qualitative task but we also made use of a quantitative approach to determine not just *where* more equitable growth was occurring but also *why* it was occurring. We specifically developed relative indices of growth and equity and explored initial correlations of different factors with these outcomes. We then generated a multivariate look at these relationships, with our growth and equity indices as dependent variables and the driving factors considered as independent variables. Because this analysis tackled only the explanation of growth *or* equity, we turned to a logistic analysis in which the dependent (or response) variable was a categorization of "growth with equity" regions based on tercile rankings of both the growth and equity indices, as well as a multinomial analysis that sought an even finer distinction.

As we will see, that quantitative analysis suggested a series of factors that were then investigated in the qualitative work as well (and that qualitative work also fed back to inform the quantitative analysis). We specifically conclude that being the state capital, having a sizeable minority middle class, and having a significant construction industry are all conducive to growth with equity. We also find that having a large percent foreign born can have a positive impact on growth but a dragging effect on equity. Education matters as well and in the expected direction: more is generally better for growth and equity. We find to the surprise of ourselves and perhaps others that a significant union presence is a negative for growth and not necessarily a clear positive for equity – and we tackle the reasons why in the conclusion.

We begin below by discussing the approach we took to using the data for initial case selection, explaining how and why we landed on twenty-five regions that we then scanned to select down to seven. We then construct a more continuous index for both growth and equity and use this to reaffirm the case selection and offer some multivariate work on the factors that might be associated with linking prosperity and inclusion. Finally, we conclude by discussing what all this means for the real heart of this project – the qualitative case studies that are profiled in subsequent chapters.

Selecting the cases: a data-driven approach

In a concurring opinion in one of the Supreme Court's most famous rulings, Justice Potter Stewart wrote about pornography that "I know it when I see it" – something that likely encouraged a generation of voyeurs to make their own first-hand determinations but also suggested that subjective determination is sometimes the best one can do.

In selecting which cases to examine qualitatively, we wanted to do a bit better. The process we decided on involved a mix of quantitative and qualitative work. Our basic approach was to use general metrics of growth and equity to determine which regions were of interest (either because of strong success or steady failure) and then to carry out a qualitative scan of those metropolitan areas to determine which might offer up particularly interesting dynamics or lessons for the project.

As usual, this was much easier to say than to do – implementing this was complex and time-consuming. We started our work by assembling a database on 192 of America's metropolitan regions – all those with a population exceeding 200,000 in 2000 – that included a wide range of statistics (from an equally wide range of sources) on economic and social performance, including estimates of income growth, job quality, the degree of concentrated poverty, residential segregation by race, the arrival dates of immigrants, and many other variables.[1] One unique aspect of the dataset was the use of uniform geographies over time – that is, we took the current metro definitions and essentially reorganized the data in the previous years to meet the new footprint, lending consistency to our time series calculations.

With a full dataset in hand, we set about to distinguish between those doing well and those doing poorly – and quickly ran into a series of complications. The first was straightforward: What exactly are the best measures of growth and equity, and how sensitive is the classification of a region as a top performer to the particular indicators one uses? The second was more methodological: to what comparison cases should a particular metropolitan region be compared? Is it fair, after all, to ask how a metro region measures up against the entire United States – or should performance be benchmarked against a set of other somewhat similar regions? For example, since the Sunbelt generally grew more rapidly than the Rustbelt, wouldn't using national comparisons miss Midwest metros that did quite well given the pressures of de-industrialization and slow population growth that afflicted most of that part of the country? The third complication had to do with timing: what about regions that did well in one period and less well in another? Were we just looking for steady performers – or were we interested in cases where there was a variation over the two decades?

We were thus well armed (perhaps overly armed) with facts but in need of making methodological choices. On the measurement side, we initially decided to focus on ten measures of growth and equity, listed in Table 2.1 (which we soon narrowed down to four). On the comparison issue, we decided to benchmark each metro region against the general census region (Northeast, Midwest, South, and West) to which it belonged rather than against the nation as a whole. And on the timing issues, we decided to not decide: we considered performance on growth and equity in the 1980s, in the 1990s, and over the entire twenty-year period, and used this to be able to also consider cases that had substantial changes in fortunes from one decade to the next.

We did *not* extend our considerations of performance into the new millennium,

Table 2.1 Indicators of growth and equity

Dimension	Variable	Years
Growth	Change in earnings per job	1979, 1989, and 1999
	Change in employment	1979, 1989, and 1999
	Change in per capita income	1979, 1989, and 1999
	Change in median household income	1979, 1989, and 1999
Equity	Change in percent below poverty	1979, 1989, and 1999
	Change in the 80–20 household income ratio	1979, 1989, and 1999
	Ratio of principal cities to suburbs poverty rate	1980, 1990, and 2000
	Poverty dissimilarity index	1980, 1990, and 2000
	African American dissimilarity index	1980, 1990, and 2000
	Latino dissimilarity index	1980, 1990, and 2000

partly because we were really looking at long-term performance, partly because some of our variables were constructed from underlying decennial census tract information, and partly because our initial case selection occurred in 2008. In the case studies, however, we do consider some of the more recent economic performance as a way of gauging the longer-term sustainability of the trajectories we identified, and the data profile we offer in each case takes us up to 2007.[2] In the last chapter, we also briefly review how the selected regions fared over the course of the Great Recession of 2008–2010, and find that our characterizations of each remain reasonably apt as a predictor of why each weathered (or did not) that economic storm.

While most of the variables in Table 2.1 should be clear to the reader, we should note a few measures that might be less familiar. The first is the change in what we call the 80–20 household income ratio. This is a measure of inequality that essentially stacks every household in the metro region by their level of income and then compares the income of the household for which 80 percent of the households are poorer with the income of the household for which 80 percent of the households are richer. The larger the ratio, the bigger the income gap in the region itself. Although there are other measures of income dispersion that could have been used (e.g. the 90–10 household income ratio), given greater volatility at the top and bottom of the income spectrum and some particular constraints with the 1980 data, the 80th and 20th percentiles were deemed to be rather stable points of the income distribution that still captured relative disparity between the top and the bottom.[3]

The second less familiar variable may be the ratio of the poverty rate in the principal cities of a metropolitan region to that in the suburbs in that region. We use that as a measure of geographic inequality but it is important to note that we use the "principal cities" definition utilized in the most recent definition of metro areas provided by the Office of Management and Budget.[4] This definition includes some large cities that many consider to be suburbs (such as Pasadena and

Glendale in the Los Angeles area) and so it is not a perfect representation of what many think of as city–suburb differences.[5] The other measures of geographic inequality are dissimilarity indices, which basically indicate what percent of a certain population (the poor, Blacks, or Latinos) would need to move to be spread across the region such that the percent in any census tract matched their percent in the metro area.

Finally, a word about the dating. In the decennial census, the data on income that are used to calculate both the change in the poverty rate and the household distribution are actually from the year before – so the 1980 census is really reporting the 1979 poverty rate and so forth. A similar dating issue affects the per capita and household income measure included on the growth side; for consistency, we collected information on the change in earnings and change in employment for those years as well. The residential dissimilarity indices are for the decadal year as they capture where people live. The twist here is that the dissimilarity index for the poor (and the ratio of principal city to suburban poverty) reflects residence in the decadal year but income in the previous year; for consistency with the ethnic dissimilarity indices, we tag this measure with the decadal year.

Doing well and doing good

Utilizing these ten indicators, we then conducted cross-tabulations to identify metropolitan regions that did well and did good – that experienced growth *and* improvements in social equity at or above the medians for their respective census regions (the Northeast, the Midwest, the South, or the West) over the 1980s, the 1990s, and the entire twenty-year period. Each tabulation had four possible quadrants, which we labeled with great normative gumption as good (fast growth and greater equity); bad (slow growth and greater inequality); and two mixed categories in which good and bad would depend on the eye of the beholder (or one's position in the local social hierarchy) – fast growth but unequal, and slow growth but equal.

With four growth measures, six equity measures, and three different time periods, we wound up with a total of seventy-two different cross-tab matrices for each of the four census regions. Presenting those results would take up much of the rest of the book – and ensure that we would generate more of a cure for a reader's insomnia than insights into inclusive growth. What we do instead is focus on the results for only two indicators for growth – the change in employment and the change in earnings – and two indicators for equity – the change in poverty and the change in our measure of household income distribution.

We chose these variables for several reasons. First, per capita and household income can be influenced by demographic change rather than economic performance. For example, Latino households are larger but also have more wage earners (who may not necessarily be part of the nuclear family) so a metro region with an influx of immigrants may experience a slip in per capita income even as median household income is growing. The change in earnings and employment seemed closer to "pure" economic measures, with employment growth preferred over, say, regional growth in gross domestic product (GDP) partly because employment opportunities are a central concern of most regional residents and partly because regional job totals involve less estimation (and less error) than regional GDP estimates.

Second, although the geographic variables involving principal city–suburb ratios and the dissimilarity indices are important, they can be shaped by political boundaries, different racial compositions, and the variety of zoning patterns and development regulations that affect the geography of housing markets, amongst other things. Although these factors are important for understanding regional dynamics – and research we and others have conducted suggest that more racially segregated places can underperform on both equity and growth (Eberts et al. 2006; Pastor 2006; Pastor and Benner 2008) – changes in poverty and changes in the overall distribution once again seemed like a "purer" measure of social equity. For example, although not likely, one can easily imagine a situation in which the circumstances of the lowest income individuals improved substantially but no one moved – in which case, the geographic measures would be stable even as economic opportunities were changing.[6]

Thus, for each of our census regions and for each of our three time periods (one being a combination of two decades), we had a total of four different matrices in which we plotted changes in earnings against changes in poverty; changes in earnings against changes in the 80–20 income ratio; changes in employment against changes in poverty; and finally changes in employment again changes in the 80–20 income ratio. We then identified metropolitan areas that fell into the following six categories:[7]

- *Consistently good*: consistently in the "good" quadrant (faster growing, improving equity) through the 1980s and 1990s.
- *Twenty-year good*: in the "good" quadrant in all four matrices for the overall twenty-year period; this included cases in which a metropolitan area did poorly in the 1980s, but performed well enough in the 1990s on all measures to overcome the deficit of the 1980s.
- *Bounce back*: consistently in the "bad" quadrant (slow growth and worsening equity) in the 1980s and in the "good" quadrant' in the 1990s.
- *Slip back*: consistently in the "good" quadrant in the 1980s and the "bad" quadrant in the 1990s.
- *Twenty-year bad*: in the "bad" quadrant in all four matrices for the overall twenty-year period (which again can include a case in which a metro area did well in the 1980s but then slipped dramatically in the 1990s).
- *Consistently bad*: consistently in the "bad" quadrant through the 1980s and 1990s. We also call these cases "stuck back."

Note that these categories are not mutually exclusive – a region could show up, for example, as both consistently good and twenty-year good, or as twenty-year good but still a slip-back case (if the slip in the 1990s was not strong enough to overwhelm the improvement in the first decade), and so on. Note further that many metropolitan areas could (and did) fail to show up in any category (e.g. if they were in a high growth but unequal quadrant or a slow growth but more equal quadrant). Finally, note that these are all relative measures, both to their broad census region and to the world as it is – surely the last few decades have been difficult given the widening gaps in inequality in the United States and doing well in this context simply means not doing as badly as the median performer.

The results of our analysis are presented in Table 2.2; again, not all metro areas are included because some failed to make the mark by showing up in the mixed categories. Also, recall the purpose of this initial cut: given constraints of time and funding, we were hoping to come up with a range of about twenty to thirty cases for which we could do a quick profile utilizing a web-based research approach and a limited set of phone interviews with experts in these regions. The idea was that these initial profiles would suggest some common themes to explore in the more in-depth case studies as well as identify a sense of particular regional dynamics (and maybe organizations and individuals) that might facilitate the final case selection.

A first look

The metro areas for which we did the initial web and expert profiles are listed below and tagged as bold in Table 2.2; note that, as a region can show up in more than one category (say, twenty-year good and a reversal if the performance in the first decade was just below the median but the performance in the second median was well above it), some regions may be bolded twice in the table. Going by broad census region, the metropolitan regions we selected for the initial profiles were:

*   *Northeast*: Atlantic City, New Jersey; Buffalo–Niagara Falls, New York; Erie, Pennsylvania;
*   *Midwest*: Cincinnati–Middletown, Ohio–Kentucky–Indiana; Cleveland–Elyria–Mentor, Ohio; Columbus, Ohio; Kansas City, Missouri–Kansas; Minneapolis–St. Paul, Minnesota–Wisconsin;
*   *South*: Atlanta–Sandy Springs–Marietta, Georgia; Chattanooga, Tennessee–Georgia; Columbia, South Carolina; Huntsville, Alabama; Jacksonville, Florida; Lexington–Fayette, Kentucky; Nashville–Davidson–Murfreesboro, Tennessee; Raleigh–Cary, North Carolina;
*   *West*: Albuquerque, New Mexico; Boise City–Nampa, Idaho; Denver, Colorado; Portland–Vancouver, Oregon–Washington; Sacramento–Arden–Arcade–Roseville, California; Salt Lake City, Utah; Spokane, Washington.

As it turns out, we also added Las Vegas, Nevada and San Antonio, Texas to the initial profile set for reasons mentioned below; neither made the final cut. In any case, the reasons for selecting these particular regions and excluding others deserve some comment.

First, we were especially interested in the "consistently good" category and so virtually all regions that fell into this category were included in this pre-case

Table 2.2 Classification of regions by just growth criteria

Consistently good	Twenty-year good	Bounce back	Fall back	Twenty-year bad	Consistently bad
Northeast					
Boston–Cambridge-Quincy, MA–NH Manchester-Nashua, NH	**Atlantic City, NJ** Barnstable Town, MA Boston–Cambridge-Quincy, MA–NH Manchester-Nashua, NH Norwich-New London, CT Philadelphia-Camden-Wilmington, PA-NJ-DE-MD	**Erie, PA** Pittsburgh, PA Scranton–Wilkes-Barre, PA	Poughkeepsie-Newburgh-Middletown, NY Trenton-Ewing, NJ	Binghamton, NY **Buffalo–Niagara Falls, NY** **Erie, PA** Pittsburgh, PA Scranton–Wilkes-Barre, PA Syracuse, NY Utica-Rome, NY	Binghamton, NY Syracuse, NY
Midwest					
Appleton, WI **Cincinnati–Middletown, OH-KY-IN** **Columbus, OH** Des Moines–West Des Moines, IA Green Bay, WI **Kansas City, MO-KS** Minneapolis–St. Paul-Bloomington, MN-WI Springfield, MO	Appleton, WI Cedar Rapids, IA **Cincinnati–Middletown, OH-KY-IN** Des Moines–West Des Moines, IA Grand Rapids-Wyoming, MI Green Bay, WI Holland-Grand Haven, MI Kansas City, MO-KS Madison, WI **Minneapolis–St. Paul-Bloomington, MN-WI** Omaha-Council Bluffs, NE-IA Springfield, MO	Akron, OH Cedar Rapids, IA Detroit-Warren-Livonia, MI Duluth, MN-WI Peoria, IL Saginaw-Saginaw Township North, MI	Fort Wayne, IN Springfield, IL St. Louis, MO-IL	Akron, OH Canton-Massillon, OH Champaign-Urbana, IL **Cleveland–Elyria–Mentor, OH** Davenport-Moline-Rock Island, IA-IL Flint, MI Peoria, IL Rockford, IL Saginaw-Saginaw Township North, MI Toledo, OH Youngstown-Warren-Boardman, OH-PA	**Cleveland–Elyria–Mentor, OH** Milwaukee-Waukesha-West Allis, WI Rockford, IL Toledo, OH

Table 2.2 Classification of regions by just growth criteria (continued)

Consistently good	Twenty-year good	Bounce back	Fall back	Twenty-year bad	Consistently bad
South					
Jacksonville, FL **Nashville–Davidson–Murfreesboro, TN** Ocala, FL	**Atlanta–Sandy Springs–Marietta, GA** Austin-Round Rock, TX **Columbia, SC** **Huntsville, AL** **Jacksonville, FL** **Lexington–Fayette, KY** Naples-Marco Island, FL **Nashville–Davidson–Murfreesboro, TN** Ocala, FL Orlando-Kissimmee, FL **Raleigh–Cary, NC**	Amarillo, TX Baton Rouge, LA Brownsville-Harlingen, TX **Chattanooga, TN-GA** Corpus Christi, TX Gulfport-Biloxi, MS Jackson, MS Lafayette, LA Little Rock-North Little Rock, AR Louisville-Jefferson County, KY-IN McAllen-Edinburg-Mission, TX San Antonio, TX Waco, TX	Charleston-North Charleston, SC **Columbia, SC** Deltona-Daytona Beach-Ormond Beach, FL **Huntsville, AL** Orlando, FL Palm Bay-Melbourne-Titusville, FL Roanoke, VA Virginia Beach-Norfolk-Newport News, VA-NC Washington-Arlington-Alexandria, DC-VA-MD-WV Winston-Salem, NC	Amarillo, TX Augusta-Richmond County, GA-SC Beaumont-Port Arthur, TX Charleston, WV Corpus Christi, TX El Paso, TX Huntington-Ashland, WV-KY-OH Kingsport-Bristol-Bristol, TN-VA Lubbock, TX Lynchburg, VA Mobile, AL Shreveport-Bossier City, LA Waco, TX	Lubbock, TX Lynchburg, VA

West

Boise City–Nampa, ID	**Boise City–Nampa, ID**	**Albuquerque, NM**	Honolulu, HI	Bakersfield, CA	Bakersfield, CA
Colorado Springs, CO	Colorado Springs, CO	**Denver-Aurora, CO**	Oxnard-Thousand Oaks-Ventura, CA	Fresno, CA	Chico, CA
Fort Collins-Loveland, CO	Fort Collins-Loveland, CO	Phoenix-Mesa-Scottsdale, AZ	Riverside-San Bernardino-Ontario, CA	Merced, CA	Fresno, CA
Olympia, WA	**Salt Lake City, UT**	**Portland–Vancouver-Beaverton, OR-WA**	**Sacramento–Arden-Arcade–Roseville, CA**	Santa Barbara-Santa Maria-Goleta, CA	Los Angeles-Long Beach-Santa Ana, CA
Seattle-Tacoma-Bellevue, WA	Santa Cruz-Watsonville, CA	Salem, OR	Salinas, CA	Visalia-Porterville, CA	Merced, CA
	Santa Rosa-Petaluma, CA	**Salt Lake City, UT**	San Diego-Carlsbad-San Marcos, CA	Yakima, WA	Stockton, CA
	Seattle-Tacoma-Bellevue, WA	**Spokane, WA**	Santa Cruz-Watsonville, CA		Visalia-Porterville, CA
		Yakima, WA	Vallejo-Fairfield, CA		

study analysis. There were, however, several exceptions. Boston, for example, was excluded from this analysis, in part because it had already been profiled as an example of a region linking equity and growth in Pastor et al.'s (2000) book *Regions That Work* and it is a region whose story has been relatively well documented. Manchester's fate seemed hard to separate from that of the larger Boston metro because of proximity and we decided to leave off both metros (and, thus, the whole Northeast) in this analysis of consistently good metros.

A number of regions in the Midwest and West were also excluded because they were small regions with a predominantly Anglo population (such as Appleton, Wisconsin; Fort Collins, Colorado; Green Bay, Wisconsin; Springfield, Missouri; and Olympia, Washington). This reflects a particular concern on our part: we were interested primarily in larger metros and in the challenges of creating pro-equity coalitions and outcomes in places with a more diverse constituency. Des Moines is somewhat larger, but also has a relatively ethnically homogeneous population; Colorado Springs has a significant Latino population, but its high concentration of defense industries makes it somewhat unique, and its experience perhaps less replicable.

A number of regions were selected for an initial profiling because they showed particularly interesting shifts in the dynamics of growth and equity. Albuquerque, Denver, and Salt Lake City, for example, moved from slower growth and below median change in equity in the 1980s to fast growth and improving equity in the 1990s, and we were interested in the reasons for turnaround. Huntsville, Alabama and Columbia, South Carolina were chosen for the opposite reason – they did much better in the 1980s than in the 1990s (although the 1980s performance was strong enough to earn both of them a tag as "twenty-year good." We also included Sacramento as a case of reversal or slip back, with the 1990s poor performance enough to drop it from meeting or beating the twenty-year (census region) medians for the variables we considered.

Given our general focus on what went well, we could have stopped there – but thought it might be important to take a quick look at what did not go well. There was, as can be seen, a whole range of cases with poor performance on both growth and equity. Many of these were in Texas and California, with California's San Joaquin Valley areas (Bakersfield, Fresno, and Merced) being stellar examples of getting it wrong and Los Angeles and Stockton managing to underperform in both the 1980s and 1990s but getting just close enough to the median in both cases to avoid being classified as "twenty-year bad." The San Joaquin Valley group is somewhat unique, with a variety of pressures from high immigration and an agricultural base addicted to cheap labor – and given that Los Angeles has been over-studied (particularly by us), we wanted to focus on other areas.

We thus selected three of the poor performers: Buffalo, Cleveland, and Erie. Of these, Cleveland was of special interest for several reasons. First, it was not just performing poorly over the twenty-year period but over each of the decades. Second, it was in Ohio, a state where other metros (particularly Columbus, a region that was eventually chosen for a case study) were in the "consistently good" category; this suggested the possibility of a comparison in which we controlled for the same state policy rules and so were better able to attribute any variation in outcomes to metropolitan dynamics. Finally, Cleveland was at that time the subject of a regionalist initiative called Fund for Our Economic Future which was attracting great attention for its dual attention to growth and equity – if being down could lead to new efforts to look up, perhaps Cleveland could offer lessons.

A final step on our selection process for the initial case studies involved looking a bit more carefully at how close various metros came to meeting the quantitative criteria. This led us to include several regions (e.g. Chattanooga) that barely missed the mark but which had interesting turnaround or growth experiences which we thought might be worth understanding in some more depth. We also decided to profile San Antonio, Texas and Las Vegas, Nevada, the former because it was in South Texas but had not performed as badly as its counterparts and Las Vegas because it was becoming increasingly known as a place where homes and employment were plentiful. Neither of these made the final cut but all of the cases provided interesting data to inform the actual selection process.

So many cases, so little time

To narrow down to the final cases, we developed brief profiles of the twenty-five regions identified through our quantitative approach and the initial sifting described above. The research for these profiles was limited to a combination of web-based investigation and select phone calls, including to academic researchers who might be able to provide a quick background analysis to make sense of trends. To make the initial profiles consistent, we developed a template that looked at the demographics of each region, the political structure and economic base, and the history of regional organizing by equity proponents and business leaders.

The demographic and economic information was mostly collected from standard national databases, and supplemented by data made available or utilized by metropolitan planning agencies or various regional civic efforts. In each of the regions, we also identified key business, public, labor, and community organizations and collected information on their various interventions, reports, and statements about the region. We were particularly interested in seeing whether there were organizations in these metro areas that embodied or were striving toward an integrated vision of growth and equity.

Each of the eventual profiles was around eight to ten pages long. We also generated a series of comparison maps showing geographic patterns of race, income, poverty, and the age and value of housing units, in order to visually represent the geographic disparities that our selection process had left behind when we focused on the "pure" economic and equity measures. We also took into account whether there were particularly interesting organizing efforts or cases in which the work of agencies or organizations went beyond standard practice – for example a metropolitan planning organization (MPO) that was going beyond the federal mandated transportation planning to engage with workforce developers, or a business leadership program that included individuals from the non-profit and/or community organizing worlds.[8]

It is from this imperfect but informative broad scan that we then narrowed down to a set of cases for our visits.Our ultimate goal was to select five to six regions for in-depth case study research – and we came up a bit short (or perhaps long) in that we wound up with seven. In sorting through which of the twenty-five regions held the most potential for case study analysis, the driving factor in our decision making was whether the case might yield insights into the processes that can lead to both growth and equity. However, we also had a preference for regions that were less profiled in the existing literature, larger in relative size, and exhibited demographic dynamics closer to what the nation is likely to experience in the near future.

The regions that were selected for in-depth case study research, and a summary of the reasons for their selection, follow:

- *Kansas City*: Despite having Kansas in its title, the Kansas City metro is mostly in Missouri, with roughly 60 percent of the metro population actually in that state. Overall, the metro experienced both above average growth and improvements in equity consistently throughout both the 1980s and the 1990s. From the initial profile, it appeared that significant initiatives linking regional growth and equity had emerged in multiple sectors, particularly in the public sector and amongst business leadership, but also to a certain extent in the non-profit/community sector. In the public sector, the MPO for the region (the Mid-America Regional Council or MARC) was well recognized for coordinating a wide range of initiatives that went beyond simply transportation planning, including evaluating quality of life initiatives, smart growth efforts, and the protection of regional natural resources; it also offered a detailed "Metro Outlook," which measures progress in the region and tracked nine other peer metros that were likely to offer lessons for Kansas City.[9] The region also seemed to have dynamic workforce development initiatives, including strong training programs in the manufacturing sector and one of the first round of the Department of Labor's Workforce Innovation in Regional Economic Development (WIRED) grants to promote training for regional clusters. All of these activities suggested a forward-looking regionalist approach along with strong outcomes – so Kansas City seemed a "go."
- *Jacksonville*: Jacksonville was also a consistently good performer on growth and equity through the 1980s and 1990s. Our profile analysis suggested that the non-profit/community sector played a strong role in leading regional initiatives, particularly in the form of the Jacksonville Community Council Inc., a non-partisan civic organization that was founded in 1975 and "engages diverse citizens in open dialogue, research, consensus building, advocacy and leadership development to improve the quality of life and build a better community in Northeast Florida and beyond."[10] The region

was also one of the first (and still few) regions in the country that achieved a city–county merger in an effort to promote better regional government. The merger was implemented in the late 1960s, and the city of Jacksonville is now the largest single city by land area in the continental United States. Our sense, particularly given previous work on the importance of municipal annexation to regional thinking stressed by David Rusk (1993, 1999) and others, was that this might provide a good case for examining the potential effects of regional government achieved through consolidation. Little were we to know how much of a role the power to annex or consolidate would play in many of our cases.

• *Nashville*: Nashville was also a consistently good performer on growth and equity through the 1980s and 1990s. Interestingly, it was also an early case of a city–county merger (in the 1960s) and provided a chance to evaluate the impact of regional government in a significant way as here the metropolitan area covers a larger number of counties than in Jacksonville (thirteen versus five). Our initial scan suggested that regional initiatives seemed less entrenched, less explicit, and more fragmented than in Jacksonville. We wondered how the region had achieved consistent performance on the growth and equity measures in the absence of prominent regional initiatives promoting growth and equity – particularly given our own bias toward a more proactive and intentional approach – and thought either that we were missing something in our initial scan or that the case might tell us something about the structural rather than the intentional elements that produce more equitable growth.

• *Columbus*: Ohio is the only state that has metros of any significant size that were in both the consistently good and the consistently bad categories for metropolitan performance on growth and equity. As noted in Chapter 1, we thought that this provided a valuable opportunity to explore a variation in outcomes in a situation in which state policy and the basic structures of local government are held constant. With Cleveland an underperformer on all counts (see below), Cincinnati and Columbus were both candidates for the "consistently good" regions in the 1980s and 1990s (again, relative to their respective census region). However, the Cincinnati metro area actually spreads across three states (with 77 percent of the population in Southwest Ohio, 19 percent in Northern Kentucky and 4 percent in southeast Indiana in 2000), meaning that this was not a good case for controlling for state policy. Moreover, the Cincinnati metropolitan area did well on the "pure" growth and equity measures we used in the selection process but ranked below median on the dimensions of geographic disparity for Blacks and the poor that we had also considered, something that is consistent with the relative slippage of the central city, which seems to be a tale familiar to those who know the area. Columbus was also a case of government consolidation through the annexation powers of the central city, a theme that, as noted, became more and more obvious to us as we hit the road to do the case studies.

Those, of course, were our consistently good cases – but we also had a series of cases that we chose in order to have a useful contrast. We chose three that represented different types of patterns:

- *Sacramento* is a "slip-back" case. After a combination of better than average growth and equity in the 1980s – fueled by an expansion of the public sector, growth in military spending, and the movement of some high-tech operations to the region – the 1990s were not so favorable. We were intrigued about why the metro had slipped and were also aware of new efforts to address regional problems. In particular, the metropolitan planning organization had driven a "regional blueprint" process in the 2000s that had won numerous awards and itself become the blueprint for a state law mandating better coordination of land use and transportation to reduce vehicle miles traveled and greenhouse gas emissions. Although there were other metros that had also experienced a slippage in the 1990s, the bulk of these were in the South and we were already doing several southern cases. And Sacramento seemed like a somewhat useful pairing with Denver: both were in the West, both were state capitals, and each had moved in different directions.

- *Denver* was a case in which the region experienced a turnaround or a "bounce back." In the 1980s, it had slower growth and worse indicators of change in social equity than the median for the West census region. This experience was turned around in the 1990s when Denver experienced more rapid growth and improvements in equity that exceeded those in its comparison census region. Although this was of general interest, the turnaround was coincident with the emergence of some prominent regional initiatives in recent years, including dynamic public sector regional efforts in workforce and economic development, a growing regional perspective within business leadership, and some emerging labor organizing around regional issues that were promising (Dean and Reynolds 2009). Denver had also put in place a regional light rail system and voters in the region had recently approved an expansion, suggesting an unusual degree of cooperation in a state normally marked by low-tax and low-investment politics. The case offered an interesting way to think about not only intentions and outcomes but also causality – did the regionalist convergence emerge after the bounce back or was it a driving force behind the bounce?

- *Cleveland* was our "stuck-back" case. As is clear from Table 2.2 – and to anyone who has spent time there – the metropolitan region has been a consistently bad performer in terms of growth and equity dynamics. At the same time, we were intrigued that Cleveland was actually in the midst of grappling with its underperformance and was the site of organizing by the business and philanthropic sector in the form of the Fund for Our Economic Future. This seemed like one of those cases in which hitting bottom – as in Alcoholics Anonymous – had actually seemed to provide the impetus for a possible turnaround (or, at the very least, admitting that you had a problem). And, heck, it was close to Columbus – always good on researchers' stretched budgets – and we were eager to contrast two cases that had the same state policy structure, something not always carefully considered in multi-metro studies.

Explaining growth and equity: a data-driven approach

Although the simple classification system above was fine for basic case study selection, we also wanted to generate a composite index that could be used to examine causal factors – providing a sort of quantitative guidance prior to entering the field.

To achieve this, we combined the percent change in earnings per job and employment into a single growth index and the percent change in the poor and the 80–20 household income ratio into an equity index. Because in this exercise we wanted to compare all the metros together but still allow for them to be benchmarked against their respective census region, we normalized the measures into regionally de-trended z-scores – that is, for each measure, we grouped metros by census region, and for each observation subtracted the census regional mean and then divided by the census regional standard deviation. We thus obtained twelve z-scores: one for each of the four variables and each of three time frames, the 1980s, 1990s, and across the twenty years. We then computed the "growth index" as the mean of the six growth-related z-scores, and the "equity index" as the mean of the other six z-scores.

We then divided the growth and equity indices into terciles. Figure 2.1 provides a cross-tab of the terciles – it tells us how many of the largest 192 metros appear in each category. Note that only thirty-three metros are in both top terciles. Moreover, only eight are best in class on equity but worst in class on

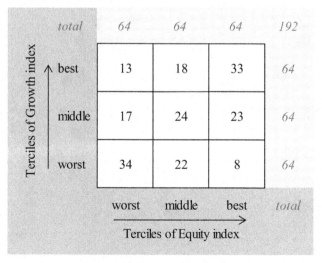

Figure 2.1 Equity and growth indices, by tercile ranking.

growth – which hints that, in practice (whatever the underlying relationship is and whatever the other determinants may be), growth and equity do in general move together. The growth–equity relationship is represented geographically in the map in Figure 2.2.

How do our case studies fall in this more sophisticated ranking system? Again, keep in mind that all of these rankings are relative to each metro area's broad census region – thus, the fact that one metropolitan region performs better than another in the comparisons below does not mean it was somehow a beacon of absolute hope but just that its improvement in growth and equity were better than the rest of its broad census region. Of the seven in-depth case studies, three of them (Columbus, Kansas City, and Nashville) rank in the top terciles for both growth and equity. Jacksonville, also considered one of our top performers, was nearly in the top tercile in growth, missing it by nine slots, and ranked fourth on the equity index. Our bounce-back case, Denver, got even closer to the top tercile in the growth index, and was safely in the top tercile for equity. The slip-back case, Sacramento, was very close to the top tercile on growth, but less so on equity (although it remained above the median for the equity index). Finally, Cleveland turns out to be safely in the worst tercile on both of the indices, solidifying its position as both "stuck back" and an interesting contrast to Columbus.

Although this more continuous measure of growth and equity is useful for reassuring ourselves about the cases, the real value is that it allows us to better test some hypotheses about what may drive our case study dynamics – that is, the circumstances in which prosperity and inclusion come together and in which they fall apart.

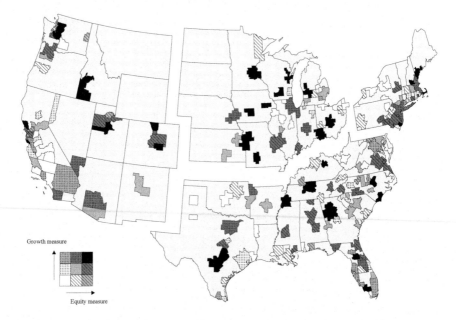

Figure 2.2 Mapping growth with equity in the 192 largest Core Based Statistical Areas.

Two qualifications are in order. The first is that we are not trying to develop complex regional growth models to assess convergence on either equity or growth (for that see Pastor et al. 2009a) or to understand the causal relationship between growth and equity (for that see Pastor 2006 or Pastor and Benner 2008). The latter task is quite complicated and involves the use of both past benchmarks as anchors for path dependence and simultaneous models in which growth is allowed to impact equity, and the other way around. Here, we are taking a more correlational approach (albeit with multivariate controls) to determine what factors are associated with growth and equity, particularly the circumstances under which they are both achieved in a region.

The second qualification is perhaps more an admission to the reader. Although we utilized this quantitative analysis to inform our case studies, it is also the case that what we learned in the case studies came back and informed the quantitative analysis. An example is the role of a minority middle class, something we had not theorized or tested in our initial data runs but which was suggested to us by respondents in the field – and lo and behold, was also important when we wandered back to our offices, our computers, and our regressions. Having a vibrant two-way information flow between quantitative and qualitative work is actually good practice, we think, and such a return to the large sample regression work after carrying out case studies is recommended for those doing the sort of "nested analysis" we undertake here (Lieberman 2005). However, laboring over the details of which variables we added when and why may be bad practice (or at least boring) in terms of writing (and reading!). Thus, we present the complete results below – that is, a full view of the quantitative work that emerged over the entire course of the project rather than a blow-by-blow of which variable got added when.

Context and correlation

Because there is not already an existing body of research on what factors are associated with growth and equity coming together (we are enthusiastic but also trepidatious pioneers on this front), we drew on the existing literature on regional economic growth and the more scarce literature on regional equity to determine four general categories of measures that have an impact on regional economic growth and the distributional – or equity – aspects of that growth:

1 *Employment and industrial composition*, including measures that attempt to capture expanding or contracting sectors, industrial diversity and firm size, labor force participation, unemployment, and degree of unionization or labor organization.
2 *Geographic and distributional dimensions*, including measures of geopolitical importance such as capital cities, complexity of political boundaries, and poverty concentration, as well as indicators of racial, political, and economic inclusion such as residential segregation and representation of minorities in the middle class.

3   *Workforce demographics and housing,* including measures such as home ownership rates and rental affordability as well as human capital variables such as immigration status, age structure, and educational attainment.
4   *Interest in regional growth and/or equity,* based on measures that capture attendance at a series of conferences put on by the business-oriented Alliance for Regional Stewardship and two Regional Equity Summits organized by PolicyLink, which have been used in earlier research ascertaining the interest of actors in regionalism (Pastor et al. 2009a).

We developed a wide range of measures within these categories, being careful to also create z-scores de-trended against the census regions as the growth and equity indicators on the left-hand side of our specification have, as described above, also been benchmarked against their census region. The variables that wound up with the most significant relationships with either one or both of the equity and growth indices are listed in Table 2.3, along with variable descriptions and sources.

Table 2.4 shows the signs and significance resulting from our first pass at the data: bivariate correlations of the variables with either growth or equity. Because we are interested in identifying how *existing* or *predetermined* regional characteristics are related to future *changes* in growth and equity, all of the measures we consider are static (rather than changes). Although we also list the 2000 measures, we are more concerned with the observed correlations in measures taken from the earlier years (1980 and 1990) because those relationships are less susceptible to reverse causality (e.g. above average improvement in the factors underlying the equity index could cause a decline in, say, the measured level of poverty concentration in 2000). Although the 1980 measures are always the best choice in this regard, some are not available in that year and so we end up relying on the 1990 measures as right-hand-side variables for the regression testing that follows.

Several interesting patterns emerge from Table 2.4, most of which make intuitive sense and are remarkably consistent across the three points in time. We start with our primary interest: measures that are correlated with *both* the equity and the growth indices, but not in opposite directions. Unemployment, for example, is associated with low growth and worsening (or at least below average improvement in) equity. Manufacturing employment is negatively related to both growth and equity, a trend that likely reflects the problems of older industrial areas struggling to survive in the context of economic transformation. Construction employment is positively associated with both growth and equity, likely because many of the jobs are middle class and because high levels of construction employment tend to occur in regions poised for economic expansion.

The presence of a state capital city in a region has a highly significant and positive relationship with both growth and equity, perhaps because such regions benefit from stable public sector employment (although the share of public administration employment is not itself significantly associated with growth, a point we touch on below). As in Eberts et al. (2006), the spatial aspects of

Table 2.3 Description of key measures

Category	Measure	Description/variable construction	Source
Employment and industrial composition	Unemployment rate	Percentage of the labor force that is unemployed	Geolytics Census CD 1980 and Census CD 1990, 2000 Census Summary File 3
	Percent manufacturing employment	Percentage of employed population in the manufacturing industry	Geolytics Census CD 1980 and Census CD 1990, 2000 Census Summary File 3
	Percent public administration employment	Percentage of employed population in public administration	Geolytics Census CD 1980 and Census CD 1990, 2000 Census Summary File 3
	Percent high-tech employment	Percentage of workers in high-tech industries using a definition of "high-tech" based on a set of six-digit NAICS codes as specified by the American Electronics Association (AEA). See http://www.techamerica.org/naics-definition/	U.S. Bureau of Labor Statistics, Quarterly Census of Employment and Wages (ES-202)
	Percent construction employment	Percentage of employed population in the construction industry	Geolytics Census CD 1980 and Census CD 1990, 2000 Census Summary File 3
	Industry diversity index	Standard entropy index calculated by share of regional employment across twelve industrial sectors (defined by two-digit NAICS codes)	Regional Economic Information System (REIS), 1969–2004
	Share of all firms that are very small (less than four employees)	Percentage of all establishments that have less than four employees	Regional Economic Information System (REIS), 1969–2004

Table 2.3 Description of key measures (continued)

Category	Measure	Description/variable construction	Source
	Percent of workers who are union members	Percentage of all workers who are union members, estimated at the CBSA level using data from Unionstats.com that were available only in the current census definitions of metropolitan areas for each year of available data, starting in 1986. To generate estimates at the CBSA level, the union membership rates were applied to all counties that were a part of each metropolitan area, and then a weighted average of the membership rates was taken across the counties in each CBSA using total employment from the REIS as weights	http://www.unionstats.com, based on data from the Current Population Survey (CPS) from the U.S. Bureau of Labor Statistics and the U.S. Census Bureau
	Labor-related community-based organizations per 10,000 people	Number of labor-related community-based organizations per 10,000 people	National Center for Charitable Statistics
Geographic and distributional	Contains a state capital city	Dummy variable equal to zero if the region does not contain a state capital city and equal to one if it does	Constructed by the Program for Environmental and Regional Equity (PERE) at the University of Southern California (USC) using web-based lists of capital cities and CBSAs
	Difference between principal cities and suburban poverty rates	Poverty rate for all principal cities combined for each CBSA minus the poverty rate for the remainder of the CBSA	Geolytics Census CD 1980 and Census CD 1990, 2000 Census Summary File 3
	Poverty concentration (percent of poor in high poverty tracts)	Percentage of people below the federal poverty level that reside in census tracts with a poverty rate of greater than 20%	Geolytics Census CD 1980 and Census CD 1990, 2000 Census Summary File 3

Measure	Description	Source
Dissimilarity index for people of color	Dissimilarity index for all people of color combined, calculated at the CBSA level using census tracts as the underlying unit of geography. For the formulas used, see http://www.census.gov/hhes/www/housing/housing_patterns/app_b.html	Geolytics Census CD 1980 and Census CD 1990, 2000 Census Summary File 3
Isolation index for people of color	Isolation index for all people of color combined, calculated at the CBSA level using census tracts as the underlying unit of geography. For the formulas used, see http://www.census.gov/hhes/www/housing/housing_patterns/app_b.html	Geolytics Census CD 1980 and Census CD 1990, 2000 Census Summary File 3
Correlation ratio for people of color	Correlation ratio for all people of color combined, calculated at the CBSA level using census tracts as the underlying unit of geography. For the formulas used, see http://www.census.gov/hhes/www/housing/housing_patterns/app_b.html	Geolytics Census CD 1980 and Census CD 1990, 2000 Census Summary File 3
Percentage of African-American households that are "middle class"	Percentage of all African-American households that are in the middle class. The middle class is defined as all households with income between 80% and 120% of the CBSA-wide median household income. For 1980, categorical data on the number of households by race and income were unavailable so families and family income were used instead	Geolytics Census CD 1980 and Census CD 1990, 2000 Census Summary File 3
Percentage of Latino households that are "middle class"	Percentage of all Latino households that are in the middle class. The middle class is defined as all households with income between 80% and 120% of the CBSA-wide median household income. For 1980, categorical data on the number of households by race and income was unavailable so families and family income were used instead	Geolytics Census CD 1980 and Census CD 1990, 2000 Census Summary File 3

Table 2.3 Description of key measures (continued)

Category	Measure	Description/variable construction	Source
Workforce and housing	Median gross rent as a percent of household income	Gross rent as a percentage of household income for the median renter-occupied housing unit, calculated at the CBSA level by summing up information on the number of renter-occupied housing units by categories of the share of household income spent on rent, and using Pareto interpolation to estimate the median	Geolytics Census CD 1980 and Census CD 1990, 2000 Census Summary File 3
	Home ownership rate	Percentage of occupied housing units that are owner occupied	Geolytics Census CD 1980 and Census CD 1990, 2000 Census Summary File 3
	Percentage foreign born	Percentage of the population who are foreign born (excluding persons born abroad with American parents)	Geolytics Census CD 1980 and Census CD 1990, 2000 Census Summary File 3
	Percentage recent immigrants (arrived in the last ten years)	Percentage of the population who are foreign born and arrived in the United States during the ten years prior to the survey	Geolytics Census CD 1980 and Census CD 1990, 2000 Census Summary File 3

	Share of population who are working age (25–64)	Percentage of the population who are between the ages of 25 and 64 (inclusive)	Geolytics Census CD 1980 and Census CD 1990, 2000 Census Summary File 3
	Percentage population age 25+ with a BA or higher level of education	Percentage of the population age 25+ who have a Bachelor's degree or higher level of education	Geolytics Census CD 1980 and Census CD 1990, 2000 Census Summary File 3
	Percentage population age 25+ with high school graduate or lower education	Percentage of the population age 25+ who have a high school graduate (or GED) level of education or lower	Geolytics Census CD 1980 and Census CD 1990, 2000 Census Summary File 3
Interest in growth/equity	PolicyLink Regional Equity Summit attendees, 2002 and 2005 combined, per 10,000 people	Combined number of attendees at the 2002 and 2005 PolicyLink Regional Equity Summits per 10,000 people	Constructed by PERE at USC using lists of attendees that included postal zip codes
	Alliance for Regional Stewardship conference attendees, 2000–2005 combined, per 10,000 people	Combined number of attendees at the 2000–2005 Alliance for Regional Stewardship conferences per 10,000 people	Constructed by PERE at USC using lists of attendees that included postal zip codes

Table 2.4 Correlations of key measures with the growth and equity indices

	Correlation with growth index			Correlation with equity index		
	1980	1990	2000	1980	1990	2000
Employment and industrial composition						
Unemployment rate	– – – –	– – – –	– – – –	insig.	– – – –	– – – –
Percent manufacturing employment (1)	– – –	–	insig.	– – –	– –	–
Percent public administration employment	insig.	insig.	insig.	+ + + +	+ + + +	+ +
Percent high-tech employment (2)	+ + + +	+ + + +	+ + + +	+ + + +	insig.	insig.
Percent construction employment	+ + + +	+ + + +	+ + + +	+ + + +	+ + + +	+ + + +
Industry diversity index	–	– – –	– – – –	+	insig.	+
Share of all firms that are very small (less than four employees)		+ + + +	+ + + +		insig.	+ +
Percentage of workers who are union members (3)	– – – –	– – – –		–		
Labor-related CBOs per 10,000 people (4)	– – – –	– –	insig.	–	insig.	– –
Geographic and distributional						
Contains a state capital city (5)	+ + +	+ + +	+ + +	+ + + +	+ + + +	+ + + +
Difference between principal cities and suburban poverty rates		– –	– – – –	+ + + +	insig.	insig.
Poverty concentration (percentage of poor in high poverty tracts)	–	– – – –	– – – –	–	– – – –	– – – –
Dissimilarity index for people of color	insig.	– – – –	– – – –	insig.	– –	– – – –
Isolation index for people of color	insig.	–	insig.	– –	– – – –	– – – –
Correlation ratio for people of color	insig.	insig.	insig.	insig.	– – – –	– – – –
Percentage of African–American households that are "middle class" (6)	insig.	+ + + +	+ + + +	insig.	–	insig.
Percentage of Latino households that are "middle class" (6)	+	+ + + +	+ + + +	–	+ +	+ + + +

Category	Measure								
Workforce and housing	Median gross rent as a percent of household income	+++	insig.	insig.	insig.	----	----	----	----
	Home ownership rate	-	+	insig.	+	+	+++	++++	++++
	Percentage foreign born	insig.	+++	++++	----	----	----	----	----
	Percentage recent immigrants (arrived in the last ten years)	++++	++++	++++	----	----	----	----	----
	Share of population who are working age (25–64)	insig.	++++	++++	insig.	insig.	++++	++++	++++
	Percentage population age 25+ with a BA or higher level of education	++++	++++	++++	+	+	+++	+++	++++
	Percentage population age 25+ with high school graduate or lower education	----	----	----	--	-	----	----	----
Interest in growth/equity	PolicyLink Regional Equity Summit attendees, 2002 and 2005 combined, per 10,000 people		insig.	insig.	insig.	insig.	insig.	insig.	insig.
	Alliance for Regional Stewardship conference attendees, 2000–2005 combined, per 10,000 people		+++	+++	++	++	+++	+++	++++

Notes

The sign "+/–" indicates a significant relationship and the direction of that relationship with either the growth index or the equity index; "insig." indicates an insignificant relationship; and a blank cell indicates that there were no available data for the measure in that year. ++++ (––––) indicates significance at the 0.01 level; +++ (–––) indicates significance at the 0.05 level; ++ (––) indicates significance at the 0.10 level; + (–) indicates significance at the 0.20 level.

General:

All of the indicated measures are figured as regionally de-trended z-scores relative to the four broad census regions: the West, Midwest, South, and Northeast. They are calculated for the largest 192 metropolitan areas (CBSAs) in the United States by subtracting the mean across all such metros in the respective census region and then dividing by the corresponding standard deviation.

Specific:

(1) Data in the 1980 column are actually for 1979.

(2) Data in the 1990 and 2000 columns are for 1990–1992 and 2000–2002 respectively. The definition of "high-tech" industries is based on a set of six-digit NAICS codes designated as high-tech industries in an article by American Electronics Association (AEA) (http://www.techamerica.org/naics-definition/).

(3) Data in the 1980 column are actually for 1986.

(4) Data shown are for 1995 and 2004 (in the 1990 and 2000 columns respectively).

(5) This measure is a dummy variable for the CBSA hosting a state capital, thus the years do not apply. It is the only one of the measures that is not represented as a regionally de-trended z-score.

(6) Middle class is defined as all households with income between 80% and 120% of the CBSA-wide median household income. For 1980, categorical data on the number of households by race and income were unavailable so families and family income were used instead.

regional poverty and residential segregation by race all tend to have a negative relationship with both growth and equity (see also Pastor and Benner 2008). The most consistently significant among the geographic factors are the dissimilarity index for people of colour and the poverty concentration, calculated as the share of the region's poor that live in census tracts with a poverty rate above 20 percent. Less significant for growth is the isolation index (the probability that a person of color will meet another person of color in the census tract in which they live) and even less significant for growth and even equity is the correlation ratio, a similar but more complex measure that is adjusted for the relative prevalence of people of color in each region (so that it will not be higher in one region just because there is a greater percentage of people of color).[11]

Interestingly, the percentage of both African-American and Latino households that are in the middle class is generally positively associated with both growth and equity. Although some of this may be reverse causality – regions with above average growth and improvement in equity over the two decades are likely to have allowed more African-American and Latino households to rise up to the middle class – there is another intriguing explanation offered by respondents in our case studies. This is that having such minority middle-class members may constitute a more empathetic – and socially influential – constituency for equitable development. Because they are positioned to benefit from growth, they support strategies that will produce it (rather than purely distributive approaches that might be counterproductive or reduce economic output) – and because they may be closer to still struggling co-ethnics (or to their own histories of struggle), they may be more supportive of policies that provide a ladder out of poverty for low-income minority communities.

As for the workforce and housing measures, the share of the population that is working age seems to have a positive relationship with both growth and equity, as does the educational attainment of a region (although the share of people aged twenty-five and older who are college educated is more significant in explaining growth than equity while the share of the population with a high school education or less is clearly a big drag on both growth and equity). This is no surprise: a highly educated workforce has long been touted as the foundation of regional economic growth, and low education levels are associated with lower productivity as well as more unequal income distribution.

As for our measures of interest in regional growth and equity, we find that attendance at the PolicyLink Regional Equity Summits has no correlation with the indices while attendance at the more business- (read growth-)oriented conferences has a positive association with both the growth and equity indices. These measures need to be interpreted differently from the others because they were actually calculated using behavior *after* the period rather than *before* the period being considered. As a result, what we might be finding is that regions that are making it – are growing and are more socially cohesive – are more likely to engage in the sorts of regional collaborations that will get them invited to the sort of meetings typified by the Alliance for Regional Stewardship. On the other hand, our case studies – as we will see – suggest the importance of developing an "epistemic community" in which there are shared understandings of the region's trends and challenges and so this may be a sign of that as well.

There are also some measures that are strongly associated with one index but not the other. In terms of employment and industrial composition, these include public administration employment, which seems to be strongly and positively associated with the equity index but shows no relationship with the growth index. Meanwhile, high-tech employment is, perhaps unsurprisingly, strongly associated with growth but is insignificant for equity – perhaps because, depending on the particular type of high-tech employment, it can provide both high- and middle-paying jobs that in turn create demand for lower-paying service sector jobs.

Interestingly, industry diversity shows up as a negative for growth and a positive for equity. Although industrial diversity is usually associated in the popular imagination with a more stable, resilient economy, it is also the case that regional economic/industrial clusters may drive growth (i.e. those that do have not clusters, and thus a more even distribution across industries, have slower growth) while regions with employment distributed more evenly across industries do better in terms of equity.[12] Perhaps as a result, the literature is actually more mixed on the impacts of industrial diversity than might be thought.[13] Having a regional concentration of very small firms (with less than four employees) appears to be strongly associated with growth while high rates of union membership are negatively associated with growth, with neither measure correlating very strongly with equity improvements.

Finally, a lack of rental affordability in 1980 is positively associated with the growth index but it is (reasonably enough) negatively associated with equity in 1990 and 2000. Home ownership appears to have a weak negative association with growth but is positively associated with equity, and a high percentage of foreign-born and recent immigrants among the population is positively associated with growth but negatively associated with equity, perhaps because of competition with lower-skilled native-born workers. Because the relationship between the immigrant population in 1980 and growth is not significant, it could be that the immigrants are following the growth in jobs rather than helping to generate economic expansion, something we discuss and test in more detail below.

Driving that train: understanding growth

Correlational analyses are a useful start but face a straightforward problem: an observed relationship between two variables, say low education levels and high inequity, could actually be due to a third variable, say a large and recent immigrant population. One way to disentangle the various relationships and better understand the strength of associations between regional characteristics and our growth and equity indices is through the use of multivariate regression analysis.

We conduct such a regression analysis below. Our strategy in this exploratory exercise was to test a variety of regression specifications using the set of variables described above, with our ultimate goal being a parsimonious model that maintained the most robust measures and explained a reasonable portion of the variation in the growth and equity indices. Given that we are attempting to identify regional characteristics with subsequent shifts in growth and equity, the optimal strategy would be to use measures from 1980, well before the time period measured by the indices. Unfortunately, we did not have data available for 1980 for several key measures and we wanted to retain consistency in our dating so we instead used data from 1990 (or as close to that year as possible). We did replicate versions of the models reported to the extent possible using 1980 data and found results very similar to those reported below.

As with the correlation analysis, all measures were transformed into z-scores that were de-trended relative to the census region. This means that the interpretation of the regression coefficients is more akin to the interpretation of standardized betas – in which one is assessing the impact on the dependent variable as measured by change relative to its standard deviation by a change in an independent variable relative to its standard deviation. In this case, the changes are relative to the broad census regions rather than the entire set of regions in the regression sample but, just as with the standardized beta, the models are essentially unit-less and thus, although the values of the regression coefficients can be compared with each other to gauge relative importance, they cannot be placed on any other scale or expressed by any other metric.

For both growth and equity indices, a variety of regression models was tested. The results reported in Table 2.5 are for the specifications that were found to be most robust, a determination we arrived at through a combination of "testing up" – that is, initially entering only the most significant measures from the earlier correlation analysis and then adding additional measures one at a time in search of those that both were significant and added explanatory power – and "testing down" – that is, entering all of the measures that were found to be significant in the correlation analysis and removing them one at a time to understand the impact on the significance of the other variables and the amount of variation in each index that was being explained. In cases in which two variables were measuring a similar regional characteristic (e.g. poverty concentration and the difference between principal cities and suburban poverty rates), we kept only the variable that added the most explanation in the model. Finally, because of missing data, only 175 of the 192 CBSAs that had all the necessary data for these analyses were included in the model.

In Table 2.5, the three columns of coefficient estimates represent three slightly different specifications of the same basic model for our growth index. The first column enters the Black and Latino middle-class variables separately; the second column combines these into a "minority" middle-class measure. The advantage of the first is that it allows for separate effects whereas the advantage of the second is that it accounts better for the fact that the size of each racial/ethnic group can vary considerably by region; although some regions may have a large share of, say, African-American households that are middle class, their share of all households may be so small that they have impacts on the body politic only in conjunction with another minority group. In the third column, the best-performing specification of the middle-class variable is maintained, and the "other" index is included on the right-hand side (i.e. the equity index is included in the growth model and the growth index is included in the equity model).

In looking at the result for the growth index model, we find a fairly good model fit with the adjusted r-squared indicating that the model explains between 59 and 67 percent of the variation in the growth index. Most of the variables and the coefficients are stable across the three specifications, with signs that match those reported in the simple correlations reported in Table 2.4. Some of the basic employment and industrial composition measures remain significant and were thus kept in the model; public administration employment was superseded by the state capital dummy variable, the concentration of labor CBOs relative to population was bumped out by the more direct union membership variable, and the concentration of very small firms had its effects muted by more dominant explanatory variables. The more important drivers (+) or hurdles (–) appear to be the unemployment rate (–), reliance on manufacturing employment (–), high-tech employment (+), construction employment (+), industrial diversity (–), and union density (–).

In terms of the geographic and distributional measures, hosting a state capital city remains positive and significantly associated with regional economic growth when controlling for many other important factors. The difference between the poverty rate of the combined principal cities and the poverty rate of the suburbs (the remainder of the region) turned out to be a more significant measure in terms of its negative association with growth than poverty concentration *per se* (though not highly significant); this suggests that even controlling for other important factors, city–suburban disparities in poverty rates are a bad thing for economic growth, something also found by other researchers (Ledebur and Barnes 1993; Savitch et al. 1993). The dissimilarity index for people of color – that is, the share that would have to move to a new census tract in order to achieve an even distribution of people of color and non-Hispanic whites across all census tracts in the region – is negatively associated with the growth index, a result very much in line with Pastor (2006) and Eberts et al. (2006).

Although the size of the Black middle class was positively and significantly correlated with the growth index in the simple bivariate comparisons in Table 2.4, it is insignificant in a multivariate setting. The size of the Latino middle class shows up as positive and significant and when the two measures are consolidated into a "minority" middle-class variable (second column), we find a positive and highly significant coefficient. However, including the consolidated "minority" middle-class variable in place of its two components seems to mute the significance of the relationships between the two geographic measures (the city–suburb poverty differential and the dissimilarity index) and growth, likely the results of collinearity between these and the more robust specification of the minority middle-class variable.

Interestingly, the only measure from the workforce and housing category that was significantly associated with the growth index and held its significance in the multivariate setting was the percentage foreign born, which shows up as positive

Table 2.5 Key drivers of the growth and equity indices

Dependent variable: growth index

Model variables	Coefficient estimates		
Intercept	−0.03	−0.03	0.00
Unemployment rate, 1990	−0.16****	−0.15****	−0.13****
Percent manufacturing employment, 1990	−0.09***	−0.08***	−0.09***
Percent high-tech employment, 1990–1992	0.19****	0.19****	0.16****
Percent construction employment, 1990	0.12****	0.11****	0.09***
Industry diversity index, 1990	−0.15****	−0.16****	−0.20****
Percent of workers who are union members, 1990	−0.25****	−0.24****	−0.23****
Contains a state capital city	0.18**	0.16**	0.08
Difference between principal cities and suburban poverty rates, 1990	−0.06*	−0.05	−0.08***
Dissimilarity index for people of color, 1990	−0.08**	−0.05	−0.03
Percentage of African-American households that are "middle class," 1990	0.04		
Percentage of Latino households that are "middle class," 1990	0.10***		
Percentage of African-American *and* Latino households that are "middle class," 1990		0.15****	0.12****
Percentage foreign born, 1990	0.10***	0.08**	0.15****
Alliance for Regional Stewardship conference attendees, 2000–2005 combined, per 10,000 people	0.12****	0.11****	0.08***
Equity index			0.40****
Adj. r-squared	0.5883	0.5998	0.6738
n	175	175	175

****$p < 0.01$; ***$p < 0.05$; **$p < 0.10$; *$p < 0.20$.

and significant in all specifications (the measure of recent immigrants was also significant but not as robust so the former was kept in the model).[14] Because it might be thought that the percentage foreign born reflects chasing growth rather than making growth, we should stress that this variable held its significance even when its 1980 measurement was entered into the current model (as well as when it was entered into a model in which as many as possible of the other right-hand side measures are also from 1980). This runs counter to what was gathered from the initial correlations in which the initial 1980 value of percent foreign born was not significantly correlated with the growth index, something that points to the power of multivariate modeling. In any case, this suggests that there is less to the

Dependent variable: equity index

Model variables	Coefficient estimates		
Intercept	−0.06*	−0.06*	0.05
Percent construction employment, 1990	0.08**	0.07*	0.02
Contains a state capital city	0.17**	0.18**	0.11
Poverty concentration (percentage of poor in high poverty tracts), 1990	−0.08*	−0.09*	−0.08*
Isolation index for people of color, 1990	0.09**	0.09**	0.13***
Percentage of African-American households that are "middle class," 1990	0.10***		0.07*
Percentage of Latino households that are "middle class," 1990	−0.01		−0.05
Percentage of African-American *and* Latino households that are "middle class," 1990		0.06*	
Percentage foreign born, 1990	−0.20****	−0.21****	−0.25****
Percentage people age 25+ with a high school education or less, 1990	−0.12****	−0.14****	−0.06*
Alliance for Regional Stewardship conference attendees, 2000–2005 combined, per 10,000 people	0.08***	0.07**	0.04
Growth index			0.29****
Adj. r-squared	0.2807	0.2713	0.3612
n	175	175	175

idea of moving to growth than to helping growth happen: a high concentration of immigrants in the base year, controlling for other important factors, is associated with longer-term regional economic prosperity.

Regional representation at the Alliance for Regional Stewardship conferences as a measure of interest in economic growth shows up as being positive and significantly associated with growth performance. However, given the time frame of this measure (2000–2005), it is easy to argue that this is likely more of an outcome of regional growth than a driver; regions that experienced relatively rapid economic growth may have become more interested in a proactive approach to regional leadership. That said, to the extent that such interest and some extent of regional leadership and cooperation in the business community existed in earlier eras within the same regions that attended the conferences (i.e. that attendance at the conferences reflected a sort of social path dependence), this may have had a part in the positive impact on economic growth that is evidenced by the regression coefficient (and it is consistent with the relationship between regional collaboration and growth that we find in our case studies).

Finally, because of our ongoing interest in the relationship *between* equity and growth, we also entered the equity index into the growth model (using the combined middle-class variable given its greater significance). We find a positive and highly significant coefficient – and although its entrance into the model causes some changes in significance levels of some of the other independent variables, the impacts are neither large nor worrisome. One interesting change is that it renders the state capital measure insignificant, perhaps because of the aforementioned impacts of state capitals and attendant employment on equity. Among the other changes in significance, the difference between principal city and suburban poverty rates becomes more important (perhaps because after adjusting for the impact of the equity index on growth, further city–suburban differences become even more important), and the percentage foreign born becomes more important as well.

All's fair? Looking at the equity index

Turning to the results for the equity index, we find that the variation in equity between regions is far more difficult to attribute to measurable regional characteristics.[15] Although a wide variety of measures are significantly associated with the equity index in the simple bivariate comparisons of Table 2.4, the most informative multivariate model we could develop explains less than a third of the variation in the equity index – about half of the variation we were able to explain in the growth index. Of course, regional equity is far less well researched and documented than regional economic growth, and so we are not entirely surprised by this result. It may also be the case that the relationship between any particular variable and social equity is more complex, involving multiple paths of causation, including policy choice and political dynamics.

Among the employment and industrial composition measures tested, we find only construction employment to be significant and positively associated with regional achievements in equity. Having a capital city in the region is a positive for equity, and, as might be expected, poverty concentration is associated with slipping into an even less equitable scenario – more so than the related measure, the difference between city and suburban poverty rates, which is why it dominates its sister variable in this regression exercise.

Counter to the initial correlations seen in Table 2.4, our measure of residential segregation, the isolation index (the probability that a person of color will meet another person of color in the census tract in which they live), is positively associated with improvements in equity. This is a seemingly odd result and it is one that merits some exploration.

Explore it we did, finding that the positive and significant association between the isolation index and the equity index is seen only after controlling for the percentage foreign born, and, to some extent, poverty concentration. When the model is run without both of those controls, the isolation index shows up as negative and significant; when it is run dropping only the percentage foreign born it shows up as negative but is insignificant. What this seems to suggest is that once we have accounted for a large share of immigrants (who tend to have less political sway) and the concentration of the poor *per se*, residential clustering of people of color tends to have a positive impact on gains in equity, perhaps because this geographic concentration facilitates social networks and social capital for political organizing. This is, of course, exactly the point of some who have argued that regionalist alliances can dilute minority political voice and their progressive perspectives (Savitch and Vogel 2004; Weir and Rongerude 2007).

Squaring to some degree with that, the African-American and Latino middle-class variables, when included separately, show that a more sizeable Black middle class is positively associated with gains in regional equity while a more sizeable Latino middle class has no significant effect; when the two measures are combined (second column) the coefficient is only very marginally significant, so we entered the two separate measures in the third column. This result is consistent with the evidence gathered from some regional interviews suggesting that a substantial Black middle class was a good thing for promoting equity – it meant that there was a population with sufficient clout and sufficient empathy to care about those who were less fortunate and structurally disadvantaged. What is fascinating here – and worthy of future exploration – is that a more sizeable Latino middle class is associated with growth while a more sizable Black middle class is associated with improvements in equity.

The percent foreign born is highly significant and negatively associated with gains in equity, which is unsurprising given that this population is disproportionately concentrated in low-skill and low-paying jobs. Despite being associated with regional economic growth, significant immigrant presence places upward pressure on poverty rates – particularly working poverty – and negatively impacts the income distribution. The percentage of people aged 25 and above with a high school education or less is also negatively associated with gains in equity. Finally, the measure of regional business interest in growth as gauged by the number of attendees at the Alliance for Regional Stewardship conferences is positively and significantly associated with the equity index. As noted above, this may be less related to causality given the timing of the variables but it does suggest that a business class thinking regionally may be more open to pro-equity elements of a regional agenda.

In the third column, we include the growth index on the right-hand side. We find that it has a positive and significant relationship with the equity index – which is as expected. Interestingly, the coefficient is smaller than the positive impact of equity on growth revealed in the earlier regression findings. The variables in these models are constructed such that their coefficients can be interpreted as standardized betas by census region – that is, how much impact a change in the independent variable by a standard deviation has on the dependent variable relative to its standard deviation – so the measures are not really comparable across dependent variables. However, it would be worth exploring whether growth might have a smaller impact on equity than equity has on growth as this would have real implications for policy choices.

Come together, right now . . .

We now turn to a quantitative evaluation of which factors are associated with equity and growth *coming together* in a metropolitan region. To do this, we use a logistical regression framework in which the dependent variable takes on discrete values, and the estimated coefficients measure how each independent variable impacts the *probability* of the dependent variable moving from one discrete value to another.

The logit framework was chosen because it allows us to combine the equity and growth indices by essentially drawing a line for each above which regions are considered to be good performers on both. The reason for this threshold strategy is simple: a single index cannot meaningfully combine growth and equity. Although the truly stellar and truly awful performers might be easy to distinguish, consider how one should compare the following three regions: a region that had slightly above average indices for both growth and equity, one that was stagnating but very equally, and one that was growing rapidly but leaving many residents behind. Despite their different dynamics, they would all show the same level if we, say, simply added our growth and equity indices together. Thinking through the various issues involved in constructing an appropriate combined index kept us up at night – until we decided to simply opt for a logit model based on achieving a threshold level in each index.

To do this, we constructed the dependent or "response" variable for the basic binomial logit based on the tercile classification scheme presented earlier in Figure 2.1 and the map in Figure 2.2. Specifically, the 192 regions under consideration were grouped into three evenly sized groups (terciles) based on their scores for both the growth and equity indices. We then defined "growth with equity regions" as those with equity and growth indices that placed them in the top third of all regions for both indices, or the top third for one index and the middle third for the other (essentially the top right corner and its adjacent horizontal and vertical neighbors in the legend of the map in Figure 2.2, something also depicted in Figure 2.3, with the categories in question represented by the gray boxes).

This resulted in a total of seventy-four "growth with equity" regions (which might also be called "equity with growth" regions). This constituted about 39 percent of all metropolitan regions, a reasonable division between the best and the rest for a logit-style regression. However, not all of these regions are created equal: thirty-three regions scored high on both equity and growth while the remaining forty-one regions did better than the rest but made the top mark in only one but not both variables. We thus also created a response variable in which we separated those who were in the top category for both indices from those who were in the top for one and in the middle for the other (see the representation in Figure 2.3 in which the box with the top performers is black and the boxes with the middle category are light gray). For ease, we call these two groups the "really high performers" and the "nearly high performers."

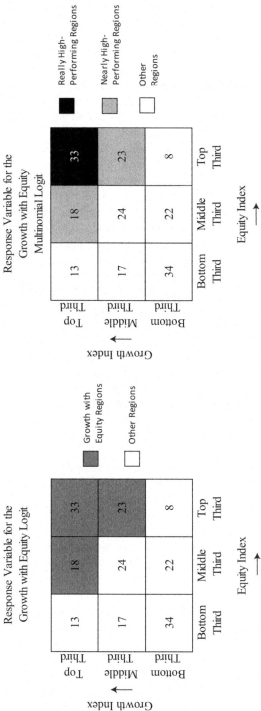

Figure 2.3 Visual representation of the response variables.

Such a neatly ordered structure for the response variable – as well as the suggestive category labels of "really high" and "nearly high" – would seem to lend itself to an ordered logit model in which the estimated coefficients measure the effect of the independent variables on moving from one discrete value of the response variable to the next highest value. In this case, that would mean moving from the white boxes in Figure 2.3 to the gray boxes and eventually to the black box. However, such a specification – which essentially assumes that we are sort of moving from less to more in a clear path – failed what is known as the test of parallel lines. This test examines whether the estimated coefficients for each of the independent variables are the same when predicting the probability of moving from one value of the response variable to the next for every step up in the response variable. Such a failure makes sense partly because the regions with high performance in one dimension and middling performance in the other could actually make it into the top northeast category in the figure by emphasizing either growth or equity. Thus, the relationship may not be as continuous as simply scaling up one dimension on the way to the best-performing category.

An alternative – and one that made more logical and statistical sense – was a multinomial logit. The multinomial approach does not necessarily assume that one category is more of another but deals with each classification – our really high-performing group or our nearly high-performing group – separately. We think that such a model is more appropriate to the task at hand and offers some useful comparisons to the results from our basic logit strategy.

We start, however, with the simple logit approach in Table 2.6. Once again, we experimented with specifications although the model we settled on generally included the set of variables that were found to be important in both of the separate models for the growth and equity indices from above. The overall fit of the models is reasonable – although the pseudo r-squared seems low, this is typical in logit models and the model is correct in predicting categorization about 75 percent of the time. Given that all of the independent variables in the model are regionally de-trended z-scores, odds ratios or marginal effects would have little intuitive meaning; hence, we simply report the regression coefficients themselves and focus here on the signs and significance levels.

We find that construction employment and hosting a capital city have a positive and significant effect on the probability of being a "growth with equity" region. High-tech employment, which was important in explaining only the growth index and not the equity index, also shows up as having a positive and highly significant effect. Although there are certainly other industries that fueled growth over the two-decade period (namely finance, insurance, real estate, and rental and leasing (FIRE), professional and business services, and healthcare), the construction and high-tech industries appear to be particularly associated with more equitable growth.

Low educational attainment among working-age people, which was significant only in the equity model and not the growth model, has a negative and significant effect on the odds of being a "growth with equity" region, as does the percentage foreign born, which was positively associated with the growth

Table 2.6 Basic logit model: probability of being a "growth with equity" region

Model variables	Coefficients	
Percent high-tech employment, 1990–1992	0.51***	0.54***
Percent construction employment, 1990	0.56****	0.50***
Percent of workers who are union members, 1990	−0.50***	−0.48***
Contains a state capital city	1.04***	1.04***
Percentage of African-American households that are "middle class," 1990	0.23	
Percentage of Latino households that are "middle class," 1990	−0.09	
Percentage of African-American *and* Latino households that are "middle class," 1990		0.25
Percentage foreign born, 1990	−0.59***	−0.67***
Percentage people age 25+ with a high school education or less, 1990	−0.48**	−0.47**
Pseudo r-squared	0.2228	0.2236
Percentage predicted correctly	75.4	75.4
n	175	175

****$p < 0.01$; ***$p < 0.05$; **$p < 0.10$.

index and negatively associated with the equity index in the earlier linear regressions. These two measures – educational attainment and percent immigrant – are certainly correlated, so the fact that the percentage foreign born remains so significant implies that it is more than the lack of human capital that is at play. We noted in the multivariate analysis of the growth index that a high concentration of immigrants in the base year seems to have a positive effect on subsequent growth; here, we see that it is by and large inequitable growth.

Union membership, which was found to be significant (negative) in the growth model, shows up as negative and significant here with a sizable effect. Given that unions have been associated with protecting workers, that may seem like a surprising result – and it is one we discuss more in the conclusion to this chapter, throughout the case studies, and in our synthetic analysis in Chapters 5 and 6.

As before, the Black and Latino middle-class variables are initially entered separately (in the first column) and then combined (in the second column) to see if allowing the group that is more prominent in any particular region to drive the minority middle-class measure has a more significant impact on the probability of being a "growth with equity" region. We find insignificance under both specifications – at least when a response variable is formulated in a dichotomous fashion. We present those results nonetheless both because the case studies suggest the importance of this factor and because the multinomial models tell a slightly more complicated story.

Table 2.7 offers the results of that multinomial specification, with separate effects reported for the two categories of interest – the really high performing and the nearly high performing.[16] The fit of the model is not quite as good as the basic logit – which is expected given the greater number of values that the response variable can take on – but the signs of the effects remain the same as in the basic logit and there are some interesting differences in their significance levels when comparing the really high performing with the nearly high performing.

There are, for example, two measures that seem more likely to land you in the nearly high-performing category versus the really high-performing category: the percentage high-tech employment and hosting the state capital. This would seem to make sense as high-tech clusters can be associated with widening wage gaps even as they promote growth, and having the state capital seems useful for equity but less so for growth. To a lesser degree, the percentage construction employment is also more associated with the nearly high-performing regions than the really high-performing regions.

Table 2.7 Multinomial logit model: probability of being a "growth with equity" region

Model variables	Nearly high-performing region Coefficients		Really high-performing region Coefficients	
Percent high-tech employment, 1990–1992	0.59***	0.60***	0.39	0.47*
Percent construction employment, 1990	0.58***	0.54***	0.57**	0.48*
Percent of workers who are union members, 1990	−0.41**	−0.41**	−0.68***	−0.61***
Contains a state capital city	1.09***	1.11***	0.92*	0.91*
Percentage of African-American households that are "middle class," 1990	0.15		0.34	
Percentage of Latino households that are "middle class," 1990	−0.16		0.06	
Percentage of African-American *and* Latino households that are "middle class," 1990		0.04		0.59***
Percentage foreign born, 1990	−0.41*	−0.43*	−1.15***	−1.40****
Percentage people age 25+ with a high school education or less, 1990	−0.28	−0.27	−0.95***	−0.94***
Pseudo r-squared	0.1868	0.1951	0.1868	0.1951
Percentage predicted correctly	67.4	66.9	67.4	66.9
n	175	175	175	175

****$p < 0.01$; ***$p < 0.05$; **$p < 0.10$; *$p < 0.20$.

Union concentration has a negative impact on the probability of a region being in either of the two "growth with equity" categories with coefficients that are nearly the same. Unlike the basic logit, here we find some significance in the minority middle-class measure, but only when the Black and Latino middle classes are combined, and the effect is significant only in making a region more likely to be a really high performer (it is completely insignificant with a coefficient close to zero in pushing a region toward just the nearly high-performing category).

The percentage foreign born is significant and negative for both our categories but has a much larger coefficient for the really high performers. The share of people aged twenty-five and older with less than a high school education level is also negative for both outcomes but significant only for the really high performers. Given that we are controlling for education, this again suggests that there is something about a larger immigrant presence *per se* that may work against achieving growth with equity. This may be the sort of negative impact hinted at by Robert Putnam (2007) in his worries about the effects of diversity on social capital and community cohesion.

Conclusion

This chapter has reviewed a wide swath of quantitative work. The first portion of this work involved narrowing down to a few variables that could guide a first cut at case study selection, followed by a more qualitative scan that yielded the seven metropolitan cases we explore in the next two chapters. The second portion of the work involved creating more continuous measures – in the form of a z-score for growth and another for equity that were both de-trended against the census regions – and then using these variables for a preliminary quantitative assessment of the factors that might be associated with achieving growth *and* equity. In the process, we conducted both simple correlation analysis and more complex multivariate analysis using both linear regressions in which the dependent was a regionally adjusted z-score reflecting *either* growth or equity, and a logistic strategy in which the dependent variable was a categorical measure reflecting both growth *and* equity.

Sorting through the procedures, we find several relatively consistent trends. In general, hosting a state capital is good for equity and moderately good for growth. Construction employment has favorable impacts on equity and growth (although it may be affected itself by growth or perhaps reflect growth potential). Having a sizeable minority middle class is important for equity, perhaps because it creates a constituency with a recent experience of the bottom of the income distribution and also stronger familial and other ties to those not succeeding economically.

Damaging to both growth and equity are concentrations of working-age people with lower levels of education (a high school degree or less). A high presence of immigrants can be positive for growth but negative for equity. High-tech employment may help growth but does little for equity. The geographic concentration of the poor hurts equity while a geographic concentration of people of color, controlling for all other factors, may actually increase equity (perhaps through enhancing political voice). Unionization seems negative for growth but not for equity but the growth effect may be large enough to kick a region out of the "growth with equity" category – obviously a worrisome result for those who think that the labor movement is crucial for social justice and can jump in and play an important role in the new regionalism (Dean and Reynolds 2009).

A few results from the linear regressions that treated growth and equity as separate outcomes are worth highlighting. First, a broad measure of regionalist consciousness by local elites – attendance at the meetings of the business-oriented Alliance for Regional Stewardship – is associated with improvements in both growth and equity. Second, various measures of social separation and segregation – as well as our direct equity measure – have a *negative* impact on growth. Growth also has a positive impact on equity but the relationship is not quite as large. This combination of results suggests that building a more equitable growth path might help with a virtuous circle of economic achievement.

As we will see, many of these themes emerge in our case study work as well – there we find that state capitals are important, that a minority middle class is indeed an equity-enhancing part of the political landscape, and that regional consciousness – what we call the creation of an "epistemic community" in which there is a shared understanding of regional problems and shared sense of common fates – is key.

A word on the union and immigrant results is in order before moving forward with the qualitative analysis. To some extent, the negative impact of unions on growth may be an artifact of the association of union workers with older (and often slipping) industries. Moreover, the fact that unionization does not correlate with equity may be disappointing but not surprising: we are focusing here on improvements for those in the bottom quintile of the income distribution and unions have traditionally targeted their efforts at those slightly higher up the income ladder. But we must also acknowledge that we are dealing with a particular time period, 1980–2000; as described by Dean and Reynolds (2009), Milkman (2006) and others, a new labor movement has emerged that focuses on organizing low-wage workers, and new institutions set up by labor have been at the forefront of regional equity efforts.

As for immigrants, although the percentage foreign born does seem to have a negative impact on equity, the remedy is not, we think, to resist the inevitable demographic change (which also has a positive impact on growth) but rather to devise new strategies for successful immigrant integration. Once again, periodization is critical: the recent mobilization of immigrants around social justice issues as well as the suggestive results linking a Latino middle class with growth suggests that immigrants can be important allies for a "growth with equity" agenda.

Finally, we should be absolutely clear about the limits to the analysis above. Too frequently in economics and other social sciences, a researcher finds a statistically significant relationship between an independent variable and some specific outcome and suggests that this provides guidance on how to make change in the real world. But knowing that, say, education makes a difference to regional economic performance does not fully tell you how and why it does nor does it explain why some regions are able to build the political coalitions necessary to support the right education and job training and others are not.

Talking to the actual actors – as messy and inelegant as that may be – is critical to a full accounting, and so this chapter (and the work it describes) is really just a platform for the qualitative analysis that makes up the bulk of this volume. It is to that qualitative analysis that we now turn.

3   Getting it right

Introduction

There is a telling joke sometimes told about statisticians. One member of the profession shows up at a bar and is persuaded, after several drinks, to join a game of darts. With money on the line, the statistician's first toss lands a foot to the left of the target – and the second toss lands a foot to the right. With the gathered crowd still eager for the third toss, the statistician instead takes the mean of the two misses and pre-emptively declares "bulls-eye!"

On average, he is, of course, right – and we are, on average, likely to be right about the characteristics we have associated with achieving regional growth and equity in the regression analysis of Chapter 2. Certainly, the structure of employment, the role of the public sector, the proportion of minority middle-class families, the metro levels of educational attainment, and even the role of immigrants are all factors that we might reasonably assume are correlated with better performance on prosperity and inclusion. And taking the sort of empirically grounded approach to both case selection and hypotheses testing is, we think, superior to the usual inductive approaches based on hunch and ideology.

But this strategy, whatever its merits, also leaves out the stories of variation – when the dart falls squarely in the "good" quadrant of growth and equity, when it lands firmly in "bad" territory, and when it hovers around the medians. It also offers very limited insights into *how* economic prosperity and social inclusion come together, specifically the political, policy and planning processes that allow that to happen. To get inside that black box of causation, we need to talk to the actors as well as look at the outcomes – and that led us to a long journey into the field that had us identifying key respondents in our case study regions, criss-crossing America to meet and talk with them, and returning to our offices better informed about what this all looks like on the ground.

Indeed, we have been too well informed: the lengths of our first case study drafts were more appropriate for a multi-volume encyclopedia than for the thinner tome we offer here. In this chapter and the next, we try to tone down and tone up – we offer a much briefer review of what we found but we also try to be consistently connected to the theoretical and policy questions we have raised thus far. And although our focus is on what explains the past, our interviews were conducted in 2007 and 2008, a time when both the present and the future were very much on respondents' minds; hence, beyond explaining what shaped their region's designation (or not) as a "growth with equity" region, we also found our respondents talking about how the previous two decades were shaping regional development patterns and decision-making processes in the new millennium.

In this chapter, we review the four cases that emerged as performing relatively well on both growth and equity in the 1980s and 1990s: Kansas City, Nashville, Jacksonville, and Columbus. In the next chapter, we review the contrast cases: Denver, which bounced back, Sacramento, which slipped back, and Cleveland, which remained stuck back. Guiding our analysis in this chapter is a series of questions: *How* have growth and equity been able to go together? To what extent has this been the result of deliberate efforts to promote social inclusion in economic development strategies, or to consider growth in anti-poverty efforts – and to what extent has this been simply luck, the unintended consequences of development patterns pursued for other reasons? What are the political relationships between growth and equity constituents in these metropolitan regions – and what are the processes that did or can bring them together in common cause?

As we note in this chapter, Kansas City, Nashville, Jacksonville, and Columbus differ quite substantially in their history, their economic and political structures, and their metropolitan development strategies. At the same time, we stress that there are some common themes among these relatively strong performers on prosperity and inclusion, including strong regional government or governance processes, stabilizing influences of public sector employment and deeply rooted private sector businesses, and diverse regional leadership with equity advocates and growth constituencies coming together in processes that build some sense of common regional destiny.

Below, we begin by explaining the methodology used to develop the case studies and then turn to the case studies themselves. For each of these four regions, we provide a brief introduction to the region, orienting the readers with both a map and a brief statistical profile that offers selected data from 1980, 1990, 2000, and 2007. We then review each region's economic, political, and social characteristics and explain the features that seem most important in explaining its patterns of growth and equity. Although we try to briefly summarize some lessons at the end of the chapter, we offer a more detailed comparison in Chapter 5 when we discuss the themes that emerged across the cases, including the slip-back, bounce-back, and stuck-back cases reviewed in Chapter 4.

Methodology

Recall that we used an empirical sorting procedure to determine potential cases, then conducted a set of quick, mostly web-based profiles of twenty-five of them, following that up with a final selection process that coupled all that information with a series of other criteria, including demographic diversity and whether a region had been studied frequently in other efforts (with our bias being for more diversity and less past coverage). Those regional profiles were the foundation for our case study work, partly because they identified some initial factors shaping patterns of growth and equity in each of our case study regions but also because they provided an initial list of organizations and regional initiatives across four broad constituencies: the private sector, the public sector (including regional planning bodies and public–private partnerships), labor unions and other labor-affiliated institutions, and community-based and non-profit organizations.

One big initial task, once we had narrowed this list of twenty-five regions to our seven case studies, was to expand our census of the various organizations in each case study area. To do this, we combined additional web research and phone calls, seeking to develop profiles of the organizations as well as the region. Of the four different types of key constituencies, community-based organizations were often the hardest to identify. As a result, we also searched the websites of national networks for local affiliates, including four major national faith-based organizing networks,[1] the Jobs with Justice network,[2] the Partnership for Working Families network,[3] and ACORN, which at the time we were carrying out our research was still the largest and strongest national network of neighborhood-based advocacy organizations (Fisher 2009; Atlas 2010). In all four sectors, our goal was to generate a list of possible key informants, and identify prominent initiatives in which the organizations were involved.

We then scheduled multi-day site visits to each case study region, interviewing as many people in each of our four broad sectors as we could fit into schedules. In each area, several respondents were not available in person but made themselves available for phone calls either before the visit or after. For both in-person visits and phone calls, we developed a detailed interview protocol that guided a discussion that lasted between one and two hours, depending on respondent availability. The questions were focused on four broad areas:

- *Structures and decision making in the respondent's own organization*, in an effort to gauge the breadth of constituencies represented in the organization, and how strategic decisions are made about priorities and focus projects.
- *Collaborative relationships*, in an effort to assess the breadth and depth of collaborative relationships cultivated by the organization with other organizations and with other constituencies that might not be their primary concern.
- *Economic growth*, in order to assess the organization's perspectives on factors shaping economic growth in the region and their own engagement with economic growth processes and policies in the region.
- *Social equity*, in order to assess the organization's perspectives on factors shaping shared prosperity and inclusion in the region, and their own engagement with efforts designed to promote equity in the region.

The specific number of interviews conducted in each region varied from ten to eighteen, with a total of 102 people interviewed; a full list of interviewees is provided in the Appendix.[4] These interviews were supplemented with detailed secondary research on regional dynamics from both web-based sources and academic literature; this research occurred both before the visits and after, particularly since the in-person interviews often raised new questions or illustrated new dynamics worth considering.

In all, this data gathering was designed to enable us to gain an understanding of regional decision-making processes, the nature of collaborative relationships, and the extent to which major growth-oriented and equity-oriented constituencies were aware of and engaged with processes related to economic prosperity and social inclusion. Obviously there are finer nuances of regional development and political dynamics in each region that we were not able to capture in the time available to us. But our goal was not to write comprehensive historical studies of any single region, but to identify broad patterns across multiple regions. We are confident in our methodology to that end.

Kansas City: homegrown opportunities in the heartland

Being in the middle often holds negative connotations: middling, middle-brow, middle-of-the-road. Indeed, noted (and left-leaning) political commentator Jim Hightower (1998) famously said, "there's nothing in the middle of the road but yellow stripes and dead armadillos."

For Kansas City, being in the 'middle' – literally the geographic middle of America – has created challenges, but also a healthy sense of community that has benefitted the region. Derided as "fly-over country" by coastal residents, the region has struggled to attract outside investment and still lacks a world-class research university. In the middle of two states – one traditionally "blue" (Missouri) and one traditionally "red" (Kansas) – and encompassing a fragmented and sprawling region, implementing a uniform vision for growth (let alone equitable growth) would seem to be a challenge (Wood 2008). (See Figure 3.1 for a map of the metro area. Note that we break up the three principal cities into the *primary* city – Kansas City, Missouri – and *other major* cities – Kansas City, Kansas and Overland Park, Kansas – using a method explained in the footnote and carried through to the other metro areas.)[5]

But for Kansas City, being in the middle has also meant stability – and homegrown opportunities. With strong community roots, major philanthropic investments, largely local business leadership, and a diversified economy rooted in the major trans-continental transportation networks that cross through the region, Kansas City has built a record of both growth and inclusion that was strong in the 1980s and 1990s, especially relative to the rest of the Midwest – strong enough to have had it land in what we termed the "consistently good" category in terms of our earlier ranking system.

A number of dynamics seem to be working together in the Kansas City area to have made this happen. One factor is the relative diversity of its economy. Without being dependent on a single industry, it was somewhat buffered from the de-industrialization that hit much of the Midwest over the past handful of decades (see the moderate decline in the manufacturing share depicted in Table 3.1).[6] There is also a unique culture of boosterism or 'giving back' within the business and philanthropic community. In part supported by the philanthropic culture,

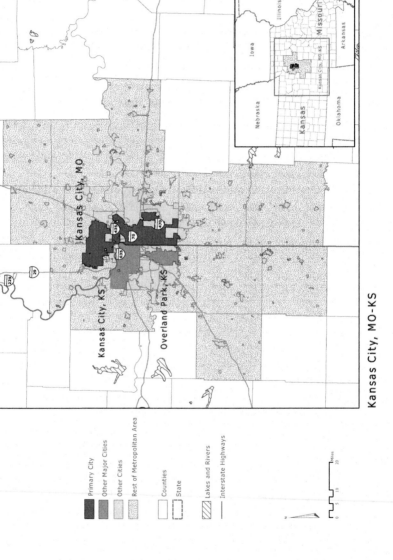

Kansas City, MO-KS

Primary City
Other Major Cities
Other Cities
Rest of Metropolitan Area
Counties
State
Lakes and Rivers
Interstate Highways

Figure 3.1 Kansas City metropolitan area.

the region has a strong history and presence of African-American community development corporations with deep-rooted traditions of community organizing.

Our sense is that the strength and comprehensive nature of public sector and regional leadership are the most important reasons for Kansas City's positive record. For example, the metropolitan planning organization (MPO), the Mid-America Regional Council (MARC), takes a somewhat unique comprehensive approach – dealing with a wide range of economic, environmental, and social issues that go far beyond the typical transportation planning on which most metropolitan planning organizations focus. The area enjoys a solid workforce development program feeding into a community college system that maintains strong partnerships with major employers in the region. The region gained a particular cohesion following a 2001 report from Citistates, a consulting firm headed by Neal Peirce and Curtis Johnson that is famous for its reports on metropolitan futures; this one focused on the challenges of sprawl and division, and the simple fact that it was commissioned by a local foundation and printed in the major regional newspaper is suggestive of what we term later an "epistemic community" – a set of shared understandings that can inform decision making in positive ways. Although these factors alone cannot explain all of the region's growth and equity patterns, they do seem to have an important and positive impact in the right direction.

Background to the region

Founded in 1853 along the Missouri River at the confluence of the Kansas River, Kansas City, Missouri saw an expanded role as a trade hub with the arrival of the railroads in the 1860s – and trade remains an important economic sector to this day. Kansas City anchors the fifteen-county metropolitan statistical area (MSA) that today straddles the Missouri and Kansas state border (see Figure 3.1). With just over two million residents in 2009, the entire region has one of the more fragmented government structures in the United States, with two states, fifteen counties, and about 160 municipalities or census-designated places.

The divides in the region – particularly between Missouri and Kansas – run deep. For example, Kansas was admitted to the union in 1861 as a free state, while Missouri remained a slave state – indicative of the "deep unresolved issues of race" that the region continues to face to this day (Johnson and Peirce 2002: 12, January 6). Within Kansas City, Missouri, particularly after 1950 when whites began leaving the city for the suburbs,[7] Troost Avenue, running south from the City's Central Business District, came to be known as "Troost Wall" – and it is still a major dividing line between African-American neighborhoods to the east and white neighborhoods to the west. In the 1990s, Mayor Emanuel Cleaver described Troost Avenue as the "Mason–Dixon Line of Kansas City" – indicative of the ways that the deep historical divides over slavery continue to reverberate in contemporary racial divides in the region (Spivak 2005: 91).

Another split: the urban core. The Missouri side is noticeably more urban: much of the regional history and the most prominent current cultural amenities

Table 3.1 Select demographic and economic data for the Kansas City metropolitan area

	Metropolitan characteristics	1980	1990	2000	2007
	Total CBSA population	1,508,283	1,636,528	1,836,038	1,980,977
	Principal cities	690,960	696,703	738,984	739,432
	Suburbs	817,323	939,825	1,097,054	1,241,545
	Race/ethnicity (%)				
	Non-Hispanic white	84	84	79	77
	Black	12	12	12	12
	Latino	2	3	5	7
	Asian/Pacific Islander (API)	1	1	2	2
	Other	0	1	2	2
	Percent foreign born	2.1	2.2	4.4	5.9
	Average annual earnings per job (2007 dollars) (place of work basis)	40,432	40,788	48,645	50,051
	Poverty rate (% persons)	9.2	10.0	8.5	10.3
	Principal cities	12.2	13.7	12.6	15.1
	Suburbs	6.5	7.2	5.8	7.4
	By percent federal poverty level				
	Below 100%	9.2	10.0	8.5	10.3
	Between 100% and 149%	7.1	7.1	6.4	7.6
	Between 150% and 199%	8.6	8.8	7.5	7.9
	Above 200%	75.1	74.0	77.5	74.2
	Poverty concentration				
	Percent of CBSA poor in high poverty tracts (poverty rate > 20%)	39	40	34	39
	Percent of CBSA poor in very high poverty tracts (poverty rate > 40%)	7	9	5	11
	80-20 household income ratio	4.1	3.9	3.7	4.1
	Income differentials (%)				
	Median Black household income relative to median white household income	62	57	60	52
	Median Latino household income relative to median white household income	87	85	75	59
	Median API household income relative to median white household income	77	87	97	100

Demography and immigration

Income and poverty

Metropolitan characteristics	1980	1990	2000	2007
Educational attainment (population 25 years and older) (%)				
Less than high school	26	18	13	10
High school only	36	32	29	30
Some college	20	27	29	29
Bachelor's degree	13	15	19	21
Graduate or professional degree	5	7	10	11
Workers by industry (total employed population 16 years and older) (%)				
Agriculture and mining	1	2	1	1
Construction	5	5	7	6
Manufacturing	17	12	10	9
Transportation, warehousing, and utilities	9	8	6	6
Wholesale trade	6	6	4	4
Retail trade	17	17	16	17
Finance, insurance, and real estate	7	8	9	9
Professional services	5	7	8	9
Health services	8	9	9	10
Information	5	6	7	6
Education	7	7	8	8
Other services	8	9	10	10
Public administration	6	5	5	4
Public sector employment	15	14	13	13
Principal cities–suburbs job distribution				
Percent of jobs in principal cities	61	57	53	50
Percent of jobs in suburbs	39	43	47	50
Job growth over preceding decade (last 7 years for 2007) (%)				
All CBSA	–	16	15	5
Principal cities	–	9	6	1
Suburbs	–	29	27	10
Spatial segregation by income and race				
Poverty dissimilarity index	36.6	39.5	38.5	31.5
African American–white dissimilarity index	77.2	73.2	70.9	52.7
Latino–white dissimilarity index	40.9	41.3	45.5	30.1
All people of color–white dissimilarity index	65.3	60.4	54.0	41.3

Education and employment

Segregation

(e.g. the museums, nightlife, and sporting events), as well as the persistent problems typical to urban areas (e.g. concentrated poverty, dismal schools, and disinvestment) are located in Kansas City, Missouri. Although Kansas City, Kansas has substantial problems of urban poverty and decay, the politics of the Kansas side of the region are driven more by suburban interests and politics, it is home to a high proportion of the region's rich and powerful families, and it is also the part of the region experiencing the most rapid growth – particularly in Johnson County in the southwest part of the region. Since 1980, nearly 90 percent of the region's population growth has been in the suburbs; the principal cities in the region were basically stable in population between 1980 and 1990, grew at about a third of the rate of the suburbs in the 1990s, and remained flat between 2000 and 2007 (see Table 3.1).

Although the metro's traditional racial divide, as in much of the Midwest, is between Black and white, the number of foreign born living in the Kansas City area more than doubled in the 1990s, with many settling directly in the suburbs (Brookings Institution 2003a). Latinos are the city's largest immigrant group, followed by Vietnamese; since the mid-1990s, refugees fleeing other civil wars and upheavals in Bosnia, Africa, and the Middle East have also flocked to the city. By 2007, the metro area's reported population was about 77 percent white, 12 percent African American, 7 percent Latino, and 2 percent Asian/Pacific Islander (see Table 3.1).

Explaining growth and inclusion in Kansas City

Given the fragmented nature of governance in the metropolitan region, the ongoing bi-state tensions, and the all too typical racial and spatial (e.g. city versus suburb) divisions in the region, it might seem surprising that the region should be able to exhibit the types of growth and equity characteristics that led to its selection as a focus for our research. Yet in our interviews with public, private, and civic leadership in the region, few of them were particularly surprised. Although they could not point to a single process or organization that had helped ensure that growth and equity went together in the region, they described a diverse set of factors and actors that have come together at different moments in time, including the diversity of the regional economy, a culture of 'giving back', and leadership in the public sector.

Economic and business leadership

In discussing the economy and the role of business, two themes came up consistently in our interviews. The first was the diverse industrial make-up of the region, something that allows the economy to adapt to single industries coming and going. The second was the fact that business leaders and entrepreneurs – more than in other regions – are from the area; being less "footloose," they are more likely to keep in mind the long-term prosperity of the region, which is also their home, not just their business location.

Unlike the auto industry in Detroit or the steel industry in Gary, there is no single industry driving the regional economy. Transportation is one major industry, as the region's central location has made it a transportation hub for both passengers and freight by road and rail. Telecommunications is also important, with Sprint being the region's largest private employer (with 12,000 workers in 2009).[8] Manufacturing is important, but specific products produced in the region span the gamut. The top twenty manufactures in the Kansas City area include well-known firms such as Ford Motor Company, General Motors, Hallmark Cards, Honeywell Aerospace, and Garmin Ltd but there is also a wide range of other lesser-known companies in industries ranging from pet food to heating, ventilation, and air conditioning equipment.

As is common in the Midwest, the region experienced de-industrialization in the early 1980s, losing some 30,000 manufacturing jobs – yet unlike much of the Midwest, the regional economy has stayed relatively strong.[9] This is in large part because the financial, government, communication, and tourism sectors of the economy have continued to grow even as the large automobile manufacturing and agribusiness sectors have declined. Public sector employment, including the federal government's regional offices of Health and Human Services (HHS), the Federal Reserve, the Environmental Protection Agency (EPA), and the Federal Emergency Management Agency (FEMA) along with state and local sector public sector employment, have had an important stabilizing effect.

Regional leaders also emphasize the deep roots of Kansas City's business leadership. The region is headquarters to a number of homegrown nationwide and worldwide companies who have retained their headquarters in the region. This includes H&R Block, founded in 1955 by Henry and Richard Bloch, which has grown to be a $3.9 billion revenue company and claims to prepare one in every seven U.S. tax returns; Garmin, the global navigation and communications devices company, founded in 1989 by Gary Burrell and Min Kao, which has since grown to have a worldwide workforce of 7,000 and an annual revenue of over $2 billion; and Hallmark Cards, founded in 1910 by Joyce Hall, which, despite worldwide success, remains a privately held family-owned firm.[10] Another prominent homegrown company is Marion Laboratories, founded in 1950 by Ewing Marion Kaufmann, which grew to have revenues of nearly $1 billion in 1989, before it merged with Merrell Dow Pharmaceuticals, a division of Dow Chemical Company.[11] The company subsequently went through a series of buyouts, first by Hoechst AG of Germany (in 1995), which kept the North American headquarters of its pharmaceutical division in Kansas City, Aventis (in 1999) and later Sanofi-Aventis (in 2004), and finally Cerner (in 2006), a $1.9 billion revenue bioinformatics company that retains its worldwide headquarters in North Kansas City (Mayer 2007).[12] What starts in Kansas City seems to stay in Kansas City.

This does not mean that regional leaders are not looking forward to economic change. Business leaders, for example, launched Kansas City's biotech sector, replete with workforce development pipelines. Jim Stowers, Jr. – who founded American Century Mutual Fund Company in 1958 – and his wife created and endowed the Stowers Institute for Medical Research with over $2 billion in the early 1990s, the largest endowment in the world solely devoted to basic life sciences research (Johnson and Peirce 2002; Mayer 2007). The Hall Family Foundation, of Hallmark Cards, and the Kauffman Foundation together pledged $150 million a year for ten years to bioscience- and life science-related initiatives, including workforce training dollars for the growing bioscience industry (Johnson and Peirce 2002). The Kansas City Area Life Sciences Institute[13] – a regional consortium – has increased the level of funding for biosciences research in the region to about $530 million a year, while generating stronger cooperation among business leaders, medical institutions, state universities, and workforce development actors (Johnson and Peirce 2002).

More broadly, the business-led civic organization – the Civic Council of Greater Kansas City – has played an important role in shaping the region's growth. The CEO-led, research-based regional organization was formed in 1964 with fifteen CEOs of large companies headquartered in Kansas City. Today, more than ninety high-ranking business executives belong to the Civic Council. Their mission is to "study, confer, develop and implement a vision" of the bi-state region that leads to a high quality of life. One example of this: the organization sponsored a revitalization study which has been credited with creating unity behind a downtown vision that has garnered local government and business support.[14]

Although the hometown character of business leadership matters for promoting growth, it can also matter for paying attention to equity. Pastor and colleagues (2000) argue that businesses may want to do more about poverty if they feel that they cannot easily run away from the consequences of neglect – and point to the anti-poverty initiatives of business leaders in Charlotte as an example. The stickier the capital, the more inclusive the growth – and capital seems to stick to Kansas City.

Philanthropy

Commitment to place is also evident in the many non-profits and foundations that business leaders have helped to create. A culture of "giving back" was strongly cited throughout our fieldwork – and Kansas City area foundations give grant money at the sixth highest rate per capita amongst the twenty-five largest metropolitan areas (Spivak 2005).[15]

The Ewing Marion Kauffman Foundation represents what is paradigmatic of Kansas City philanthropy – a foundation with money from a homegrown industry, giving back in a big way to the region. The Kauffman Foundation was established in the late 1960s to advance education and entrepreneurship and today's dense philanthropy network continues to focus in those areas and other targeted initiatives. Another example is the Hall Family Foundation (from the Hallmark Company), which had nearly $750 million in assets in 2009. Similarly, local banker William T. Kemper also left a legacy of two philanthropic funds as seems to be common for the estates of prominent local businessmen. As a result, the Greater Kansas City Community Foundation has gone from a base of small donor funds to the seventh largest community foundation in the country, with over $1.1 billion in assets.[16]

The philanthropic community and its close ties with business leaders often results in support for each other's initiatives. For example, following the substantial donations that led to the founding of the Stowers Institute for Medical Research, the business leaders in the Civic Council of Greater Kansas City came together to see how they could leverage this into expanding the life sciences cluster in the region – the result was the Kansas City Life Sciences Institute, a regional consortia of universities and health centers with a $1 million annual budget financed by grants from a range of local foundations and which has made substantial strides in its goal of making the Kansas City region a nationally recognized center for life sciences research, development, and commercialization. In a similar example of coordinated philanthropy, the Kauffman Foundation has championed an aggressive agenda to fund urban education while others are working to fund higher education and workforce development initiatives. Philanthropy, in short, is not in short supply – and it is often directed to areas that can help both growth and equity.

African-American leaders and community organizations

Another factor in Kansas City's development is the presence of a strong African-American leadership network. Although the region has a history of racial discrimination, it also has a history of resistance, including by neighborhood and community-based groups that were initially nurtured by federal programs, the Community Development Block Grant program, and the generosity of local foundations. Strikingly, one of the leaders emerging from that milieu, Reverend Emanuel Cleaver, was elected as Kansas City's first Black mayor – a significant event partly because it occurred when the city was still only about 30 percent African American. Although a tribute to the cross-constituency appeal of Cleaver, it also suggested the openness of the city and the ways in which the city has created opportunities for Black leadership.

This is not to say that discussion about the direction of Kansas City has been without conflict. In the early 1980s, the agendas of community-based groups often conflicted with the growth agenda of the business leaders, especially around the emphasis of business leaders on downtown development (e.g. AT&T Town Pavilion[17]) and large capital projects (e.g. airport development and professional sports facilities) versus funding for small capital improvements (e.g. sidewalks, park improvements, sewers, etc.) and basic services, including along Troost Avenue, the symbolic (and historically residential) dividing line between Black and white in Kansas City (Gotham 2002).

Former mayor and subsequent congressman Emanuel Cleaver is credited with galvanizing the power of Black churches to participate in these debates. But he was not alone: former NFL football stars and community activists Jim Brown and Curtis McClinton founded the Black Economic Union of Greater

Kansas City (BEU), the oldest of Kansas City's thirteen community development corporations.[18] Finally, Communities Creating Opportunity (CCO), founded over thirty years ago, has leveraged more than $20 million in housing and community investment and continues to train leaders across twenty-four congregations and communities representing 18,000 people throughout Kansas City.[19]

Black leadership has been important in other venues as well. Once the receptionist, in 1997 Bridgette Williams became president of the Greater Kansas City AFL-CIO Central Labor Council at the age of twenty-eight. The first African-American woman to head a metropolitan-wide Labor Council in the United States, she supported capital investments in the city but on the condition that downtown development initiatives would involve union labor. To accomplish this, she and the labor council sought to "elect and recruit elected officials that are driving a working people's agenda."[20] She also built partnerships with atypical partners, such as the Kansas City Area Chamber of Commerce – and was able to leverage her relationships to rally business support to defeat a proposed ballot measure that would have banned affirmative action in the state of Missouri (Gross 2008). Further evidence of both her skill and the fluidity of relationships: in 2009 she stepped down from the Labor Council and became deputy director of the Heavy Constructors Association of the Greater Kansas City Area, a business group.

In short, the African-American community has championed the causes of its neighborhoods and communities and has worked to focus attention on the needs of long-time residents, marrying the need for downtown development and regional economic growth with some attention to equity. As we will see, such Black activism seems to be crucial to striking a similar balance in several of our other cases as well.

Planning the region

One of the more striking institutional features in the Kansas City region is the impressive level of comprehensive planning carried out by the area's MPO. The Mid-America Regional Council serves as the association of city and county governments and the MPO for the bi-state Kansas City region.[21] As the MPO, it is responsible for delegating federal transportation funds – but it does much, much more. Crossing its own jurisdictional boundaries, MARC takes on a host of issues, including transportation, childcare, aging, emergency services, public safety, and environmental management, that go well beyond the province of most MPOs, producing reports and monitoring data on current conditions, challenges, and progress in the region.[22]

Consider MARC's Metro Outlook project. This initiative was designed to develop a unified understanding of the challenges facing the Kansas City region, and to develop a comprehensive strategy for addressing them. The first Metro Outlook report, published in 2001, collected a variety of indicators on everything from time for family, poverty levels, and charitable giving, to economic productivity, regional exports, and job growth. It developed four main conclusions: (1)

that concentrated poverty – particularly in the African-American community – was creating problems not only in the urban core but also increasingly in surrounding areas; (2) that suburban expansion was costly to everyone, including the urban core, first-ring suburbs, developing suburbs, and the natural environment; (3) that public spending on new infrastructure helped to improve the region's innovative capacity but was being resourced by a limited budget; and (4) that without such infrastructure investments the economic outlook for the region was uncertain (MARC 2001). These findings were reinforced by other reports that appeared in subsequent years – most prominently a major study conducted by the Citistates Group (Johnson and Peirce 2002) and another by the Brookings Institution (2002).

In both the initial report and a 2007 update, MARC offered an explicit model that integrates an analysis of three intertwined systems – eco-system processes, social networks and trust relationships, and entrepreneurship and business development – into a comprehensive model for the region. Figure 3.2 shows the model: for those who are very linear, this may seem way too confusing. Perhaps, but the fascinating take-away from this volume is the emphasis on social capital and communities in a model seeking to determine the elements of growth. Typical of the tone of the 2007 report is the following:

> Fragmentation hurts when the region's disadvantaged students are clustered in urban school districts with high poverty and crime in their surrounding communities, so that many middle-income families feel they have no choice but to move out to developing suburbs. As a region, this causes us to spend more on police than most of our peers, to less effect, and build new roads faster than we can maintain them . . . at best our fragmentation makes us inefficient. At worst, it diminishes our opportunities and competitiveness.[23]

Moreover, the overall policy recommendations are a fascinating mix: boost the region's innovation capacity, create more focused growth, break down racial disparities in incomes and assets, and organize for success, particularly across traditional divides. MARC also developed indicators in seven different broad areas not only to track the region's progress, but also to benchmark it against nine other peer regions.[24]

In a highly politicized metro region, MARC creates a neutral space where leaders can convene. Drawing on its regional network, which includes the business-oriented Civic Council, philanthropic foundations, workforce development agencies, public schools, and others, MARC has developed a range of other initiatives designed to improve governance and the quality of life. These initiatives include "Creating Quality Places," a set of guiding principles for quality development; a "Natural Resources Inventory," providing planners and developers with detailed maps of natural assets and ecological features; "Smart Moves," a regional plan for improved transit; and the First Suburbs Coalition, which brings first-ring suburbs together to address the common challenges facing these older communities with aging infrastructure and lack of greenfields for development.[25]

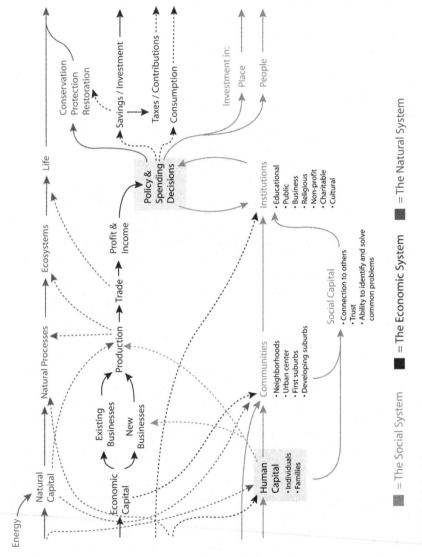

Figure 3.2 Metro Outlook 2.0 model.

MARC is not a full regional government – this isn't Portland – but rather a regional coordinating body. Local jurisdictions retain their control over land use decisions and collaborate with MARC to varying degrees depending on the issue.[26] Nonetheless, MARC is a high-functioning metropolitan organization focusing on a broad range of issues, advocating cooperation among several initiatives, and shaping the growth of the region through its efforts at knowledge building and advocacy. The Brookings Institution cites MARC as a strong example of proactive regional leadership that other places in the United States should try to emulate because of its ability to spur regionwide discussions on issues ranging from open space to childcare (Katz 2007).

Working for success

Workforce development programs in the Kansas City region are also exemplary – producing effective programming that helps meet the skilled workforce training needs of business. According to one informant, after a visit from former president Bill Clinton, Kansas City became one of the models for the creation of Workforce Investment Boards (WIBs), a key feature of the Workforce Investment Act of 1998.[27] One example of workforce innovation in the region was the creation in 1994 of the Business and Technology Center, an initiative of the region's Metropolitan Community Colleges, as an economic and workforce development arm that provides consulting, development, and training for Kansas City area businesses and organizations. In 2002, the Center expanded its facilities, nearly tripling in size, and became a full college, the Business & Technology Campus (BTC). BTC has developed strong partnerships with prominent area employers, including Harley-Davidson, Honeywell, Sprint, Ford Motor Company, and others. The partnership with Harley-Davidson, for example, had resulted at the time of our interview in an eleven-year relationship of contract training in which Harley-Davidson had donated custom machinery to make the BTC machine tools shop state-of-the-art, and counted on BTC to not only provide training but also handle job applications and other employment assessments (e.g. team-building skills and basic math and reading abilities) to the point that reportedly all new hires at Harley-Davidson were coming directly from BTC training programs.[28]

The development of a self-sustaining call center by BTC in collaboration with regional businesses is another example that shows the ability of the region to adapt for new growth with an eye for inclusivity. In the 1990s, the project was developed to both fill a gap in industry – as a major location for call centers, there was a shortage of customer service representatives in the region – and provide jobs for economically and educationally disadvantaged individuals (Ream et al. 2001). AT&T, Lucent Technologies, Gateway, Sprint, DST, Citibank, and the Missouri Departments of Workforce Development and Elementary and Secondary Education contributed equipment and funding for the state-of-the-art call center training facility at the BTC. Training dollars were provided by the Full Employment Council (for welfare participants) and the Missouri Department of Elementary and Secondary Education. Workers with barriers to employment were sent by Project Refocus and the Kansas Private Industry Council – both organizations contributing funds as well. With such a network of participants and stakeholders, the Call Center Training Program at the BTC became well known and received awards, including the 1999 American Association of Community Colleges/U.S. Department of Labor Workforce Development Award and the Vision 2000 Model of Excellence Award (Ream et al. 2001).

Kansas City has also paid attention to training for manufacturing and was one of thirteen regions in 2005 to receive a first-generation grant from the Department of Labor's Workforce Innovation in Regional Economic Development (WIRED) program. Meanwhile, Project Prepare is a pre-apprenticeship program to draw more minorities and women into construction work that is a joint effort of the Full Employment Council, Kansas City area unions and contractors, the Kansas City AFL-CIO, and the City.[29] This regional workforce capacity is not a surprise – it is quite consistent that a region with a "give back" attitude and homegrown business leaders would tend to invest in the local workforce.

Summing up: Kansas City in it together

We do not mean to make too much of KC's success: after all, the comparison Midwest metros against which it is benchmarked include some of the metropolitan areas most devastated by the de-industrializations of the 1980s and 1990s: Detroit and Flint, Michigan; Cleveland and Youngstown, Ohio; Gary, Indiana; and Peoria, Illinois. But to the extent that Kansas City did score better – and more stably – on encouraging growth and improving equity, some of the reasons seem clear.

For one thing, the region has a favorable environment in terms of industrial diversity, a solid base of public employment, and innovative workforce development programs. We would contend, however, that there are other less tangible features of the region's political economy that are equally important, including a strong, stable, and reliable business leadership with deep roots in the area; although this leadership may be driven too much by an "old boys" network, at least these "boys" (and now some girls) have a sense of social responsibility and demonstrated philanthropic generosity. Kansas City also has a committed African-American leadership, with a solid network of community development corporations and organizing groups and a history of commitment to neighborhood investment – and as African Americans rose in political prominence, this helped to fortify the voice for equity.

An even less tangible – and perhaps more important – factor is the region's MPO. In contrast to most MPOs, which are generally considered weak and ineffectual, partly because of jurisdictional limitations on the decisions they can make, MARC has been able to step out of the transportation straightjacket, consider a wider range of issues, and convene actors together for a broad regional vision. This is not just the province of the public sector – regional business and philanthropic leaders have also been critical to the development of a regional consciousness – and such a regional consciousness does not mean agreement by all actors on every principle and policy. But it does mean that there is broad acceptance of a common destiny and this, we argue later, is one of the fundamental building blocks of "just growth" – we need to think that we're all in this together to make sure that policies are such that we prosper together.

Nashville: consolidation and collaboration in the Music City

> Large enough to be a big city, and small enough to know everyone. Everyone is expected to be involved.
>
> (Jerry Williams, Leadership Nashville)[30]

Music is often described as an international language – the "universal language of mankind" in the words of Henry Wadsworth Longfellow (1835: 4) – with the ability to bring people together across cultures, backgrounds, and beliefs. Perhaps Nashville, nicknamed the Music City and the second biggest music production center in the United States, has taken this characteristic to heart. The region's patterns of prosperity and inclusion – one of only three southern metropolitan regions to show positive patterns of growth and equity in both the 1980s and 1990s – suggest a region making important connections.

We do not mean to make too much of the success. Talk to folks in Nashville and you will hear that poverty remains high, racial and income inequality are substantial, city and suburb divisions remain significant, and new tensions are emerging as the immigrant population grows in this historically two-toned metro. Yet – and we try to square this in what follows – the poverty rate declined from 11.8 percent in 1980 to 10.3 percent in 2000, and the 80–20 income ratio decreased from 4.1 in 1990 to 3.9 in 2000, placing it squarely as a better performer in a tough census division for equity (see Table 3.2).

The reasons are complex. Nashville, like other cities in the south, benefitted from manufacturing plant relocations from the north. This and the strong music industry and the large public sector – Nashville is the state capital of Tennessee – has produced economic growth numbers that are the envy of many competitor regions. Nashville's city–county consolidated government – one of the closest approximations of a regional government – has allowed for better management and investment in the large urban core. The region's strong Black middle class, often attributed to the presence of historically Black colleges and universities in the area, serves as a bridge between equity and growth concerns. Finally, a number of regional associations help ensure that advocates for growth and activists for equity are communicating with each other in substantive ways.

Background to the region

Founded in 1779 and named state capital in 1843, much of Nashville's early growth and development was due to its strategic location on the Cumberland River. Eventually a rail hub as well, during the Civil War Nashville was the first southern state capital to fall, in part because the transportation networks made it

Table 3.2 Select demographic and economic data for the Nashville–Davidson–Murfreesboro metropolitan area

Metropolitan characteristics	1980	1990	2000	2007
Total CBSA population	913,076	1,048,176	1,311,789	1,521,751
Principal cities	488,496	533,296	615,675	687,906
Suburbs	424,580	514,880	696,114	833,845
Race/ethnicity (%)				
Non-Hispanic white	83	83	79	76
Black	15	15	15	16
Latino	1	1	3	5
Asian/Pacific Islander (API)	1	1	2	2
Other	0	0	2	1
Percent foreign born	1.3	1.7	4.5	6.7
Average annual earnings per job (2007 dollars) (place of work basis)	35,441	38,160	46,733	49,827
Poverty rate (% persons)	11.8	11.7	10.3	11.8
Principal cities	12.8	13.7	13.6	12.9
Suburbs	10.6	9.7	7.7	10.6
By percent federal poverty level				
Below 100%	11.8	11.7	10.3	11.8
Between 100% and 149%	9.2	7.7	7.3	8.3
Between 150% and 199%	10.4	9.3	7.9	8.6
Above 200%	68.7	71.3	74.5	71.3
Poverty concentration				
Percent of CBSA poor in high poverty tracts (poverty rate > 20%)	35	39	31	45
Percent of CBSA poor in very high poverty tracts (poverty rate > 40%)	16	14	7	8
80–20 household income ratio	4.3	4.1	3.9	4.1
Income differentials (%)				
Median Black household income relative to median white household income	62	58	65	60
Median Latino household income relative to median white household income	70	94	74	71
Median API household income relative to median white household income	100	98	98	115

Demography and immigration

Income and poverty

Metropolitan characteristics	1980	1990	2000	2007
Educational attainment (population 25 years and older) (%)				
Less than high school	37	27	20	15
High school only	31	29	29	31
Some college	16	23	25	25
Bachelor's degree	12	14	17	19
Graduate or professional degree	5	7	9	9
Workers by industry (total employed population 16 years and older) (%)				
Agriculture and mining	2	2	1	2
Construction	6	6	7	8
Manufacturing	18	14	12	11
Transportation, warehousing, and utilities	6	6	6	5
Wholesale trade	5	5	5	4
Retail trade	16	17	17	17
Finance, insurance, and real estate	7	7	7	8
Professional services	4	6	9	9
Health services	8	9	9	10
Information	5	5	5	4
Education	8	8	8	8
Other services	8	10	10	11
Public administration	6	4	4	4
Public sector employment	14	12	10	10
Principal cities–suburbs job distribution				
Percent of jobs in principal cities	67	70	67	62
Percent of jobs in suburbs	33	30	33	38
Job growth over preceding decade (last 7 years for 2007) (%)				
All CBSA	–	28	28	13
Principal cities	–	34	22	5
Suburbs	–	17	41	30
Spatial segregation by income and race				
Poverty dissimilarity index	31.4	35.3	33.2	38.8
African American–white dissimilarity index	65.0	61.3	58.1	65.8
Latino–white dissimilarity index	21.8	37.9	46.0	48.9
All people of color–white dissimilarity index	60.7	56.2	50.4	48.4

Side labels: Education and employment · Segregation

a strategic location. After reconstruction, Nashville became a center for printing (e.g. National Baptist Publishing Board), education (e.g. Vanderbilt University and Fisk University), and distribution (Nashville Public Library 2011). Today, Nashville has several nicknames: "Athens of the South," reflecting its multiple universities; "Buckle of the Bible Belt," reflecting its large Christian community, including the publishing arms of the Southern Baptist Convention, the United Methodist Church, and Thomas Nelson (the world's largest producer of Bibles); and "Music City," reflecting the region's strong music industry.

The Nashville–Davidson–Murfreesboro metropolitan statistical area, comprised of thirteen counties, is one of the fastest-growing areas in the central South (see Figure 3.3 for a map of the area and Table 3.2 for data on population). Demographically, the region has been mostly white and Black, but immigrants have been increasing the diversity of the region. As of 2007, 76 percent of residents were white; 16 percent were African American; 2 percent were Asian; and 5 percent were Hispanic/Latino. The percentage of the regional population who are foreign born has risen from only 1.3 percent in 1980 to 6.7 percent in 2007, with the share of foreign born in the city of Nashville several percentage points higher. Latin Americans constitute the largest foreign-born population in Nashville, with Mexico the largest sending country to the region (more than a quarter of all immigrants) (Lotspeich, Fix et al. 2003). Other significant immigrant-sending regions include Asia (at about one-third, including the Middle East), Europe (16 percent), and Africa (8 percent).

Nashville is a pioneer in consolidated metropolitan governance. As early as 1915, a city commission in Nashville recommended massive annexation and the formation of a single city–county government (Hawkins 1966). In 1962, a solid majority of voters – from both the city and outside the city – voted for the creation of a consolidated city–county government. A blue city in a red state, since 1963 all of Nashville's mayors have been Democratic – and in 2008 Barack Obama carried Nashville with 60 percent of the vote while John McCain won the state by fifteen points.

Nashville's economy is primarily driven by healthcare, education, and retail and wholesale trade – all areas with generally solid growth. Healthcare and education have the added benefit of being less sensitive to economic cycles. There are an estimated 250 healthcare companies with operations in Nashville that work at the multi-state, national, or international level (i.e. not just locally serving health centers). One of the most prominent of the public healthcare companies in the region is HCA (originally the Hospital Corporation of America), co-founded in 1968 by former Republican Senate Majority Leader Bill Frist's father Dr. Thomas Frist Sr. A 2010 economic impact study reported that the healthcare sector contributed $29.2 billion total to the Nashville area economy and accounted for 113,453 direct employees and another 97,606 indirect and induced jobs. The entire cluster of healthcare-related industries represented about 15 percent of the region's employment, and 26 percent of all job growth between 2004 and 2008, making the cluster larger than any other non-governmental economic sector (Arik 2010).

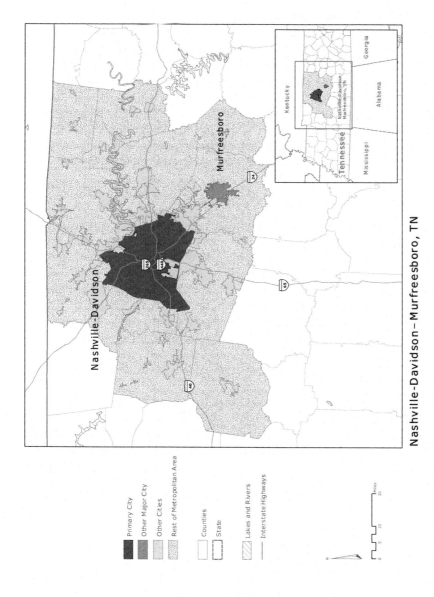

Figure 3.3 Nashville–Davidson–Murfreesboro metropolitan area.

The area has been successful in attracting other headquarter operations, including Shoney's, Nissan North America, Mars Pet Foods, Tractor Supply Company, MedSolutions, Corrections Corporation of America, Life Point Hospitals, and others.[31] Manufacturing remains strong in the region, due to the enduring presence of the automotive industry, with major Nissan, Bridgestone, and TRW Automotive plants in the area.[32] The region also has a high degree of entrepreneurialism: an estimated 20.8 percent of workers in the region were self-employed, a higher rate than comparatively sized Midwest and Southern metropolitan areas (Lotspeich et al. 2003). Finally, the education sector is vast – with twenty universities and colleges within or near the Nashville CBSA.[33] The city of Nashville itself houses Vanderbilt University and three prominent histori-cally Black colleges and universities (HCBUs): Fisk University, Tennessee State University, and Meharry Medical College. In addition to being less sensitive to economic cycles, these educational institutions have been valuable in helping to create a Black middle class, a point to which we return below.

Explaining growth and inclusion in Nashville

The structural elements for Nashville's solid growth seem clear: as a state capital it has recession-resistant public employment, its large healthcare industry has grown over the past three decades, while education, music, and manufacturing have rounded out the diverse employment base. To explain the more inclusive nature of that growth, we identify several factors, including the consolidated government, a strong Black middle class, the comprehensive perspectives of regional business leadership, and the development of strong, cross-constituency civic leadership.

Government consolidation and collaboration

The City of Nashville and Davidson County began operating as a single govern-ment in 1963, and, although a substantial portion of the metropolitan region has grown beyond the boundaries of Davidson County, consolidation seems to have aided in avoiding bureaucratic duplication, developing an integrated regional economic strategy, and reducing the city–suburb divisions and inequality that characterize many other regions.[34] Most U.S. metros do not consolidate their governments at all, and even in Nashville it took a few attempts before, in 1962, a majority of the city and county voters in the Nashville area favored the change.[35]

Business leaders strongly favored consolidation because it would enable them to work with a single governing body, target industries more effectively, and bring in more jobs to the region. Judging by contemporary opinions, the busi-ness leaders of the 1960s were right. One of today's prominent businesswoman explained: "I just feel very blessed that we had the sense to do it [consolidation] . . . and it works."[36] The consolidation *does* seem to have limited job sprawl: in 1980 two-thirds of the jobs were in the principal cities and the figure was identical in 2000 (although job sprawl did seem to occur between 2000 and 2007; see Table 3.2). Although the gap between city and suburban poverty widened between 1980 and 2000, it closed again by 2007. Ralph Schulz, president and CEO of the Nashville Area Chamber of Commerce, said that "Nashville is one of the first cities to consolidate and that created a really stable platform that created for equitable growth." He worries that as the Nashville metro has out-grown its consolidated boundaries, the region will need a renewed commitment to "breaking down governmental fragmentation."[37] But there clearly is greater spatial equity in the Nashville region than in many other parts of the South, and consolidation likely has helped.

Civil society and the rise of a Black middle class

The historically Black colleges and universities have been key to educating – and employing – a substantial African-American middle class. Fisk University was founded in 1866 immediately after the end of the Civil War.[38] With alumni such as W. E. B. Du Bois and Booker T. Washington, Fisk has developed intel-lectual, artistic, and civic leaders within the African-American community. Meharry Medical College, founded in 1876 and now the country's largest pri-vate, independent Black academic health center, has graduated nearly 4,000 predominantly African-American physicians, nearly 2,000 dentists, and nearly 200 Ph.Ds. in biomedical and biological services.[39] Founded in 1912, Tennessee State University has since grown into a truly national university with over 8,000 enrolled students from at least forty-three states and forty countries; famous alumni include Oprah Winfrey, although Dallas Cowboys fans will be more likely to remember Ed "Too Tall" Jones.[40]

Nashville was also one of the first Southern cities to try to integrate public schools. One does not want to paint too rosy a picture – the gradual integra-tion program was faced with bombings and agitators – but the city steadily progressed in granting African Americans educational equality before the law (Booth 1963) – and Nashville was highly ranked by Black Enterprise in 2007 among the nation's best cities for African Americans – fifth behind Washington, DC, Atlanta, Raleigh-Durham, and Houston.

Interestingly, two of our other case studies, Columbus and Jacksonville, were ranked nine and ten, while Charlotte, an example of equitable growth profiled in Pastor et al. (2000), was ranked at number seven (see Table 3.3).[41] In Table 3.3 we have also added a comparison group by taking those metro areas out of the 100 largest that have a Black share of the population in excess of 10 percent (just a bit more than half of the top 100). As can be seen, the metros that were highly ranked by Black Enterprise had about the same proportion of the population who are Black as the comparison groups but had much higher income and educational attainment, and lower unemployment. In short, they had a strong middle class.

In our qualitative research, not only in Nashville but also in our other regions with strong African-American leadership, interviewees suggested that a growing number of African-American business leaders and executives in the region are able to access new opportunities in the regional economy – but that, having recently emerged from more disadvantaged communities, these same leaders potentially have a stronger commitment to reinvesting public and private resources in the communities from which they have emerged. Some are representing those interests more directly, with the Black community on the forefront of faith-based organizing efforts that also played an important role in bridging Black and white congregations; this has increased the political influence of the religious community – generally a pro-equity voice – in the region.[42]

Comprehensive private sector leadership

The Nashville Chamber of Commerce coordinates private sector leadership, representing more than 2,500 businesses in a ten-county area and maintaining two affiliates – the Nashville Healthcare Council and the Nashville Technology Council. In 2005, the Chamber developed a five-year regional economic development blueprint, tied to a public–private partnership called Partnership 2010, seeking to attract new business to the region. As mentioned above, leaders of the Chamber say that government consolidation and regional cohesion are useful in marketing the region to potential investors. Whatever the specific reason, the partnership is credited with successfully landing a range of major corporate plant relocations or office developments, including Dell Computer, Saturn Corporation, the HCA headquarters, Caterpillar Financial, Ford Motor Credit, and more than 350 other relocations and expansions.

But private sector leadership has had more on its mind than simply growth: the Chamber has taken on social concerns, including poverty, education, and immigration. In 2008, for example, the Chamber hosted a major summit on poverty.[43] It has also developed its own Public Benefits Foundation that dedicates full-time attention to social issues that are important to business but outside of the day-to-day operations of a Chamber.[44] The Chamber has also played a role in immigrant rights advocacy, opposing a 2009 ballot measure that would have required all government publications and communications to be in English only – and rallying other sectors, including labor unions and public officials, to successfully block the measure.

Finally, private sector leadership in Nashville has also been important in the so-called "Smart Growth" movement that calls for better land use planning, including limits to sprawl. The non-profit organization Cumberland Region Tomorrow, founded in 2000 with strong private sector involvement, is one of the more prominent Smart Growth organizations, bringing together multiple constituencies to promote quality growth and improved planning, focusing on the intersection of land use, transportation, and the preservation of rural landscapes. It seems to have been an important convener, bringing together multiple constituencies that might on their own be more rooted in only a growth or equity perspective.

Table 3.3 *Black Enterprise* ranking of top ten metros for African Americans, 2007

Metropolitan area	Black Enterprise survey ranking, 2007	Total population, 2007	Percent Black, 2007	Black median household income, 2007	Percent Black households with income > $100,000, 2007	Percent Blacks with Bachelor's degree or better, 2007	Black unemployment rate (%) (for those aged 25–64), 2007
Washington, DC	99.73	5,306,125	27	$59,794	25	29	6
Atlanta, GA	95.88	5,271,550	32	$42,865	12	25	8
Raleigh-Durham, NC	93.77	1,049,674	21	$37,306	10	25	6
Houston, TX	91.18	5,629,127	17	$34,866	10	20	8
Nashville, TN	87.79	1,521,751	16	$32,912	8	21	9
Dallas, TX	80.82	6,144,489	15	$38,815	11	21	8
Charlotte, NC	80.54	1,650,667	24	$38,318	9	21	9
Indianapolis, IN	78.21	1,697,964	15	$34,159	8	17	10
Columbus, OH	74.67	1,754,337	15	$34,013	8	18	10
Jacksonville, FL	74.49	1,296,676	23	$35,308	6	15	7
Average for Black Enterprise top ten	—	3,132,236	21	$38,836	11	21	8
National average for largest metros with > 10% Black	—	2,240,818	20	$33,603	8	17	9

Cross-constituency civic leadership development

To understand the role of the Chamber and business leaders in unexpected social issues, it is important to see this as part of a broader tapestry of leadership development in the region – and key to that tapestry has been Leadership Nashville.

Founded in 1976 and now one of the oldest leadership programs in the United States, Leadership Nashville is an independent, executive leadership program focused on issues, not training. Each incoming class is carefully constructed – there are about 250 applications for only forty spots – to represent a diverse mix of industry, race, gender, religion, age, international origin, political persuasion, sector (i.e. unions, non-profit, business, etc.), and geographical location within the region. Each cohort is designed to replicate the diversity of the Nashville community – and thereby to expose participants to views and issues unlike their own. Moreover, because there is no pressure to develop specific positions, Leadership Nashville creates a "safe space" to be honest and open to other perspectives.

The curriculum is designed to give leaders exposure to new experiences and issues. The nine-month program opens and closes with a two-day retreat where participants choose topics for the year, including social and economic challenges facing the region. Through the year, the cohort has seven day-long meetings, makes on-site visits around the region, hears from over 100 speakers, and works in study groups to investigate the topic at hand and present a report in their final meeting. In addition, participants work on the program committee for the next incoming cohort.

Leadership Nashville alumni have, since graduation, gone on to form organizations that build bridges between regional constituencies. In 1989, alumni created Leadership Music, whose mission is to link the music scene with the larger community. In 1993, new CEO alumni initiated Nashville's Agenda, a broad consultative effort to gauge what is needed to "make Nashville the best it can be" (Nashville's Agenda 2007: 1). This initial effort, involving thousands of Nashville residents through survey questionnaires and community meetings, produced twenty-one ambitious goals for improving the city's future, resulting in new initiatives and developments, including the Frist Center for the Visual Arts and the Nashville Housing Fund. This regionwide goal-setting process was renewed in 2007 with a similar process, involving more than 3,000 residents in developing priorities for development in fields ranging from education and youth development, to housing and safety, to transportation and economic development (Nashville's Agenda 2007). Leadership Nashville alumni were also responsible for founding the Davidson Group, devoted to improving race relations in Nashville (Johansson 2007). Their driving belief is that familiarity breeds understanding and respect, and so they promote dialogue and interaction between people of different backgrounds.[45]

Without much fanfare, for over three decades, Leadership Nashville has connected regional leaders and given them broad insight and understanding on local issues and challenges. And because the program has been active for many decades, it has built a base of leaders who may think more collectively about problem-solving.[46] In concert with government consolidation, the strong Black middle class, and coordinated private sector leadership, the region is evolving into a community where diverse constituencies frequently come together to make decisions and address issues.

Summing up: Nashville talking together, acting together

During our site visits to several other regions, interviewees often expressed surprise that their region had been identified for our study. As we will see, for some of them it was the fact that things had not gone as well since 2000 as they had before – and the recent experience was more present in their thinking. But it's also a matter of perspective: when you're striving to get better, often how you're coming up short dominates your perspective. In Nashville, however, stakeholders generally responded with simple acceptance: they were aware that they were growing and felt that, despite continued social challenges, they had made progress in addressing social inequalities over the past few decades.

A strong sense of regionalism seems to permeate Nashville. The city/county merger in the 1960s symbolizes this sentiment and the Chamber of Commerce emphasized the cohesive nature of the region as a means of attracting new businesses. Moreover, the link between growth and equity seems more explicit in Nashville. The Nashville Area Chamber of Commerce has played an important role in identifying and addressing equity-related threats to economic growth – especially economic and educational inequality – and has built infrastructure to address them. Interviewees stressed the role of Black business leaders and the Black middle class, arguing that this constituency also helped direct work toward a type of growth that would benefit disadvantaged communities.

But what began to resonate for us in Nashville was that the boundary crossing forced into being by city–county consolidation was being matched by a commitment to creating leaders who could cross other sorts of divides. Leadership Nashville, for example, had a very conscious selection and development strategy that brought together people across sectors, and community organizations that had started in the Black church were reaching across lines of race and faith. The idea that a shared understanding of the region was critical began to emerge more clearly as a potential common factor in achieving a more inclusive sort of prosperity.

Jacksonville: consolidation, community and the Navy

Ask most people what they think of when they hear "Jacksonville" and you are likely to get a blank stare. A quiet backwater; just a few exits off of I-95 that soon recede far in the rearview mirror for eastern and mid-western tourists heading for Disney World or the warm beaches of southern Florida (Figure 3.4). More like Southern Georgia than the rest of sun-bleached Florida, it has been easy for the region to be eclipsed in the public imagination by tourist meccas such as Miami or Orlando.

Yet despite its relative anonymity – or maybe because of it – over the past twenty-five years, Jacksonville has found a way to grow faster and more inclusively than nearly all other metro regions in the South. Employment and earnings growth outpaced the rest of the South in the 1980s and 1990s, and, although inequality is far from absent in the region, the poverty rate declined from 15.1 percent in 1980 to 10.7 percent in 2000, while the 80–20 income ratio declined from 3.95 to 3.82 over the same period (see Table 3.4). From 2000 to 2007, Jacksonville saw poverty remain stable and inequality rise just slightly, a much better performance than the rest of the country. According to the Brookings Institution, Jacksonville was the tenth best metro area in the United States (amongst the 100 largest metros) at preserving its middle class; although the share of middle-class households dropped by an average of 10.7 percentage points between 1970 and 2005, in Jacksonville it declined by only 3.9 percentage points.[47] And as we will see in Chapter 6, Jacksonville weathered the Great Recession better than any other major metro area in Florida.

The relative success in Jacksonville involves a combination of public, private, and civic dynamics that can shape processes of growth and equity. One key factor in this case is the city–county consolidation, a governance feature that seems to provide the formal structure for another key factor – a culture of collaboration that seems to be *embedded* within the region's decision-making processes. That culture first gave birth to the consolidation and has continued to provide important participatory processes at key moments in the region's development, with the Jacksonville Community Council Inc. (JCCI) being a key institutional manifestation. In that context, it may be no surprise that the private sector has aggressively focused on both high-road job growth and working with other sectors to build strong and agile workforce development pipelines.

Background to the region

Incorporated in 1822 on the banks of the St. Johns River, harbor improvements starting in the late nineteenth century have made Jacksonville a major military and civilian deep-water port. By land area, it is the largest city in the continental United States and serves as the county seat of Duval County. In 2010, the Jacksonville metropolitan statistical area, which includes the surrounding counties of Baker, Clay, Nassau, and St. Johns, had over 1.3 million people.

Jacksonville and Duval County enjoy a single, consolidated government and are part of a larger Northeast Florida Regional Council that covers a total of seven counties and their twenty-seven municipalities.[48] Historically, Jacksonville has been led by elected officials from the Democratic Party; when John Peyton was elected mayor in 2003, he was only the second Republican in 100 years to be elected to that office, although the city has been trending Republican since the early 1990s.[49]

Demographic change and growth in the region has been mostly the result of in-migration of newcomers from other parts of the United States – half of the population growth is due to relocation, rather than natural growth. Although the

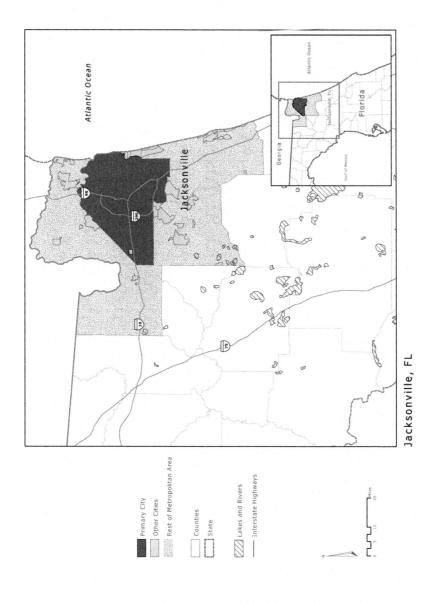

Jacksonville, FL

Primary City
Other Cities
Rest of Metropolitan Area

Counties
State
Lakes and Rivers
Interstate Highways

Figure 3.4 Jacksonville metropolitan area.

Table 3.4 Select demographic and economic data for the Jacksonville metropolitan area

	Metropolitan characteristics	1980	1990	2000	2007
Demography and immigration	Total CBSA population	735,640	925,213	1,122,750	1,296,676
	Principal cities	540,920	635,230	735,618	808,526
	Suburbs	194,720	289,983	387,132	488,150
	Race/ethnicity (%)				
	Non-Hispanic white	76	76	71	68
	Black	21	20	21	22
	Latino	2	2	4	6
	Asian/Pacific Islander	1	1	2	3
	Other	0	0	2	2
	Percent foreign born	2.8	3.3	5.3	7.1
	Average annual earnings per job (2007 dollars) (place of work basis)	38,001	40,201	44,943	46,839
	Poverty rate (% persons)	15.1	11.9	10.7	10.9
	Principal cities	16.0	13.0	12.2	12.6
	Suburbs	12.8	9.5	8.0	8.2
	By percent federal poverty level				
	Below 100%	15.1	11.9	10.7	10.9
	Between 100% and 149%	10.7	8.7	7.8	8.1
	Between 150 and 199%	11.0	10.0	8.7	9.1
	Above 200%	63.1	69.4	72.8	71.9
	Poverty concentration				
	Percent of CBSA poor in high poverty tracts (poverty rate > 20%)	47	40	29	37
	Percent of CBSA poor in very high poverty tracts (poverty rate > 40%)	17	11	7	10
	80–20 household income ratio	4.6	3.9	3.8	4.0
Income and poverty	*Income differentials (%)*				
	Median Black household income relative to median white household income	53	55	65	60
	Median Latino household income relative to median white household income	81	85	81	78
	Median API household income relative to median white household income	86	113	111	113

Metropolitan characteristics	1980	1990	2000	2007
Educational attainment (population 25 years and older) (%)				
Less than high school	33	23	17	12
High school only	33	31	29	32
Some college	20	27	31	30
Bachelor's degree	11	13	15	17
Graduate or professional degree	3	6	8	9
Workers by industry (total employed population 16 years and older) (%)				
Agriculture and mining	2	1	2	1
Construction	7	7	8	9
Manufacturing	10	8	7	6
Transportation, warehousing, and utilities	8	8	8	8
Wholesale trade	5	5	4	3
Retail trade	18	18	19	18
Finance, insurance, and real estate	11	12	11	10
Professional services	5	7	8	8
Health services	7	8	8	9
Information	4	4	4	3
Education	7	7	7	7
Other services	9	9	10	10
Public administration	7	6	5	6
Public sector employment	23	19	13	12
Principal cities–suburbs job distribution				
Percent of jobs in principal cities	82	80	76	74
Percent of jobs in suburbs	18	20	24	26
Job growth over preceding decade (last 7 years for 2007) (%)				
All CBSA	–	45	20	26
Principal cities	–	40	15	22
Suburbs	–	63	39	38
Spatial segregation by income and race				
Poverty dissimilarity index	32.5	34.4	31.4	39.2
African American–white dissimilarity index	67.5	58.1	53.9	63.8
Latino–white dissimilarity index	22.0	25.4	26.6	50.8
All people of color–white dissimilarity index	59.9	49.4	43.8	43.6

Education and employment

Segregation

foreign-born population is increasing – it grew from 2.8 percent in 1980 to 7.1 percent in 2007 – the racial discourses and divergences in Jacksonville follow the traditional Black–white binary, with the metro's population 68 percent white, 22 percent African American, 6 percent Latino, and 3 percent Asian/Pacific Islander in 2007.[50]

The mix of industrial manufacturing, transportation, consumer goods, information services, financial services, healthcare, and military employment has helped keep Jacksonville's economy stable. Major employers reflect this diversity, including the Naval Station Mayport and Air Station Jacksonville, Duval County Public Schools, the City of Jacksonville, Baptist Health Hospital, Bank of America, Blue Cross & Blue Shield of Florida, Mayo Clinic, Citi, and the Bank of America.[51] Jacksonville's deep-water port – the largest on the South Atlantic coast – has kept it a leading location for automobile imports and the Navy.

The area's four military bases employed more than 56,000 people in 2009, with a combined annual payroll of $1.59 billion, translating into an annual economic impact of $6.1 billion for the local economy.[52] An estimated sixteen of every 100 Jacksonville-area residents are connected with the Navy, either through active or reserve duty, or as a retiree, civilian employee, or member of a military family.[53] Even with all of the funding reductions, reorganizations, and base closure and realignment actions during the 1990s, Jacksonville's Naval Air Station was able to grow.[54]

Explaining growth and inclusion in Jacksonville

Jacksonville is no Mecca of social inclusion: racial divides remain strong, poverty is still too widespread, and economic worries persist. Still, the region performed relatively well on our growth and equity measures, with growth seemingly due to the diverse structure of the economy and the stabilizing effect of public employment. The fact that this came with some degree of equity seems to be related to the consolidated city–county structure, the culture of collaboration, and private–public partnerships that promote inclusive growth.

Consolidation and its contents

Like Nashville, Jacksonville is one of the few cities in the United States that was able to consolidate its city and county under one government. Partly as a result, the county and city have managed to stay central to the metro region as a whole: in 1980, nearly three-quarters of the region's residents and over 80 percent of its jobs were contained within the boundaries of Jacksonville City, and even by 2007, 62 percent of the population and 74 percent of jobs in the region were still within city boundaries (see Table 3.4).

Consolidation stemmed from a sense that Jacksonville in the 1960s had become wrought with problems such as dismal schools, serious pollution, blatant racism, and escalating racial and political tensions (Bartley 2000). Emerging business elites, whose purpose was more focused on economic vitalization, took advantage of the extremely low public approval rating of government (Crooks 2004) and garnered the support of a diverse but disgruntled populace, promising that consolidation could bring an effective, accountable, and prosperous city. In the summer of 1967, almost 65 percent of the voters supported consolidation.

In 1974, after the dust of consolidation had settled, business leaders organized what became known as the Amelia Island Conference – an event paradigmatic of the growing spirit of collaboration in the region. The nearly 100 delegates represented businesses, activist organizations, government, and organized labor. In coming together to establish goals, priorities, and a vision for Jacksonville, they agreed that the conversations and plans initiated during the campaign had to continue if the newly consolidated region was to succeed. As a result, they created a non-profit organization, the Jacksonville Community Council Inc., with the goal of spurring citizen participation. Since then JCCI has reported on issues of popular (and not so popular) concern – from air pollution to transgender issues – and spurred a spirit of collaboration and civic participation that has had an enduring impact on the present-day civic culture.

Local civic culture: culture of collaboration

Using a consensus-based approach, JCCI has spurred numerous initiatives, actions, and – perhaps its greatest strength – public–private partnerships addressing citizen concerns. The organization's numerous reports have covered topics such as mass transit, teenage parents, services for ex-offenders, affordable housing, and future workforce needs. But what is more remarkable than the range of topics is the process by which JCCI has chosen issues, researched them, come to consensus, and persuaded others to collaborate for regional change.

A practice that evolved over time, each year JCCI identifies community problems through a wide network of volunteers and then selects two issues for concentrated study. A diverse group of community members is then invited to join study committees on the issues. Over six months, the committees meet with stakeholders and experts in order to gain a thorough understanding of the problem. Recommendations are then developed and chosen through a consensus-based process – not a majority vote. If a recommendation to which there are objections is chosen, the objections are of a limited enough scope or scale such that committee members do not block the process. Recommendations are then written into a report and brought to local leaders in government, business, and non-profits, where JCCI volunteers advocate for change. As the president of JCCI explained, "for 30 years we have invested 2 years worth of advocacy for every community study we have done."[55] At the same time, "When we advocate, we don't take the action. We convince the Mayor's office to take action, we convince the court authority to do something, we convince the community to do something to convene."[56]

One illustrative example: a report on race relations that emerged out of a collaborative community study process and was published in 2002.[57] "Beyond the Talk: Improving Race Relations" (JCCI 2002) was then followed by a range of advocacy efforts and initiatives, including formal announcements of support by the mayor and the City Council and the development of an annual report card on race relations that tracked racial disparities in education, employment and income, neighborhoods and housing, health access and outcomes, justice and the legal system, and political processes and civic engagement. The 'Race Relations Progress Report' was modeled after JCCI's annual 'Quality of Life Progress Report,' an indicator project that has served as a model throughout the nation since it was initiated in the 1980s.[58]

JCCI has also been instrumental in building regional processes beyond the boundaries of Jacksonville City. Its 2000 report, "Improving Regional Cooperation in Northeast Florida" (JCCI 2000) contributed to the Cornerstone Economic Development Partnership (the economic development arm of the Jacksonville Chamber) expanding into six counties and spurring the Northeast Florida Regional Planning Council to create a shared regional database. JCCI continued to work with the Council on a visioning process and developing quality of life indicators for the seven-county region.

Private–public partnerships for a strong economy

Jacksonville has also worked to develop public–private partnerships aimed at building strong industries and adaptable and comprehensive workforce development pipelines. The Chamber of Commerce, in collaboration with public agencies, has been innovative in strategies to attract "high-road" jobs. Moreover, it has worked closely with community colleges and secondary schools to make sure the upcoming workforce has skills demanded by the current mix of industry.

Business leaders in the region have steadily become more strategic in the type of growth they are willing to accept. In the past, much of the Chamber's focus was simply on attracting any jobs and external investment. In 1999, however, the Chamber redefined exactly what kinds of jobs they wanted to bring in; according to one Chamber executive, "We [are] no longer interested in all jobs and just growth for our region. We are only interested in focusing on good, meaningful, higher-wage job growth for our region."[59] These are not just words – the compensation of the Chamber's staff became tied to their ability to attract these types of jobs. One concrete outcome of the Chamber's focus on good jobs has been deliberately to *avoid* developing a tourism industry. Part of this decision may be related to the difficulty of competing with neighbors to the south, but, with less tourism, the region does not have to grapple with the challenges of the sort of part-time and low-paid jobs that are embedded in the tourism sector. Indeed, in 2005, the region reported its fastest growth in some of the best-paying jobs, including aircraft mechanics, computer software engineers, loan officers, and surveyors (JCCI 2006).

In addition to attracting good jobs, the public–private partnership was instrumental in changing public policy to incentivize paying workers well. The Cornerstone Economic Development Partnership works with public economic development agencies in the seven-county area. Together, they changed the rules behind subsidies and other incentives given to companies to relocate in the Jacksonville region, requiring that such efforts be restricted to companies paying at least 115 percent of the state's average wage.[60] Despite what many might view as the handicap of requiring a high baseline wage, in 2008, the region outcompeted Nashville and Charlotte in bringing German-based financial services giant Deutsche Bank to the region using such an incentives package.[61] The bank at that time projected 1,000 new, full-time jobs – 900 of which would be local hires – with salaries averaging $49,200 plus benefits (Witkowski 2008).

The Jacksonville Chamber also crafted the "Blueprint for Prosperity" in collaboration with the City of Jacksonville (City of Jacksonville 2007). The initial goal for the Blueprint was to raise per capita and median income in Jacksonville. Planners conducted twenty-nine focus group meetings with 355 participants, fourteen community meetings with 580 participants, and twenty task force meetings with 382 participants and found that getting to increased income would mean tackling community-identified obstacles (City of Jacksonville 2007: 3). The top six priority areas were education, economic development, quality of life, infrastructure, leadership, and racial opportunity and harmony.[62]

Although primarily concerned with economic growth, the attention that business leadership has shown to social issues over the past decades is unusual; the Chamber of Commerce, for example, explicitly talks about strategies to achieve "racial opportunity and harmony" and "eradicate structural and institutional racism." The high priority placed on race relations is reflective of JCCIs report on race relations – developed just three years prior to the Blueprint – and of the way in which actors and agencies influence each other across the region.[63]

Regional actors have also created a workforce development pipeline that is agile and well connected to regional industry. WorkSource, the regional workforce investment board, was described as working "hand in glove" with the private sector.[64] In the Duetsche Bank case, WorkSource directly screened all applicants and took applications for the bank. These collaborations also include the community college system, and the president of the Florida Community College at Jacksonville (FCCJ) serves on the board of the Chamber of Commerce. Moreover, FCCJ is vigilant about insuring that its degree programs match up with industry needs, regularly reviewing its degree offerings, funding labor market research to that end, and including forty-seven industry-based standing advisory committees to provide advice in the curriculum development process. As a result, between 2001 and 2008, FCCJ deactivated 188 existing degrees that were not geared toward meeting current labor market needs and activated 156 new degrees. Better yet, although in 2001 about 20 percent of degrees granted by the institution were in high-wage high-skill occupations, in 2008 the figure was about 60 percent.[65]

The Chamber of Commerce (through the Cornerstone Economic Development Partnership), WorkSource, and FCCJ have also been working in secondary schools to develop Career Academies – schools-within-high schools that offer focused technical skills in particular industries.[66] Academies operate through small learning communities that combine rigorous academics with career-specific skills meant to match up with the region's industries, including healthcare, information technology, finance, and aviation. Since being launched in 2001, the region has more than forty Career Academies with nearly 8,000 high school students participating each year (CREDP 2010).

Summing up: building community in Jacksonville

Good experiences can begat further good experiences. Cities and regions have a particular history and set of experiences "with conflict and/or cooperation as well as the social structure that go into the making of local culture" (Savitch and Kantor 2004: 45). For Jacksonville, a successful city–county consolidation experience was followed up with the development of some degree of popular access to decision-making processes and led, as in Kansas City, to a "local culture" of collaboration that facilitated public–private partnerships and encouraged elites to legitimize their actions and gain public approval.

Regionalists often talk about the "ties that bind" or "interwoven destinies" (Cisneros 1993; Savitch et al. 1993). Jacksonville represents an extreme case in which destinies have indeed been interwoven by both formal governmental structures and less formal research and policy-making processes. Although the consolidation of city and county governments was and is important, it was reflective of a civic impulse that has found its way into the Jacksonville Community Council, a series of workforce decisions, and other joint efforts of the public and the private sectors. In Jacksonville, key actors learn together, act together, and develop policy together; the process does not eliminate conflict or difference but it does seem to have led to a more intentional and inclusive prosperity.

Columbus: annexation and the ties that bind

With its many colleges and universities, as well as its historically diverse economy, Columbus, Ohio has been touted as one of the most steadily growing economies in the United States. Although it obviously did well enough to make it into our case study sample on the growth side, it also had moderate improvements in both the proportion of people in poverty from 1980 to 2000 as well as the 80–20 income ratio, placing it above average for the Midwest census region (Table 3.5). From 2000 to 2007, employment growth was in the top fifth for the Midwest and earnings growth was in the top half; as we explore further below, it did less well on equity in this period but Columbus nonetheless remained a reasonable choice as a case study – and it was especially attractive because of the opportunity to contrast dynamics here with dynamics in Cleveland.[67]

On the surface, the most obvious difference between the two metropolitan regions is Cleveland's heavy dependence on manufacturing, and Columbus' economic base in a more diversified set of industries and thus ability to adjust to de-industrialization more readily. But a more in-depth examination of dynamics in Columbus suggests a more nuanced understanding of economic restructuring, and a more complex set of dynamics around regional governance and social relations that help explain Columbus' ability to do better than its sister metro in Ohio at promoting inclusion along with economic growth.

We specifically suggest that the region's strong metropolitan planning organization and the power of annexation – which has helped to avoid interregional competition – make a difference. There has also been a long history of collaborative regional stewardship by Columbus business leaders, which has helped build a sense of common destiny in the region. We also note that Columbus does not seem to carry as many of the scars of racism and segregation as Cleveland, and many informants attribute this as a key factor to its success in creating an environment for people to work together; indeed, as in the Kansas City and Nashville regions, the presence of a strong middle-class African-American community establishes a constituency that is interested in both prosperity and justice. Finally, as in many of our cases, there is a strong commitment to workforce development within the metro's community college system that has helped expand opportunities for disadvantaged workers.

Background to the region

Columbus was founded in 1812 in an effort to situate the Ohio state capital in a location more accessible to its citizenry and more centrally located to the entire state. On the Scioto River and centrally located with access to trade routes, Columbus has grown substantially over the years, spurred on by a range of public sector investments, including a state prison, a school for the blind, and multiple universities, along with all the trappings of the state government (Keating 2005). Today, the Columbus MSA, also referred to as the Central Ohio region, is comprised of seven counties: Delaware, Fairfield, Franklin, Licking, Madison, Pickaway, and Union (Figure 3.5).

With a population of 1.8 million people in 2007, the relative size of the central city – the City of Columbus held 42 percent of the metro's population and 54 percent of the metro's jobs as of the same year – is a testimony to the annexation power that Columbus used in the 1960s and 1970s to expand the city aggressively into surrounding areas. This annexation allowed for new malls, office buildings, and general commercial development to occur within city boundaries, thereby increasing the tax base. Some studies have argued that this growth may still have been at the expense of the poorer neighborhoods that remain in the older central core areas, as 90 percent of those moving to outer neighborhoods and suburban areas in the 1990s were white residents (Brookings Institution 2003b). But the period from 1980 to 2000 was marked by a falling rate of poverty in the principal city that was roughly on pace with what was occurring in the metro overall.

Demographically, Columbus has become more diverse in recent years, partly as the result of an influx of Latino immigrants, Somali refugees, and more international students attending area universities (Brookings Institution 2003b). Since the 1940s, Columbus has overshadowed Cleveland as a destination for newer immigrant streams, and by 2000 it had the largest foreign-born share (6.7 percent) of any large city in Ohio (Otiso and Smith 2005). Growth of immigration

Table 3.5 Select demographic and economic data for the Columbus metropolitan area

Metropolitan characteristics	1980	1990	2000	2007
Total CBSA population	1,269,408	1,405,193	1,612,694	1,754,337
Principal cities	565,021	632,910	713,418	732,974
Suburbs	704,387	772,283	899,276	1,021,363
Race/ethnicity (%)				
Non-Hispanic white	88	86	81	78
Black	11	12	8	14
Latino	1	1	2	3
Asian/Pacific Islander (API)	1	1	2	3
Other	0	0	6	2
Percent foreign born	2.2	2.6	4.5	6.3
Average annual earnings per job (2007 dollars) (place of work basis)	38,638	40,601	47,085	47,455
Poverty rate (% persons)	11.0	11.8	9.9	7.3
Principal cities	15.7	16.5	14.4	10.2
Suburbs	6.8	7.4	6.0	5.2
By percent federal poverty level				
Below 100%	11.0	11.8	9.9	7.3
Between 100% and 149%	7.7	7.0	6.7	7.1
Between 150% and 199%	9.5	8.6	7.3	7.9
Above 200%	71.7	72.6	76.0	77.7
Poverty concentration				
Percent of CBSA poor in high poverty tracts (poverty rate > 20%)	48	48	41	53
Percent of CBSA poor in very high poverty tracts (poverty rate > 40%)	17	24	13	19
80–20 household income ratio	4.0	3.9	3.9	4.5
Income differentials (%)				
Median Black household income relative to median white household income	64	62	63	61
Median Latino household income relative to median white household income	70	83	74	62
Median API household income relative to median white household income	88	88	97	105

Demography and immigration

Income and poverty

	Metropolitan characteristics	*1980*	*1990*	*2000*	*2007*
Education and employment	*Educational attainment (population over 25 years and older) (%)*				
	Less than high school	28	20	14	11
	High school only	35	33	31	31
	Some college	17	24	25	26
	Bachelor's degree	13	15	19	21
	Graduate or professional degree	6	8	10	11
	Workers by industry (total employed population 16 years and older) (%)				
	Agriculture and mining	2	2	1	1
	Construction	5	5	6	5
	Manufacturing	18	13	10	8
	Transportation, warehousing, and utilities	5	5	6	6
	Wholesale trade	5	4	4	3
	Retail trade	17	19	19	18
	Finance, insurance, and real estate	8	9	10	11
	Professional services	6	7	8	9
	Health services	8	8	8	10
	Information	4	4	5	4
	Education	9	9	9	9
	Other services	8	8	9	10
	Public administration	7	6	6	5
	Public sector employment	18	16	14	14
	Principal cities–suburbs job distribution				
	Percent of jobs in principal cities	58	56	53	54
	Percent of jobs in suburbs	42	44	47	46
	Job growth over preceding decade (last 7 years for 2007) (%)				
	All CBSA	–	26	20	2
	Principal cities	–	21	13	5
	Suburbs	–	32	29	0
Segregation	*Spatial segregation by income and race*				
	Poverty dissimilarity index	39.9	43.1	40.8	40.4
	African American–white dissimilarity index	72.2	66.9	63.4	61.2
	Latino–white dissimilarity index	26.0	38.8	36.9	47.1
	All people of color–white dissimilarity index	64.6	57.8	50.1	45.9

Columbus, OH

Figure 3.5 Columbus metropolitan area.

in Columbus has partly been shaped by its employment structure, with greater concentrations in growing service and retail sectors and less dependence on declining manufacturing industries, but also partly by U.S. refugee resettlement policies, which have resulted in Columbus becoming by 2000 the home of the second largest concentration of Somalis in the United States (Otiso and Smith 2005: 136).

Despite the influx of immigrants, Columbus remains a primarily white–Black metro, and the central city has a much higher percentage of African Americans than the metro as a whole (26 percent in 2007 for the city versus 14 percent for the metro). In 2007 the city was ranked as the ninth best city for African Americans according to *Black Enterprise* magazine; and the second best place for Black families to live according to Black Enterprise Television.[68] Although some informants suggested that this has more to do with having a Black mayor and other Blacks in high-level positions, rather than the conditions facing lower-income Black families, it is exactly this middle class that may be essential to our other cases and many key informants in both Columbus and Cleveland pointed to the lower incidences of racial tension and segregation in Columbus as contributing to a healthier community.[69]

The political landscape in Columbus is also somewhat less fragmented than in other areas of Ohio. For example, there are 280 local and special district governments in Columbus, less than the 383 in Cleveland, 345 in Cincinnati, and 360 in the average U.S. metro.[70] In addition, the City Council of Columbus functions as an at-large system, rather than the neighborhood-based ward system in Cleveland. Although ward systems can improve minority representation, they can also encourage fiefdoms and localism. The at-large system in Columbus, some suggest, means that Council people tend to work on initiatives that might improve the plight of all residents of Columbus, rather than simply meet the specific needs of constituents in certain neighborhoods.

Columbus has a generally stable and diverse economy, with strong employment in government, education, retail, and finance companies. The economy has tended to grow at a steady and predictable pace despite what Ohio as a state has experienced. In fact, until the 2001–2003 economic downturn, Columbus had never experienced job losses in times of national downturns. One important feature of the economic landscape: Columbus has never relied on the manufacturing sector as much as other regions of Ohio, most notably Cleveland. For example, at the peak of manufacturing employment in Columbus, in 1960, it represented only 25 percent of overall employment compared with nearly 41 percent in Cleveland the same year (Otiso and Smith 2005). In 1980, manufacturing was 18 percent of the workforce and it declined to 8 percent by 2007; the shift in Cleveland over the same period was 28 percent to 15 percent. Many of our informants pointed to this and essentially argued that Columbus had de-industrialized earlier than Cleveland; as a result, Columbus was moving quickly on building a new economy while Cleveland was still clinging to the old economy.

This notion of economic flexibility is only part of the story – although it makes for a confidence-boosting vision of the region. Another key factor is the opposite of flexible: government is the largest employer in the region and that lends stability to the underlying labor market. Although the federal government is important, with one of the largest processing centers for the Defense Finance and Accounting Service located in Columbus, the single greatest employer is the State of Ohio, followed by Ohio State University. A number of other universities are in the area, employing many residents and serving approximately 100,000 students.

Of course, the private sector is important and the region is home to several important retail headquarters (such as Limited Brands, Express, Victoria's Secret, and Bath and Body Works). Recent efforts have been made to increase the technology base of the region by strengthening research and technology along the 315 Corridor. The 315 Corridor is one of the largest research-based sites in the nation with about 10,000 acres of dedicated land and 50,000 employees. The area houses over twenty technology-related organizations, including businesses, non-profits, and schools.[71]

Explaining growth and inclusion in Columbus

Some places have original sin, others have original grace. Part of Columbus' good fate is that it was created to be a state capital and has thus been blessed since birth with a more stable economy, rooted in large public sector employment. But the area has also seen less political fragmentation then other regions, driven by the central city's annexation efforts that have benefitted the entire region. Its economic diversity has allowed for growth in different sectors while business leadership has a long tradition of collaborative regional stewardship. It has a strong presence of universities as well as community colleges preparing the workforce. And its history of racial segregation and racial tension is less marked than in other areas such as Cleveland, something both due to and reflected in a relatively large African-American middle class. Each of these factors, we argue, have helped ensure that growth in Columbus was shared more broadly in the 1980s (although the performance in the 2000–2007 period is less exemplary, as we note below).

Public sector ties

The public sector has played a critical role in shaping growth and equity patterns across the region. Part of this contribution is simply in the public sector's large role as an employer in the region, and the stabilizing effect that this has on the region's growth. Also important, however, has been Columbus' ability to grow over time, annexing surrounding areas rather than having them fall to suburban districts with entirely separate tax revenues and land use planning. Although Columbus' experience with annexation falls short of the kinds of city–county mergers that Nashville and Jacksonville achieved in the 1960s, from the 1950s through 1980s it still played an important role in stemming suburban flight (as well as retaining jobs; note that the share of jobs in the principal city fell from 58 percent in 1980 to 54 percent in 2007, an extraordinarily modest slippage in the context of overall job sprawl in the United States; see Kneebone 2009).

Two major components of Columbus' annexation policy were critical. The first was implemented in 1954, when the city imposed a freeze on water and sewer service extensions. Residents of unincorporated areas contiguous to Columbus who wanted to incorporate their own municipal governments had to petition Franklin County Commissioners, but approval of these petitions was always contingent upon the ability of the receiving municipality to provide services. Columbus had a quasi-monopoly on water and sewage provision at the time (in contrast to Cleveland, which did not have such a monopoly), forcing expanding communities on Columbus' periphery to petition for annexation rather than self-incorporation in order to gain access to needed municipal services. The result? Between 1954 and 1960, the land area of Columbus more than doubled through annexation.

Columbus added a second component to its annexation policy in the mid-1960s, when it began entering into water and sewer service contracts with other surrounding municipalities in Franklin County. These contracts allowed for some growth in suburban areas, but the suburban contract services areas were restricted in size – thus limiting the suburban municipalities from developing a tax base sufficient to invest in their own competing utility systems. Columbus also negotiated growth corridors linking to these suburban neighbors, allowing for future growth of the central city. Again, the result was that between 1965 and 1974 the land area of Columbus grew an average of close to ten square miles a year (Jonas 1991).

One of the reasons why this aggressive annexation policy did not meet significant resistance was that it did not include transfer of school district territory, which remained under the jurisdiction of the Ohio State Board of Education. This minimized potential opposition to annexation from area residents, who saw the value of being annexed for accessing municipal services without threatening either the school district tax bases or the districts themselves. Thus, while the City of Columbus expanded, the city school district did not; indeed, by 1980, 40 percent of the land area of the City of Columbus was within suburban school districts (Cox 2010: 222). Once municipal and school district annexations were recoupled in 1986 – combined with the white flight from Columbus schools following desegregation in the 1970s – Columbus' annexation process dramatically slowed (Jonas 1991).

Public sector efforts

This then is a complicated legacy: ties that bind but not too tightly, with the most ticklish issue of sharing educational systems left to one side. Another linking system has been the region's metropolitan planning organization, the Mid-Ohio Regional Planning Commission (MORPC). Founded more than sixty years ago – long before federal transportation policy required the creation of MPOs – MORPC is an association of forty-four local governments dealing with a wide range of issues, many beyond the transportation planning that is typically core to many MPOs. At the time of our research, for example, MORPC was leading a coalition on dealing with foreclosures and participating in an energy group focused on reducing energy costs for low-income residents. Its executive was serving on the governor's Anti-Poverty Taskforce and the mayor's 2012 Commission, and chairing the United Way's Board of Trustees.

As with the annexation, MORPC has sought to bring city and suburb together, even as it recognizes the real political limits to such bridges. For example, MORPC accepts the regionalist argument that a tax-sharing system would be good for the region (Orfield 1997) but also knows that adequate suburban support for this is still lacking. MORPC leaders have thus been convening conversations to help leaders from the suburbs and the central cities understand how such initiatives have the potential to result in a win-win situation.[72] Still, it is rare to see an MPO engage – let alone advocate for – tax-base redistribution.

The public sector higher education complex in the region has also played an important role in lifting up equity issues in the context of the region's economic growth. Institutions of higher education create a stable economy, to be sure, and are widely recognized for their contributions to science and technology development and related economic growth opportunities. But their value is also in the ways in which their research can highlight key issues and challenges as well as prepare the workforce. The Ohio State University, for example, is home to the Kirwan Institute for the Study of Race and Ethnicity, one of the most prominent equity-based research centers in the nation, with a reach that includes affected communities, academia, and government.[73] The University System of Ohio is the largest integrated state university system in the country, including fourteen campuses, twenty-four regional branches, and twenty-three community colleges. It also includes an adult workforce education and training system with 200 adult workforce centers spread throughout the state.[74]

The Ohio Skills Bank, run from within the University System of Ohio, focuses on integrating workforce and economic development activities.[75] Much like the aggressive targeting done by the Florida Community College in Jacksonville, the Ohio Skills Bank identifies priority growth sectors, directs state resources to those sectors, and aligns higher education programs with the needed skills. This involves labor market analyses, education resource analyses, and the formation of employer panels in each region. Although the program is certainly a model for supporting high-growth, high-wage industries, it could do more to focus on lower-skilled, lower-paid groups.[76]

Meanwhile, the Columbus State Community College has partnered with the private sector, state government, local government, foundations, industry-specific organizations, high schools, career centers, and other universities to create both credit and non-credit programs for workforce development. Non-credit programs focus on career readiness, workshops, training, continued professional education, General Educational Development (GED, or high school equivalency diploma), and more to train students and supply workers for local companies. The College also develops relationships with other four-year institutions in the state, helping to provide pathways for low-income students to access higher education. Both students and employers benefit from these programs.[77]

Finally, Columbus' role as the state capital also means that it benefits from certain leadership initiatives emerging from the state legislature and governor's office. One example that was very prominent during our field visit was an Anti-Poverty Task Force that was spearheaded by the governor in 2008 to focus on short- and long-term strategies to reduce poverty. This was particularly critical because Ohio as a whole saw a dramatic increase in poverty in the 2000s, and, although Columbus outperformed seven other Ohio metropolitan regions in terms of the growth in jobs and earnings better 2000 and 2007, it was near the bottom in terms of worsening poverty and income distribution.[78] The Task Force consisted of thirty members including state agency representatives, faith-based and community non-profit leaders, business and labor leaders, and key anti-poverty stakeholders from around the state, including several Ohioans living in poverty. Over 300 Ohioans participated directly in five working groups of the Task Force, and over 1,800 people participated in one of twenty-two regional conversations on reducing poverty. The work resulted in targeted short-term and long-term priorities in four broad focus areas: economic advancement; provision of basic needs; investment in children and young adults; and ensuring transparency, accountability and leadership.

Although the focus of the Task Force was on statewide strategies to address poverty, many of the Task Force members were from the Columbus area and the fact that it was initiated from the governor's office meant that it has high visibility in discussion of regional development as well. This has been in keeping with a general role of the public sector, as represented by the Mid-Ohio Regional Planning Council, government, and educational institutions, to keep equity issues as at least one important part of the regional conversation.

The nature of the economy and business leadership

Columbus enjoys a diverse economy: finance and insurance, retail, logistics and manufacturing have all been important employment sectors along with government and education. Aside from the headquarters of retail companies, including Victoria's Secret and Bath and Body Works, Columbus also hosts the central offices for Bank One and Nationwide Mutual Insurance Company in the financial sector and Rickenbacker and Honda's U.S. headquarters in the logistics and manufacturing sectors. Honda located its first automobile plant in the United States in 1982 within the Columbus metropolitan area, with nearly 7,000 employees. Columbus' location as a transport hub is a critical plus for company location and trade in general. According to the Mid-Ohio Regional Planning Commission, the region is within a one-day truck drive of 58 percent of the U.S. population, 50 percent of the Canadian population, 61 percent of U.S. manufacturing capacity, and 80 percent of U.S. corporate headquarters.[79]

But it's more than just the economic structure itself. Leadership within the private sector has long played a role in building a collaborative regional vision.

As early as 1945, major private sector employers in Columbus helped to create a Metropolitan Committee for Jobs and Progress that formulated plans on a metropolitan-wide basis, and in fact endorsed a metropolitan-wide income tax proposal in 1947 (although this was never passed). Later, it played a critical role in trying to bring about intergovernmental cooperation, and was at least partly responsible for the 1950 creation of the Franklin County Regional Planning Commission, precursor to the Mid-Ohio Regional Planning Commission. Another regional business initiative was the Development Committee for Greater Columbus, which was incorporated in 1956 to provide technical advice and support for local governments throughout the region on behalf of private employers. In 1958, the Columbus Area Chamber of Commerce endorsed a statewide referendum, ultimately unsuccessful, which sought to make metropolitan government in Ohio more feasible. These relatively early examples of collaborative business leadership, as in Jacksonville, created a sort of path dependence: it was easier for Columbus' private sector leadership to build on a tradition of regional stewardship (Jonas 1991; Cox 2010).

Private sector concern for the region, and not just the narrow bottom line, has continued in more recent times. CEOs of major companies in the region came together in 2002 to create the Columbus Partnership, a civic organization of business leaders whose goal is to improve the economic vitality of Central Ohio. Key goals of the initiative include working with the public and non-profit sectors to develop a common agenda, balance residential and commercial development in an effort to ensure the vibrancy of the downtown, engage in regional solutions to problems of economic and workforce development, and improve education and technology's role in the regional economy.

In order to create a baseline understanding of dynamics in the region, the Partnership funded a study to create metropolitan benchmarks across four areas: economic growth in the region, population vitality, personal prosperity (which includes many measures of equity), and community well-being. The Columbus region was compared with thirty metropolitan areas in the United States, including Cincinnati and Cleveland, some "usual suspect" regions (those that have similar growth patterns), but also more "aspirational" regions (those that are faring much better than Columbus and serve as good models). The resulting "Benchmarking Central Ohio" reports were published in 2007, 2008, and 2009, and have been widely read and discussed in the region (and by interested academics like ourselves).[80] These reports and the Partnership's leadership were an important stimulus for the creation of Columbus 2020, a broad public–private effort that includes leadership from the Mid-Ohio Regional Planning Commission and the City of Columbus and Franklin County, as well as the Columbus Partnership, the Columbus Chamber, and TechColumbus (an association of more than 700 technology-related businesses and organizations in the region).[81]

Community leaders

Although the role of regional governance processes and a more collaborative private sector emerged as the most important factors in the Columbus story, non-profit and community initiatives were somewhat important as well, particularly in shaping a common knowledge base of poverty conditions in the region. However, it may be the less prominent presence of pro-equity actors that helps to explain why Columbus slipped so dramatically on poverty and inequality in the 2000s.

For example, the labor movement in Columbus has been relatively weak, at least compared with other manufacturing strongholds throughout the Midwest. Part of this was due to state law that undermined public sector unionization – the 1947 Ferguson Act banned public employee strikes, provided for dismissal of strikers, and stipulated that any striker who was rehired would get no pay raise for a year and would be on probation for two years. The law was repealed in 1984, but its impact on unionization levels is clear – in 1986, only 33 percent of public sector workers in the Columbus MSA were unionized, ranking Columbus 137 out of 246 metropolitan areas. In the private sector, historically the strongest union in the state had been the United Steelworkers, but this was always much stronger in Cleveland than in Columbus – only 10.7 percent of Columbus area private sector workers were union members in 1986 (compared with 18.1 percent in Cleveland), and by 2000 this had declined to 7.2 percent.[82] Much of the labor activities through the 1980s and 1990s were focused on defensive struggles, rather than broad-based organizing efforts (Van Tine et al. 1998; Dixon 2004).

Faith-based organizing is ongoing but is mostly focused on community issues and community development, particularly in African-American neighborhoods, rather than regionwide advocacy. For example, the Black Baptist Pastors' Conference (BBPC) has served since the 1950s as an important network of African-American church leaders and their engagement in municipal politics, but its focus has primarily been on education and economic empowerment specifically in African-American neighborhoods (Alex-Assensoh 2004). BREAD, an affiliate of the DART network, has a wide reach, working with fifty member congregations through annual Nehemiah Actions and periodic house meetings to strategize the most pressing and winnable issues for the year. From these conversations, BREAD has pushed the city and county to create an Affordable Housing Trust Fund, influenced the city and county to require businesses that receive tax abatements to hire at least 50 percent of their non-salaried workforce through the one-stop employment service provider, Central Ohio Workforce Investment Corporation, and pushed for policies to reduce truancy within the Columbus schools. These are all important issues and initiatives, but they do not seem to have risen to the level of substantially shaping metropolitan equity dynamics that we've seen in other regions (Pastor et al. 2009b).

One of the most prominent recent non-profit organizations to emerge in our research – and one certainly tackling regional issues – was Community Research Partners (CRP). Originally formed in 2000 by the United Way of Central Ohio, CRP provides current economic, social, and demographic data that inform discussions of economic vitality and social equity within the policy, public, non-profit, and philanthropic communities. For example, CRP staff sit on the Financial Stability Committee of the United Way where they help examine workforce development, debt reduction, increasing assets, and financial literacy. In addition, at the time of our interview, CRP was preparing a brief for the more left-leaning Policy Matters (discussed in the Cleveland case study) around green collar jobs and growing opportunities and jobs for middle-skill positions and with Greater Ohio around vacant and abandoned properties.[83] The role of CRP was crucial in creating a shared understanding: its widely acknowledged strength in gathering and analyzing data helps to create a base of shared knowledge that can guide business, philanthropy, and progressive policy organizations as they shape policy and development strategies.

Greater Ohio Policy Center markets itself as the state's smart growth organization, with the mission to build a vibrant economy, improve quality of life, and provide for the common good by focusing on people, land, and prosperity. In 2008, the organization and the Brookings Institution unveiled "Restoring Our Prosperity: The State Role in Revitalizing Ohio's Core Communities" at a summit that included more than 1,000 business, community, and political leaders throughout the state.[84] The report included short-, medium-, and long-term recommendations for building assets, reforming government, and engaging federal government that draw on the expertise of the public and private sectors, philanthropies, educational institutions, and non-profits. From this report, Greater Ohio has developed its leading initiative – "Restoring Prosperity" – in an effort to build a state-based competitive agenda, with multi-sector coordination, to transition Ohio into a new export-oriented, lower-carbon, and innovation-fueled economy. Although this is a statewide effort, there are, as noted above, spill-over effects into the conversations in Columbus itself.

Meanwhile, the United Way of Central Ohio (usually the most business-oriented of formal philanthropic efforts) has demonstrated its own commitment to equity through investments in five pilot neighborhoods. At the time of our research, the United Way had selected the neighborhoods in which to focus work to reduce crime and the number of vacant and abandoned properties over a ten-year period. The plans included building Neighborhood Impact Councils and providing each with about $50,000 a year plus one full-time staff, with the Councils slated to involve community organizations, local corporations, and other non-profit organizations. The United Way is also engaged in providing many small grants to grassroots organizations in the region to focus on building trust and engaging constituencies.[85]

Summing up: ties that bind – but not too tight

Columbus was a shoe-in as a leader in the Midwest simply because of its strong economy. The public sector and large higher education complex is a stabilizing force that supports the range of other industries providing important growth opportunities. But Columbus has also annexed substantial areas around its historical boundaries, leaving it with fewer of the city–suburb divides that characterize other Midwestern cities. Clear racial differences remain between the city and the rest of the region, but these differences are less than in many other Midwestern cities – especially less than in the Cleveland metropolitan area – and the result has been a strong African-American middle class with interest in both equity and growth.

Columbus, in short, has ties that bind. They are, as we have noted, not too tight: school districts were not annexed along with suburban territory. Still, there is a legacy of collaboration and cooperation that is reflected in the local metropolitan planning authority, business leadership efforts, and public–private partnerships. This has all contributed to a strong growth record (relative to the Midwest) and, at least until recently, a decent record on poverty and income distribution. However, the labor and community sectors seem weaker than business and the government, and this may contribute to downplaying the equity side of the growth equation. Still, Columbus offers important lessons – and a sharp contrast to the dysfunction and tension that characterize the Cleveland metropolitan area we explore in the next chapter.

What a long, strange trip . . .

Kansas City, Nashville, Jacksonville, and Columbus – as attractive as these places may be to their residents and others who know them well, they are far from the top of any list of popular urban destinations in the United States. Perhaps more importantly, these places have rarely emerged in studies that have formed the mainstream of urban studies and urban theory in the United States.

Our largest cities, of course, serve as icons of – or stand-ins for – major trends in understanding urban development. Chicago gave birth to urban sociology and our understanding of concentrated poverty, New York is emblematic of world cities and high finance, and Los Angeles is often cast as the proto-typical postmodern city. Other cities have served as important case studies of important trends affecting a broad swath of urban areas. Think, for example, of studies of Detroit, Pittsburgh, and Cleveland as iconic of broader paths of, first, early twentieth-century industrialization and, later, decentralization, white flight, and central city decay. Las Vegas, Miami, and Phoenix have served as exemplars of iconic sun-belt cities, while Silicon Valley, Boston, and Raleigh-Durham are known for their technology-led growth. Other smaller cities have become well known for innovative urban governance and development practices, such as Portland for its urban growth boundary, Minneapolis–St. Paul for regional tax sharing, or Charlotte and Chattanooga for innovative urban revitalization efforts.

Kansas City, Nashville, Jacksonville, and Columbus have no such visibility, either in the popular imagination of the broader public or the less popular musings of us and our academic colleagues. Seeming to pass under the radar – at least until someone, namely us, took a numbers-driven approach to generating cases – these regions built enviable records of solid, sustained growth and consistent improvements in social equity over the 1980s and 1990s. Can these case studies become the icons of a newly recognized metropolitan growth trajectory? Can they provide the elements of a model for bringing growth and equity together in a more sustainable fashion?

Fortunately, the cases do yield a few key lessons, such as the importance of governmental consolidation or annexation, the key role of a collaborative business community, and the potential significance of a politically important minority middle class. Unfortunately, they do not yield a single silver bullet that can be easily transported across metropolitan America – and they also generate a series of research questions for which interested academics will now seek new grants and create new teams to explore.

For example, are businesses in Kansas City really more rooted in the region than their counterparts in metros across the Midwest? It seems so, but it would take a large comparative survey of business leaders across multiple regions and their attitudes toward regional investment and long-term regional stewardship to be sure, perhaps also combined with more quantitative measurements of business 'foot-looseness' or 'rootedness' beyond the measure of business headquarters that is often used as a proxy for assessing business commitment to staying in a region. Are the collaborative leadership building processes in Nashville and Jacksonville, as impressive as they are, really that much more effective than somewhat similar leadership programs that exist in many metropolitan regions around the country? Again, it would probably take a large-scale comparative study specifically devoted to understanding the differences in such leadership programs and their broader effects in order to definitely make conclusions about their importance in shaping growth and equity trajectories. And is the relative slippage in the equity performance in Columbus since 2000 really due to the weakness of the pro-equity constituencies or simply to the broader forces ravaging the Ohio economy? Again, this would require a more careful political economy study over a much bigger set of cases.

What does seem to cut across the cases, however, is the role of building common knowledge about regional challenges and opportunities across diverse constituencies, a factor that could not have surfaced in a quantitative study alone. It was a long trek from city to city, region to region, far from our offices, our computers, and our ability to simply play with the data. The journey brought surprises but perhaps the most striking was this sense of a shared knowledge base in these regions – of a shared "epistemic community" in which it was expected that facts counted and that who knew them mattered.

But before making any definite conclusions about what was working, we knew we wanted to also understand what wasn't. So the bags did not stay unpacked long before we headed out to three regions that have had varying experiences of good fortunes lost, or bad circumstances reversed, or prosperity and inclusion enduringly sought with little success. Sacramento, Denver, and Cleveland were next on our whirlwind tour of U.S. metros, and the following chapter takes up that phase of our journey.

4   Slipping, reversing, stuck

Introduction

Only highlighting the best in class does not necessarily tell much about the field. What about those regions that seem sure to make it – then do not? What about those that make a comeback but leave us wondering for just how long? And how about those long-struggling places that finally look like they are about to break through?

This chapter turns to the other side of the equation – to those regional contestants that may have been bounced off "American Idol" well before the finals, and even one that might not have made it past the initial audition. As noted in Chapter 2, Sacramento showed strong growth and improvements in social equity in the 1980s, but had a sharp reversal of fortunes in the 1990s. Denver was just the opposite, with sluggish growth and relative deterioration of social indicators in the 1980s, but rapid growth and inclusion in the 1990s. Meanwhile, Cleveland was stuck in sluggish growth and relative deterioration of social equity indicators throughout the 1980s and 1990s – stemming from even longer periods of industrial decline and social conflict – but seemed to be showing signs of improved regional collaboration (although not much movement in real economic indicators) in the new millennium.

What do these cases tell us about the factors that can promote prosperity and inclusion – and the potential threats that might undermine positive growth and equity trajectories? What are the opportunities for reversing patterns of decline and growing social disparities toward more robust trajectories? And for those deeply entrenched in poor performance, what hope is there for breaking out in ways that can expand social inclusion while building the economy?

In what follows, we examine the experience of three regions in some depth, labeling one the "slip-back" case, one the "bounce-back" case, and one the "stuck-back" case. As in the previous chapter, we provide background on the region, a description of dynamics and processes of regional collaboration, and our assessment of the processes that likely shaped their varying growth and equity trajectories. These cases reinforce many of our conclusions in Chapter 3, including the importance of public sector employment and investment, the value of collaborative research, planning, and decision-making processes amongst diverse constituencies, and the contributions of particular groups of people that can bridge between growth coalitions and equity advocates. Yet what also emerges from these cases is the particular value of more recent thoughtful attempts to link economic growth and social equity across broad constituencies that may reflect that these regions are beginning to learn from the experiences of others.

Sacramento: vibrancy and vulnerability in California's capital city

Despite being the capital of the eighth largest economy in the world, the Sacramento region is often overshadowed by the more urbane Bay Area with its high-tech Silicon Valley and the glittery, post-modern metropolis of Los Angeles to the south. Much of Sacramento's growth and development can be understood by its service to other regions – from its origins as the restocking site for gold miners seeking their fortunes in the Sierra foothills, through its more recent incarnation as a low-cost back-office to firms seeking to escape the sky-high real estate prices of Silicon Valley in the 1990s. But being in the shadows has led to a bit of an inferiority complex: high-profile Sacramento mayor and former NBA star Kevin Johnson once complained to the *Wall Street Journal* that its national weather map did not even include Sacramento, despite its being the state capital.[1]

Yet despite the lack of visibility, Sacramento provides valuable lessons for how to link prosperity and inclusion. Through the 1980s, Sacramento showed strong patterns of above median growth with substantial improvements in equity as well. In the context of economic restructuring in the 1990s, it reversed this pattern, with social inequality increasing and growth slower than in much of the rest of the West. Interestingly, there seems to have been a positive reversal once again in recent years – with the poverty rate actually declining between 2000 and 2007 and the city–suburb poverty differential narrowing (Table 4.1), perhaps as a result of some conscious policy efforts that we explore below.

However, there are two major trends at the heart of the earlier slippage that reinforce some lessons from our quantitative research and the other case studies. First, in the 1980s, the region benefitted from a strong military presence amidst a rapid expansion in defense spending. This all disappeared in the 1990s as the region was disproportionately affected by base closures and other forms of military downsizing. Not only did this result in slower growth, but the large number of African Americans previously employed by the military became more susceptible to growing poverty. Second, in the 1990s, parts of the region experienced substantial high-tech employment growth, particularly hardware design, as established Silicon Valley companies expanded operations into the nearby region to take advantage of lower land and housing prices. This contributed to population and economic growth – the Sacramento metro population grew by 35 percent in the 1980s and 21 percent in the 1990s – but inequality actually worsened in the second of these two decades, as incomes at the top of the income distribution rose while those at the bottom stagnated.

On the other hand, the crisis of the 1990s gave rise to a range of regional initiatives that have helped build a basis of strong regional collaboration – a promising sign for regional recovery. Led by strong public and private sector initiatives, the collaboratives have strong growth agendas. But signs of equity-led regionalism are emerging, along with perhaps a growing awareness among public and private sector leadership that equity matters for growth and the region's future. The region's continued vulnerability to broader economic forces – most recently to the foreclosure crisis – underscores the continued importance of deliberate efforts to include both growth and equity in regional development strategies.

Background to the region

In 1848, when gold was discovered fifty miles east of Sacramento, in Coloma, the region emerged as the place where both ocean-bound immigrants arriving in San Francisco and overland travellers from the east converged before seeking their fortunes in the gold fields – frequently returning to reassess their futures when their efforts proved less remunerative than their dreams (Holliday 1981; Eifler 2002). Strategically located at the confluence of the Sacramento and American Rivers (Figure 4.1), the city became a major trading center, although San Francisco, eighty miles to the west, remained the dominant financial and trade center for the state (Brechin 1999).

Sacramento became the state capital in 1854, beating out San Luis Obispo and Santa Barbara in the south and Benicia, Stockton, San Francisco, and Vallejo in the north (Avella 2003: 41). A major transportation hub, it was first the end point of the Pony Express, and later a terminus of the Transcontinental Railway. The Sacramento railyards became the largest railroad facility west of the Mississippi River, combining both Central Pacific and Southern Pacific locomotive repairs, general maintenance, and locomotive construction. In the early part of the twentieth century, the railyards reportedly employed one-third of all Sacramento workers (Datel and Dingemans 2008).

Like most of the United States, Sacramento experienced substantial slippage in manufacturing and urban sprawl in the post-war period, particularly in and after the 1950s. One thing that remained central was the role of public employment: in 1990, 30 percent of employment in the four-county metro area – which includes Sacramento, Placer, Yolo, and El Dorado Counties – was in public sector employment, with state employment alone accounting for nearly 14 percent of total employment. In the same year, 4.2 percent of all employment was in the federal government, including the Department of Defense.[2]

Growth and inclusion in the 1980s

In the 1980s, two trends shaped the region. The first was a growth in military spending, something that helped alleviate the effects of the worst national recession since the Great Depression. The second was the "discovery" of the region by rapidly expanding Silicon Valley firms attracted to Sacramento's proximity, low costs, quality of life, and seismic stability.

In the 1980s, Sacramento had four large and thriving military bases. The largest

Table 4.1 Select demographic and economic data for the Sacramento–Arden-Arcade–Roseville metropolitan area

Metropolitan characteristics	1980	1990	2000	2007
Total CBSA population	1,100,836	1,481,796	1,796,857	2,091,120
Principal cities	471,777	624,425	738,075	846,142
Suburbs	629,059	857,371	1,058,782	1,244,978
Race/ethnicity (%)				
Non-Hispanic white	79	73	64	59
Black	5	7	7	7
Latino	10	11	15	18
Asian/Pacific Islander (API)	5	7	9	12
Other	1	1	5	4
Percent foreign born	7.3	9.5	14.5	17.3
Average annual earnings per job (2007 dollars) (place of work basis)	42,253	43,549	49,632	52,874
Poverty rate (% persons)	11.2	11.9%	12.7%	11.1%
Principal cities	12.6	13.7%	15.6%	12.4%
Suburbs	10.2	10.6%	10.8%	10.4%
By percent federal poverty level				
Below 100%	11.2	11.9	12.7	11.1
Between 100% and 149%	9.3	8.0	8.4	8.0
Between 150% and 199%	9.3	8.2	8.1	8.4
Above 200%	70.2	71.9	70.8	72.5
Poverty concentration				
Percent of CBSA poor in high poverty tracts (poverty rate > 20%)	27	39	50	41
Percent of CBSA poor in very high poverty tracts (poverty rate > 40%)	1	6	5	4
80–20 household income ratio	4.3	3.9	4.1	4.2
Income differentials (%)				
Median Black household income relative to median white household income	67	69	68	59
Median Latino household income relative to median white household income	75	80	75	73
Median API household income relative to median white household income	107	86	88	107

Demography and immigration

Income and poverty

Metropolitan characteristics	1980	1990	2000	2007
Educational attainment (population over 25 years and older) (%)				
Less than high school	22	17	15	13
High school only	30	24	22	24
Some college	28	35	35	33
Bachelor's degree	13	16	18	20
Graduate or professional degree	7	8	10	10
Workers by industry (total employed population 16 years and older) (%)				
Agriculture and mining	3	3	2	2
Construction	7	8	7	9
Manufacturing	7	7	7	5
Transportation, warehousing, and utilities	6	5	5	5
Wholesale trade	4	4	3	3
Retail trade	18	17	16	18
Finance, insurance, and real estate	7	8	8	9
Professional services	4	7	8	8
Health services	7	7	8	9
Information	4	4	5	4
Education	10	8	8	7
Other services	8	10	11	12
Public administration	17	12	11	9
Public sector employment	30	25	22	21
Principal cities–suburbs job distribution				
Percent of jobs in principal cities	48	57	56	53
Percent of jobs in suburbs	52	43	44	47
Job growth over preceding decade (last 7 years for 2007) (%)				
All CBSA	–	47	18	–2
Principal cities	–	75	15	–8
Suburbs	–	21	21	5
Spatial segregation by income and race				
Poverty dissimilarity index	24.9	33.2	36.6	34.6
African American–white dissimilarity index	57.9	56.9	57.9	55.4
Latino–white dissimilarity index	36.7	37.6	40.3	50.7
All people of color–white dissimilarity index	38.3	40.0	40.4	47.3

Education and employment

Segregation

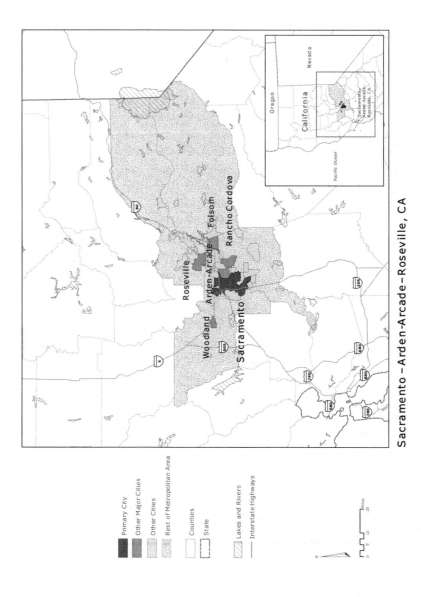

Legend:
- Primary City
- Other Major Cities
- Other Cities
- Rest of Metropolitan Area
- Counties
- State
- Lakes and Rivers
- Interstate Highways

Sacramento – Arden-Arcade – Roseville, CA

Figure 4.1 Sacramento–Arden-Arcade–Roseville metropolitan area.

was McClellan Air Force Base, primarily a site for logistics and maintenance for military aircraft and equipment. Opened in 1936 and expanded dramatically with the start of World War II, it employed over 22,000 people at its peak – and was one of the region's largest employers of women (Avella 2003).[3] Mather Air Field was operated from 1918 through 1932, and then was reopened again in 1936 because of the lobbying by Sacramento elected officials that resulted in the establishment of McClellen. In the 1950s, Mather became a major training facility and a base for the Strategic Air Command, employing some 7,000 people – though with more military than civilian wage earners. The Sacramento Army Depot opened in 1942 to relieve congestion as a spin-off from facilities in the San Francisco Bay Area and employed some 4,000 (mostly civilian) employees through the 1980s. Finally, Beale Air Force Base, located about forty miles north of the city of Sacramento, was also established in 1942. Originally a training facility, it became a reconnaissance and intelligence gathering site providing combat support, and is the home to approximately 4,000 military personnel.[4]

Military contractors complemented the military bases. Sacramento shared in the largess of defense spending that went to California from the 1960s to the 1980s – nearly one-quarter of national defense spending poured into the Golden State (Clayton 1962; Markusen et al. 1991). Headquartered in the area, Aerojet designed, built, and tested rocket engines and was a major beneficiary, with the company reaching $1 billion in sales in 1988.[5]

During the 1980s and early 1990s, the region also became an important node in global information technology industries, including hardware manufacturing as well as expanding in software, telecommunications, and internet services. Silicon Valley-based high-tech firms saw Sacramento as a low-cost manufacturing center that was only a few hours drive from corporate headquarters. Hewlett-Packard first established operations in the region in 1979, followed by Intel in 1984 and Apple in 1992. Semiconductor firms such as Intel (1984), NEC Electronics (1983), and Level One Communications (1985), whose operations were becoming increasingly sophisticated at a micro scale, were especially attracted to the region's seismic stability, in contrast to the tremor-prone Bay Area.[6] As housing and land prices skyrocketed and traffic congestion worsened in Silicon Valley, companies increasingly saw the Sacramento region as an attractive site for expansion around a wide range of activities.

The Sacramento region's improvement in both social equity and growth in the 1980s seems to have been driven by the quality of jobs at the time, rather than by any explicit attempts to promote equity, regional or otherwise. For example, public sector jobs are highly unionized and typically pay middle-class wages – and in the mid-1980s, 57 percent of public sector jobs in the Sacramento metropolitan statistical area (MSA) were covered by a union contract.[7] Even wages at the bottom end of the income distributions were relatively higher because unemployment rates were low throughout the period – and the unemployment rate, more than skill level, drives wage bargaining in this part of the workforce (Blanchflower and Oswald 1990). With military-related employment also sustaining mid-skill occupations, this muted the inequity effects so common with high-tech growth.[8]

Economic and social shocks of the 1990s

Sacramento's pattern of growth and inclusion in the 1980s was dramatically reversed in the 1990s, primarily as the result of the government's cuts in defense spending and three military base closures. Surprisingly, the Sacramento regional economy actually grew – employment still grew by 17.5 percent during the decade – but this was much lower than the 46.9 percent growth in the 1980s, and was accompanied by growing poverty and growing inequality. Essentially, as military spending left the region, the economy became more bifurcated as high-tech and service work became more prevalent.

The post-Cold War decline in the military presence in Sacramento began in 1988 with the closure of Mather Air Force Base, followed by the Sacramento Air Depot in 1991, and McClellan AFB in 1995. Nearly one-third of the military bases closed in the 1988 round were in California,[9] and the state's share of Department of Defense spending, which was as high as 23 percent in 1984, was just 14 percent of defense contract expenditures by 2003. In the Sacramento/ Central Valley region, base closures resulted in the loss of an estimated 16,848 jobs, including 3,673 direct military jobs and another 13,175 civilian jobs on military bases (Freedman and Ransdell 2005). Aerojet saw its total employment in the region decline to an estimated 1,700 in 1999.[10]

Meanwhile, the Silicon Valley attention to Sacramento also brought the attention of a different set of suitors. By the late 1990s, Sacramento had garnered a reputation as something of a "call center city." Franklin Templeton was one of the first financial companies to expand operations in Sacramento, attracted in part by the substantial fiber-optic cable infrastructure in the region, the result of early investment by state government agencies with substantial data processing needs. Templeton's expansion led a number of other Bay Area-based firms to expand into the Sacramento area. By the late 1990s, the Highway 50 corridor east of downtown had become a major hub for call centers, back office operations, and financial processing firms. But these new jobs were poor substitutes for the solid middle-class ones provided by military spending. The call center jobs paid substantially lower wages, and the high-tech jobs were mostly out of reach for laid-off military base employees, with African Americans disproportionately impacted by the military slowdown.

The increasing bifurcation took a spatial form. Employment growth in the 1990s and 2000s was most dramatic in the region's eastern suburbs, but the majority of the region's low-income residents were concentrated in the core. For example, in 1998 in Sacramento County, 22 percent of the population were eligible for MediCal, while in El Dorado and Placer Counties only 8 percent were eligible;[11] a full 11 percent of Sacramento County residents received TANF assistance, compared with only 3 percent in El Dorado and Placer Counties.[12]

The silver lining: new collaborative regional responses

Although Sacramento slipped into underperformance on prosperity and inclusion in the 1990s, the economic restructuring catalyzed a number of broad, regional, collaborative initiatives that have continued through the new millennium. The strongest are at an elite level – major public and private sector leadership networks – and have a strong focus on growth. Equity-oriented coalitions are less prominent, but are making progress in creating a line of communication between growth and equity constituencies. Together they are creating a strong culture of collaborative visioning and implementation.

Military base closure offered an opportunity for joint conversations about postbase use. Years of notice were given for the closure – leaving plenty of time for deliberation. In one case, this went poorly: at Mather Field, Sacramento County offered to buy up housing to add to the affordable housing stock, the Air Force would not lower its price, and in the end the housing was destroyed (Freedman and Ransdell 2005). In contrast, early on in the closure process, Packard Bell expressed interest in moving its manufacturing to the soon-to-be-vacated Sacramento Air Depot. At the urging of the governor's office, the Sacramento Area Trade and Commerce Agency (SACTO), a private sector regional marketing and attraction agency, partnered with the City of Sacramento and the Sacramento Employment and Training Agency (SETA), a public sector-funded workforce development agency, to help close the deal. Negotiating accelerated conversion of the site and providing substantial training and hiring assistance, the collaboration resulted in – at its peak – employment for close to 5,000 people and in a location relatively close to a poor neighborhood in need of economic revitalization.[13]

The SACTO–SETA partnership catalyzed other collaborative work. Together they created START (Sacramento Training and Response Team) as a partnership of regional economic development, business, education (including community college and higher education), labor, and government.[14] Its focus is on developing a highly trained workforce throughout the whole region as a means of making it easy for business to locate or expand in the region.[15] SACTO has been working with local economic development departments to encourage regional business attraction efforts rather than interjurisdictional competition. The six counties and twenty-three cities involved have broadly recognized that they are better off marketing the region as a whole and growing the overall regional economic pie rather than fighting over which slice they will get. Any jurisdiction that gets a prospective new business immediately shares it with SACTO to give the business the best possible chance of locating somewhere in the region.[16]

In 1994, Valley Vision was founded to create an objective, non-partisan, and impartial organization that could bring people from different sectors together to address long-term regional challenges and opportunities. A 1999 "regional compact" resulted in virtually every city and county in the region officially agreeing that many public policy and community issues can be solved only at the regional level and that cooperation among jurisdictions is crucial to enduring solutions. Valley Vision's 2006 Partnership for Prosperity initiative brought together thirty-four prominent organizations in the region to develop a common economic development strategy, with a growing focus on the region's substantial clean and green energy industry. Other regional initiatives are working to protect open space and agricultural land from sprawl, to bring together minority business leaders, and to tackle health disparities.

Since the late 1990s, the region has also experienced strong levels of public sector collaboration throughout the region, led largely by the Sacramento Area Council of Governments (SACOG). Starting in 2002, SACOG, with Valley Vision's support around public participation, began a long-range regional planning process to develop a common vision for land use and transportation infrastructure through 2050. The process of developing a regional "blueprint" compared a base case scenario of sprawling and uncontrolled urbanization against other scenarios designed to promote denser development and expanded mass transit. SACOG has received multiple national awards for the content of the blueprint – but also for the process that produced it. Throughout the region, more than thirty neighborhood-scale workshops (involving more than 1,000 citizens) were held to discuss development scenarios. Following this, countywide discussions were held in five of the six counties. More than 1,400 people participated in a final regional forum on April 30, 2004. Through this process, "regionalism" became popularized.

After the initial blueprint process began, Legal Services of Northern California (LSNC), ACORN, and other community organizations started educating and mobilizing residents to ensure that equity principles would be reflected more strongly in subsequent planning. Starting in February of 2003, LSNC coordinated neighborhood meetings with leaders from more than forty-one different community-based organizations. Together, they convinced SACOG and Valley Vision to include three diversity sessions in future blueprint planning. But, in essence, equity advocates were playing catch-up, primarily reacting to initiatives rather than developing their own. So in 2007 they formed the Coalition for Regional Equity (CORE), a coalition of affordable housing developers, environmentalists, advocates focused on transportation, the homeless, and poverty, social service providers, labor, the faith community, civil rights leaders, and health groups. CORE has clearly impacted SACOG's attention to equity, which is more central in their 2010–2011 update efforts, and they have made a way for building ongoing communication between equity and growth coalitions (Pastor and Benner 2011).

Another community-led regional equity initiative emerged in the early 2000s, led by ACORN. Working with a broad coalition of community groups, the focus here was on mobilizing support for California State Assembly Bill 680, which would have allocated sales taxes from new growth throughout the region in a tax-sharing formula that would have taken account of population needs and smart growth projects and planning. Passed in the Assembly, it lost in the Senate, largely because of opposition from outside of Sacramento – city officials and others who had concerns that tax-base sharing would spread past Sacramento.

Although the Sacramento metropolitan region has one of the highest regional unionization rates in the United States, the labor movement has been only modestly involved in regional efforts.[17] This is because the largest unions have been focused on statewide policy and bargaining issues, rather than Sacramento regional dynamics – one of the cross-cutting effects of being in a state capital. The Sacramento Central Labor Council (CLC), although strongly integrated into the region's workforce development system and involved in the Partnership for Prosperity, lacks the kind of regional research and policy capacity associated with other CLCs that comprise the Partnership for Working Families, a network of organizations that includes the Los Angeles Alliance for a New Economy, Working Partnerships USA, and other such configurations.

So although there are strong regional collaborations tackling growth in a deliberate manner, voices for equity have been less prominent in the Sacramento region. Still, the region did perform better on these measures in the 2000–2007 period, ranking in the top quarter for the Western census region in terms of employment growth, poverty reductions, and shifts in income distribution. Perhaps the efforts of various regional collaboratives at forging common understandings and commitments are starting to pay off.

Prosperity, inclusion and deliberation

As we complete the writing of this book in spring of 2011, Sacramento is frequently in the national news, but not for the reasons we would hope. For the third year in a row, the State of California is facing record budget deficits, and the strategies to balance the budget rest on drastic cuts to social services and public education. California has been at the center of the explosive crisis of the Great Recession and Sacramento is where the big decisions about how to deal with the budgetary fall-out get made (Walker 2010).

Partly because it is the center of state politics, the challenges of the Sacramento region itself often remain invisible to the national eye. Although the period from 2000 to 2007 brought progress as well as an increasing regional consciousness about the need to move forward on growth and equity, Sacramento has been deeply affected by the national and state crises. Unemployment has been above 10 percent for more than three years. Median home prices in the Sacramento MSA plunged more than 50 percent from their bubble-induced peak.[18] Foreclosures in the region are among the highest in the nation. A return to the 1980s golden years of both prosperity and inclusion seems far away.

Still, Sacramento's experience suggests a few lessons in comparison to our other regions. Sacramento has significant public sector employment, but this clearly cannot guarantee stability against external economic shocks. It did find a way to kindle some growth even as the military base closures rocked the region in the 1980s. But with growth occurring in suburban job centers away from central city residents and with the growing high-tech sectors bringing bifurcation by income and race, Sacramento sagged.[19]

Public and private sector organizations in Sacramento have shown impressive leadership since the mid-1990s in building strong regional collaborations to tackle the issues of spatial fragmentation and economic slippage. While successful in engaging regional economic and environmental issues, they have been much less so in engaging equity. In the wreckage of the housing crisis, one wonders whether a stronger regional focus to address unaffordable housing and stagnating wages might have helped stem the worst of the property bubble.

Denver: the mile-high comeback?

We chose Denver because it seemed to be an example of a region bouncing back – and in an intentional way. When the regional economy went bust in the 1980s, regional actors were quite purposeful about taking a more regional approach, including promoting a new airport, a new light rail system, and new downtown developments. Through the 1990s, the poverty rate fell and the 80–20 housing income ratio went to 3.6, the best of all our case study regions for that year.

When we conducted our site visit to Denver, however, interviewees were surprised to learn that the region had improved in quantitative equity measures. We thought that this was partly because the history of the 1980s bore heavily on the region and partly because they perceived Denver as a boom–bust town in which the worst was soon to return. They were right about the latter: between 2000 and 2007, Denver's economy performed on average as compared to the Western census region but its equity measures – the changes in poverty and the income distribution ratio – were among the worst (Table 4.2).

Interviewees were also quite insistent about a story behind the favorable numbers of the 1990s: the "Colorado Paradox" in which many highly educated workers in the region come from out-of-state while many poorly educated workers are native, creating an overall picture of improvement while gains from growth really accrue to newcomers. Despite this, many did note that the growth of the 1990s stemmed from the region's willingness to invest in public infrastructure, the coordination of businesses, and the emergence of a multi-jurisdictional metro identity. Harnessing that to address equity remains a challenge for the regional future.

Background to the region

With the mythos of the California gold rush still in the air, a small group of prospectors found gold at the base of the Rocky Mountains in 1858 – and travelers quickly flocked to soon-to-be Denver. In short order, a town sprang up along the banks of the South Platte River, with the population surging, then receding when gold was periodically found in the nearby mountains. Precious metals drove another boom when the Kansas Pacific Railroad was routed through Denver and a miner struck silver. But in keeping with the inevitable boom–bust cycle, in 1893, silver was demonetized and the region was forced to diversify its economy to include livestock, wheat farming, and sugar beet production, among other land-based industries.

In 1902, the City of Denver consolidated with the newly formed county by the same name (Riley and Noel 2006) (Figure 4.2). In the first half of the twentieth century, progressive politics filled the air, from hosting the 1908 Democratic national convention, to being a center of the Social Gospel movement, to being entangled in a free speech fight (Brundage 1994; Denton 1997). After World War II, the Denver regional economy flourished because of the oil industry. In the 1970s, the population doubled during a building boom and Denver emerged as a business hub, tourist playground, and the economic and cultural capital of the Rocky Mountain West.

From bust to boom: Colorado's economy in the 1980s and 1990s

In short, Denver has historically had a boom-and-bust economy – and the 1980s–1990s era was no exception. Since its founding in 1858 as a mining town, the economy has been tied to the status of Colorado's predominant commodity at the time, be it gold, silver, beaver furs, cattle, or, more recently, oil shale. The recession tied to oil in the 1980s was the worst that the state has experienced since the Great Depression (Blount 1998). In 1982, Exxon abruptly abandoned its $5 billion Colony Project in Western Colorado, triggering a chain of events that left the state in distress – 2,200 Exxon workers unemployed and other firms following suit by leaving the state (Williamson 1999). The mainstay of the regional economy was gone.

The oil bust was the center of a larger collapse that deeply impacted Denver and the surrounding region. In aviation, Frontier Airlines laid off 3,500 workers, most in the Denver area. Manufacturing workers took a hit when firms such as Storage Technology Corporation and MiniScribe Corporation laid off thousands (Blount 1998). Given the drop in jobs, the region's foreclosure rate grew to approximately 2.4 percent in the 1980s – a rate comparable to those seen in the 2008 real estate crash (2.5 percent in the first quarter) (Silverstein 2008). These compounding events rippled throughout the state and resulted in some of the most difficult times in Colorado's history.

The difficult climate of the 1980s was followed by a dramatic boom in the 1990s. The bust town once again became a boom town; this time with a more diversified economy that no longer relied on a single commodity for its fortunes. The prosperity of the 1990s was often described by our interviewees as the tide that lifted all (or at least many) boats. Denver leaders attribute the return of prosperity in that era to three things: public investment in major infrastructure and development projects, private sector leadership in diversifying the economy, and the overall improvement in the U.S. economy.

Former mayor Peña (1983–1991) was committed to the idea that, if Denver invested in infrastructure, businesses would come. In 1989, residents approved the $3 billion Denver International Airport (DIA) project and in 1990 taxpayers both voted for a stadium tax to fund the new Coors Field and completed the new $126 million dollar Convention Center (Leonard and Noel 1991). The DIA was the largest and most important of the three projects.[20] It provided long-term, stable employment and many of the jobs created improved equity because they were unionized (or at least paid prevailing wages). While others regions were trying to lure businesses with tax *breaks*, Denver was *spending* money on these infrastructure projects as well as on schools, roads, and parks to improve the city.[21] These public investments laid the foundation for the private sector to diversify the regional economy.

Table 4.2 Select demographic and economic data for the Denver-Aurora metropolitan area

Metropolitan characteristics	1980	1990	2000	2007
Total CBSA population	1,465,575	1,666,973	2,179,365	2,466,591
Principal cities	651,274	689,713	830,140	898,762
Suburbs	814,301	977,260	1,349,225	1,567,829
Race/ethnicity (%)				
Non-Hispanic white	81	79	71	67
Black	5	6	5	5
Latino	11	13	18	22
Asian/Pacific Islander (API)	2	2	3	4
Other	0	1	2	2
Percent foreign born	4.5	4.9	10.8	12.4
Average annual earnings per job (2007 dollars) (place of work basis)	43,274	43,461	55,731	57,571
Poverty rate (% persons)	8.2	9.7	8.0	11.5
Principal cities	11.7	14.0	12.4	17.9
Suburbs	5.4	6.7	5.2	7.8
By percent federal poverty level				
Below 100%	8.2	9.7	8.0	11.5
Between 100% and 149%	6.4	6.6	6.0	6.9
Between 150% and 199%	7.8	7.7	6.8	7.2
Above 200%	77.6	76.0	79.2	74.5
Poverty concentration				
Percent of CBSA poor in high poverty tracts (poverty rate > 20%)	28	38	28	47
Percent of CBSA poor in very high poverty tracts (poverty rate > 40%)	7	7	1	4
80–20 household income ratio	3.9	3.8	3.6	4.3
Income differentials (%)				
Median Black household income relative to median white household income	66	60	64	61
Median Latino household income relative to median white household income	69	71	69	58
Median API household income relative to median white household income	89	84	89	92

The left margin contains two vertical bracketed labels: *Demography and immigration* (covering the upper portion of the table) and *Income and poverty* (covering the lower portion).

Metropolitan characteristics	1980	1990	2000	2007
Educational attainment (population over 25 years and older) (%)				
Less than high school	19	14	13	12
High school only	30	25	22	24
Some college	25	31	29	28
Bachelor's degree	18	20	23	24
Graduate or professional degree	8	9	12	13
Workers by industry (total employed population 16 years and older) (%)				
Agriculture and mining	3	2	1	2
Construction	7	5	8	10
Manufacturing	14	10	7	6
Transportation, warehousing, and utilities	7	7	6	6
Wholesale trade	6	6	4	3
Retail trade	16	17	17	17
Finance, insurance, and real estate	8	8	9	9
Professional services	7	9	11	11
Health services	7	8	7	8
Information	4	6	8	7
Education	8	7	7	7
Other services	8	10	10	10
Public administration	6	5	4	4
Public sector employment	15	14	11	11
Principal cities–suburbs job distribution				
Percent of jobs in principal cities	61	52	46	44
Percent of jobs in suburbs	39	48	54	56
Job growth over preceding decade (last 7 years for 2007) (%)				
All CBSA	–	20	30	4
Principal cities	–	2	14	0
Suburbs	–	48	48	8
Spatial segregation by income and race				
Poverty dissimilarity index	36.3	40.5	39.0	40.4
African American–white dissimilarity index	69.1	65.6	64.3	61.2
Latino–white dissimilarity index	48.8	47.1	50.2	47.1
All people of color–white dissimilarity index	46.4	43.3	44.0	45.9

Left margin labels: Education and employment; Segregation

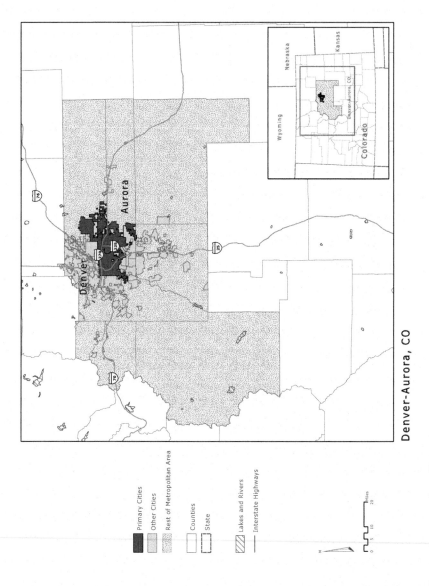

Denver–Aurora, CO

Figure 4.2 Denver–Aurora metropolitan area.

The private sector, particularly the Greater Denver Corporation (GDC), played a major role in the success of public infrastructure projects. The GDC was formed in 1987 amidst the state's recession to act as the economic development arm of the Denver Metro Chamber of Commerce, with its goals being diversifying the economy, attracting new high-tech jobs, and encouraging new business start-ups. The GDC was active in the successful campaign to annex land in Adams County for the new airport. Subsequently, the GDC's involvement in the referendum to publicly fund airport construction is believed to have swung voters, who were originally narrowly divided on the issue, to a two-to-one win (Delaney and Eckstein 2003).

GDC also helped boost the regional economy by garnering public support to build a new, publicly funded baseball stadium in Denver that attracted the Colorado Rockies baseball franchise. In 1989, former governor of Colorado Ray Romer approached the GDC about pulling together an ownership group to begin the franchise application process. The GDC, along with other stadium proponents, invested $500,000 into supporting a referendum to fund the stadium with tax dollars. The public was generally divided on the referendum because there were no guarantees of a team coming to Denver; however, the passage of the referendum in August of 1990 helped to convince the National League to award Denver with the baseball franchise in 1991. Construction began in 1992 and Coors Field was completed by 1995.

GDC also went on to establish a truly metropolitan economic development program called the Metro Denver Network. The network was a collaboration of economic development agencies, funded by participating cities and counties. Denver's vision, which originated with Mayor Federico Peña, was that Denver should be marketed as a six-county economic engine (McCormick 2006). This emphasis on Denver as a region, rather than a stand-alone city–county, initiated a tradition of collaboration across jurisdictional lines. Economic development corporations in local jurisdictions throughout the region began to share their leads on companies looking for sites with others in the Metro Denver Network, and then to collectively send their corporate proposals together in order to maximize the potential attraction of the region.[22]

Of course, in some ways, the bust in Colorado in the 1980s had set up Denver for the boom to follow. Economists have cited speculative real estate development in the early 1980s as one of the causes of that recession; however, the upside to the abundance of vacant office buildings was that by 1990 the region boasted very cheap office space. At $13 per square foot, the office rental rate compared quite favorably to Atlanta, where office space ran for $21 per square foot, and New York, which had the country's most expensive lease rates at $45 per square foot (Blount 1998). These cheap rents presented an opportunity for employers looking to settle in the region to secure long-term affordable rental contracts. Meanwhile, workers were increasingly attracted to Denver because of its high quality of life, good weather, access to the mountains, and affordability (relative to other large cities). The attraction of workers resulted in employers following suit.

The exodus of thousands of the region's residents during the 1980s also had a beneficial impact on workers' livelihoods in the recovery of the 1990s. One interviewee recalled such a labor shortage in the 1990s that McDonald's was offering signing bonuses; another described employers recruiting people out of parking lots. Employers did everything they could to get people to come and to stay in the region. All of this – the booming economy, the labor shortage, and rising wages – led to positive changes in growth indicators, as well as in the seeming well-being of Denver residents.

Did Denver really improve?

But did Denver residents really benefit? Although it is likely that they did, it is also the case that the attraction of migrants from other states can obscure the picture. Colorado ranks amongst the top five most educated states in the country, based on the number of degree holders per capita. But interviewees urged us to separate native Coloradans from the largely educated workforce that moved into the region during the 1990s. We did just that for Denver: approximately 35 percent of the region's population had a Bachelor's degree or higher in 2000, but that rate for those born in another state is higher at 41 percent.[23] This is the so-called "Colorado Paradox": native Coloradans have lower high school graduation rates and lower rates of higher education attainment despite the state's high overall ranking, and so may not be as well positioned to benefit from growth.

The redevelopment of the Stapleton Airport is another example of the region's uncertain record with regard to equity in the 1990s. Before the opening of DIA in 1995, Stapleton served as the region's major airport. Stapleton's closure presented the region with an opportunity. The undeveloped land at the old airport allowed civic groups and city leaders to think critically about how redevelopment could benefit the surrounding community, which was predominantly Latino, African American, and low income. Social equity became one of five guiding principles of the Stapleton Master Development Plan, along with environmental responsibility, economic opportunity, physical design, and implementation.

In 2000, Denver named real estate developer Forest City as the master developer for the project. Forest City would purchase the 2,900 developable acres and would be held responsible for infrastructure while the city would demolish the old airport buildings and clean up the site – in addition to providing hundreds of millions in incentives, including a $294 million tax increment financing package (Montgomery 2005). In return, Forest City would connect the development to the surrounding community, apportion 13 percent of the housing stock as affordable housing, and hire minority workers. By 2008, Stapleton had become a prime example of growth in the area – a bustling community with businesses, retail shops, six schools, and over 7,000 residents.

Although Stapleton's redevelopment plan explicitly endorsed social equity as a goal, its success on that front is not so clear. Housing prices are higher than the average Denver resident can afford and the development is not an integrated, mixed-use urban community. Tony Robinson, Associate Professor at the

University of Colorado, Denver, has suggested that, if Stapleton is receiving $300 million in public dollars, the project should better reflect the needs of the local community (Montgomery 2005). Piton Foundation Senior Research Associate Terri Bailey notes that in the region there are plenty of examples of developments with both growth and equity goals but, in practice, only one usually wins out; the Stapleton project, some argue, has evolved into a wealthier and gentrified neighborhood.[24] On the other hand, Carol Hedges of the Colorado Fiscal Policy Institute said that, compared with the redevelopment of Lowry Air Force base in the same time period, Stapleton is a success story for blending equity and growth.[25]

Risking the future?

Denver's dramatic turnaround from the 1980s to the 1990s was certainly impressive – but, as noted in the introduction to this case, it may also have been just another twist in the boom–bust cycle. For example, the 80–20 household income ratio jumped from 3.61 in 2000 to 4.24 in 2007 – which is even worse than the 80–20 household income ratio in the 80s (3.82). Meanwhile, poverty rose from 8 percent to 11.5 percent by 2007. The economic growth figures were middling for the Western census region but these equity figures were pretty much near the bottom. Meanwhile, jobs continued to sprawl outward: the share of jobs in the principal cities declined from 61 percent to 46 percent between 1980 and 2000, and fell an additional two percentage points between 2000 and 2007.

Addressing the equity challenge will be difficult because there is no strong regional governing body – and few actors committed to social issues on a regional scale. The Denver Regional Council of Governments, the body designed to foster regional cooperation amongst county and municipal governments in the Denver metropolitan area, has a limited presence and is not widely viewed as a regional leader. The voluntary Metro Mayors Caucus has limited capacity, as do the thirty-seven allied mayors – none of whom are full time except for Denver's.

There have been calls for collaboration. Former Denver City mayor and now Colorado state governor John Hickenlooper called in his 2004 State of the City address for "building innovative partnerships based on the understanding that the future prosperity of each of our communities is inherently linked" (McCormick 2006: 90). One of the more influential efforts initiated under Mayor Hickenlooper's tenure was the Economic Prosperity Taskforce. The Taskforce brought together public sector and community representatives (from labor, philanthropy, non-profits, and the private sector) to discuss what it means to be prosperous, thriving, and financially self-sufficient in the City.

The culmination of the Taskforce's year of study was a set of five recommendations to the administration, City Council, and City.[26] Participants we interviewed noted that one of the most valuable things to come out of the taskforce was a shared understanding between the various stakeholders of how the interaction between government, individuals, and the private sector creates opportunities or challenges to progress toward economic prosperity. A number of our interviewees commented on how rare an opportunity it was to have the space to share different perspectives and have tough conversations about what it means to be prosperous and the roles of the different players in individual economic growth. The results of their efforts are not yet in, but it may be a start for developing the kind of regional consensus that economic prosperity for all individuals will result in economic prosperity for the region.

The business community has been more successful at building a regional consensus and creating ongoing regional organizations to carry forward the work of economic development, including the Greater Denver Corporation, the Metro Denver Network in the mid-1990s, and the more recently formed Metro Denver Economic Development Corporation (EDC). EDC is a non-profit entity whose primary functions are to create new jobs and to promote Denver as a cohesive region to attract businesses. There was a consensus from interviewees that EDC has played an important role in attracting businesses and in branding Denver as a well-functioning, cooperative region.

Yet Denver stands in stark contrast to Jacksonville and Nashville in the low level of engagement of business leadership with social issues. One of the more telling examples: although immigrants comprise a substantial share of the population (approximately 13 percent in 2007), very few interviewees touched on issues affecting the immigrant community. In 2006, Colorado passed a slew of anti-immigrant workplace legislation, leading to increases in deportations, raids, and employer aggression against undocumented workers.[27] Yet business leadership in Denver, unlike in Nashville, was silent (George 2004).

As for labor, Colorado has historically been an anti-union state. The evolution of the Denver Area Labor Federation (DALF) since the late 1990s helped to establish labor as a powerful voice in the region. With the election of Leslie Moody to the Central Labor Council in 1998, DALF had set out to transform its role and presence in electoral politics, labor community work, policy movement, and coalition building (Luce and Nelson 2004). Although union density in the region remains low – around 7–8 percent – DALF won a living wage campaign in 2000 and influenced a series of elections: the 2000 State Senate elections, the 2003 Denver City Council elections, and the 1999 election of two school board members who convinced their colleagues to grant organizing rights to service workers.

In 2002, Leslie Moody and Carmen Rhodes (political director at the time) further grew DALF's reach by developing the Front Range Economic Strategy Center (FRESC), an organization that acts as a bridge between unions and community organizations through research and policy development. FRESC has been steering regional economic growth toward equity as its leaders have pushed for accountable development and kept equity alive in the discourse on growth. In their Campaign for Responsible Development, FRESC won a community benefits agreement, including a "first source" hiring agreement, living wage provisions, affordable housing, and other community benefits for a publicly subsidized redevelopment initiative being undertaken by the Cherokee Denver company at the former Gates Rubber Factory.[28] Several interviewees viewed FRESC as pivotal in changing the perception of labor, partially because its leaders do not talk about the need to unionize, but the need to provide good jobs and strengthen the economy.

Denver has been home to minority leadership, perhaps ahead of the curve. Federico Peña was the city's first Latino mayor, from 1983 to 1991. Residents subsequently elected Wellington Webb for two terms, the city's first Black mayor, from 1991 to 2003. But despite interesting organizations and initiatives under way, the community sector in Denver overall seems to be quite weak. There are some interesting (albeit modest) community-based initiatives. The Colorado Fiscal Policy Institute, for example, has been trying to educate regional workforce development actors around minimum income thresholds. It promotes the Self Sufficiency Calculator to demonstrate what it takes to survive based on where employees live and their family situation.[29] Metro Organizations for People (MOP), a member of the faith-based PICO Network, organizes in the region and focuses its work on fiscal and budget issues.[30] The Piton Foundation funds and provides technical support to these and other non-profit organizations. Still, Karen Lado of Enterprise Community Partners characterized community-based organizations in the region as having a thin infrastructure of support.[31]

Stopping the roller coaster

Denver bounced back in the 1990s, posting above median gains in both growth and equity. But there are questions whether the fruits of the improvement really trickled down to long-time Denver residents – the 2000s saw growth remain moderately robust even as the equity measures slipped dramatically.

There are some hopeful efforts to bring together growth advocates and equity advocates, with Denver's Economic Prosperity Taskforce being a prime example. The need to link development initiatives with equity efforts has been established in specific private sector-led and publicly subsidized development initiatives such as the Stapleton redevelopment effort. And it is increasingly making its way into the public discourse through the efforts of civic organizations such as FRESC and the Colorado Fiscal Policy Institute; leaders from the various sectors we interviewed all acknowledged that there were segments of the population (e.g. low-wage workers, immigrants, native Coloradans, the homeless) that have been left behind and that would need to be included if the region was to truly reach its economic potential.

But Denver may be a warning about what happens when a region does not take deliberate action to make inclusion key to prosperity. Its business and civic leaders did act with intention and purpose to promote regional growth, with business organizations working hard to generate public support for investments in needed economic infrastructure such as the airport. But with little attention to and limited constituencies pushing an equity agenda, inclusion was bound to slip – and slip it did in the boom and bust cycle of instability, insecurity, and inattention.

Cleveland: been down so long

In our efforts to identify those metropolitan areas with strong growth and notable improvements in social equity, we were intrigued by the contrast in fortunes of metropolitan areas within the state of Ohio. Columbus, as we saw in Chapter 3, had moved the needle positively on growth and equity even as most of the metropolitan regions in the state – places such as Toledo, Dayton, Youngstown, Akron, and Cleveland – showed up in the bottom half of our growth variables and performed worse on our equity indicators than other metro areas in the Midwest. The long experience of de-industrialization and racial inequality in the state seemed to keep some stuck back – and few metros seemed more mired than Cleveland.

The differences between Cleveland and Columbus – and how they might impact prosperity and inclusion – are not difficult to identify. Cleveland was always much more reliant on manufacturing than Columbus, and thus more vulnerable to the slippage of America's industrial base. Columbus' ability to annex surrounding land and, thus create a more inclusive tax base, contrasts with the extreme levels of sprawl and fragmentation in Cleveland. Leaders in both communities suggest that there is a stronger legacy of racial inequality and conflict in Cleveland, further undermining the ability of the region to respond to economic challenges in a coordinated and strategic way.

At the same time, as we were beginning our case selection, Cleveland was being noted for a regional philanthropic effort called the Fund for Our Economic Future (Pastor and Benner 2008; Pastor et al. 2009b). An initiative to revitalize both the Cleveland metro and the larger Northeast Ohio area (Figure 4.3), the Fund was paying specific attention to both equity and growth, and had commissioned research that demonstrated that equity was among the factors that could explain sustainable growth. If Cleveland, a place where things had fallen apart so dramatically, was trying to pick itself up again through a focus on both inclusion and economic growth, then perhaps we might find clues to how other regions could become unstuck from the glue of stagnation and social conflict.

Background to the region

Settled in the early 1800s, Cleveland's waterfront location on Lake Erie proved to be an important advantage in contributing to economic growth. When the Ohio and Eric Canal was completed in 1832, making a key link between the Great Lakes and the Ohio River, Cleveland was strategically connected to both the Atlantic Ocean (via the Erie Canal and St. Lawrence Seaway) and the Gulf of Mexico (via the Ohio and Mississippi Rivers). With numerous transportation routes and large deposits of coal and iron ore, it became an attractive place for businesses and businessmen to settle. John D. Rockefeller and his partners began the Standard Oil Company in Cleveland during the 1860s and Samuel Mather began steel production; by 1880, 28 percent of Cleveland's workforce was employed in the steel mills. The region boomed in the late nineteenth and early twentieth centuries, and at one point Cleveland was the sixth largest city in the United States (Warf and Holly 1997).[32]

An important industrial center by the dawn of the twentieth century, on the cusp of the Great Depression, Cleveland was second only to Detroit in the

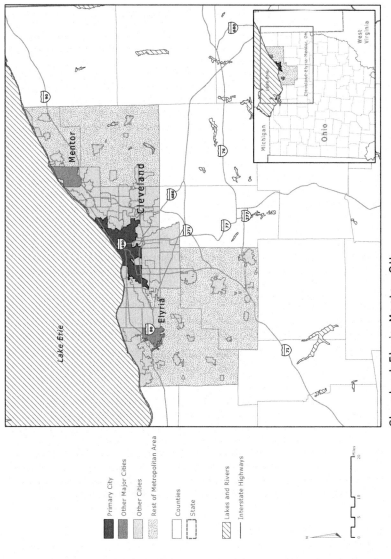

Cleveland–Elyria–Mentor, OH

Figure 4.3 Cleveland–Elyria–Mentor metropolitan area.

percentage of workers engaged in manufacturing. Like other industrial regions, it suffered during the Great Depression; by 1933, roughly one-third of Cleveland's workers were unemployed. Although industry recovered with the war and the post-war boom, recovery was not as sustained or dramatic as in the rest of the country and the region was battered as de-industrialization proceeded across the country in the 1970s and 1980s.

Job loss has led to a continual decline in population as well. The City of Cleveland reached its population peak in 1950 at 914,808 and has been losing population ever since; by 2000, the city's population had fallen by nearly half to 478,403, with further shrinkage to 396,815 by 2007.[33] The region as a whole remained more or less stable in the population count, but the hallowing out of the core and expanded suburban sprawl (in terms of both population and jobs) have gone hand in hand with economic stagnation and growing social disparities (see Table 4.3). As of 2007, the leading sectors in the Cleveland area were educational services and healthcare (21 percent), while employment in manufacturing has declined to only 15 percent (see Table 4.3).

No growth, no justice

Why has Cleveland remained such a poor performer on both growth and equity? Why did the slow descent not lead to a reconsideration and resurrection? We would point to several factors: reliance upon and subsequent loss of manufacturing; a history of racism and segregation; political fragmentation and continued sprawl; and an inadequate educational system.

Cleveland's economy suffers from a lack of much-needed diversity and competitiveness in the global market. For many decades, manufacturing was relied on as the sole economic driver. Although it remains a major factor in the economy of the region, its importance has continued to decline on an annual basis (Lamoreaux and Levenstein 2008). Employment in manufacturing in the Cleveland metro area fell from 280,000 in 1979 to less than 190,000 in 1994 – a drop of 40 percent in just fifteen years. The list of companies closing plants in the Cleveland area during that time reads like a "who's who" of U.S. manufacturing: U.S. Steel, General Motors, Westinghouse, General Electric (which shut down six factories in the region), Firestone, and Goodyear (Warf and Holly 1997).

Despite the obvious changes going on in the employment base, education and workforce training programs remained focused primarily on the manufacturing sector, creating a workforce ill prepared for potential future opportunities in other industries. According to Joe Roman from the Greater Cleveland Partnership (GCP), previously there were few incentives for people to go to college because there were plenty of jobs in the steel mills that did not require higher education.[34] The mills may be gone but it has taken a few generations to shift expectations and direct people to new pathways into quality occupations – particularly when those new occupations are only being slowly developed by an economy still staggering from de-industrialization and a populace often wishing that the better times of the past would simply return.

Meanwhile, segregation and racial disparities in the region have been dramatic. Before World War I, most of the migrants to Cleveland's booming industries were from Europe, but this shifted dramatically with the war and the great migration of Southern African Americans to the north (Wilkerson 2010). In a single decade, from 1910 to 1920, Cleveland's Black population increased 308 percent, from 8,448 to 34,451 (Krumholz and Berry 2007: 134). Most of the Black population settled on the city's east side and racial segregation took root (Kusmer 1978). By 1980, the Cleveland region had the fifth highest level of Black–white residential segregation of all metropolitan regions in the country.[35] In the city of Cleveland itself, the Black–white dissimilarity index was 86.5 in 1990, indicating that more than 86 percent of all Blacks in the city would have to move to a different neighborhood for every neighborhood to have the same white/Black racial distribution as the city on a whole.

The racial divisions also contributed to ongoing sprawl as whites, and later middle-class Blacks, have fled the growing poverty in the central city, leaving more concentrated poverty in their wake (Keating et al. 1995). Race riots in the 1960s accelerated the exodus, but the flight to better schools and amenities has continued the momentum (Krumholz and Berry 2007). In addition to contributing to racial disparities, sprawl also damages economic competitiveness as year in and year out infrastructure dollars find their way into progressively farther suburbs and provide very little investment for the inner city or even the older suburbs. Accompanying this outward extension is the proliferation of inter-urban, municipal competition.

Interviewees were quick to comment that Cleveland is politically fragmented. One reason for this is the city's utilization of the ward system, in which council members represent small geographic areas of the city. Although the number of City Council wards has recently been reduced from thirty-three to twenty-one, council members are charged with the responsibility of meeting the needs of neighborhood residents and improving the infrastructure in their particular area.[36] Many interviewees commented on this as potentially divisive and argued that it inhibited local leaders from collaborating for the common good. And it has been accompanied by city–suburb splits that further impede the realization of a regional vision.

Cleveland is also affected by "brain drain," as the lack of local employment opportunities leads youth who are able to leave to pursue opportunities elsewhere in more attractive markets. It is a statewide problem: although Ohio has a strong university system, it has a relatively low educational attainment level – Ohio ranked fortieth of all states, and the Cleveland metro area ranked sixty-ninth of the top 100 metro areas in the proportion of the adult population with a Bachelor's degree in 2000.[37] And it is not just the higher education system. Local observers comment on the relatively weak skill and employability levels of the area's young adult population. Local school board members, administrators, and teachers understand the need to work with local companies to better understand the core skills and competencies that they covet. But making this happen – and then convincing investors that it happened – remains a central challenge for the region.

Table 4.3 Select demographic and economic data for the Cleveland–Elyria–Mentor metropolitan area

	Metropolitan characteristics	*1980*	*1990*	*2000*	*2007*
Demography and immigration	*Total CBSA population*	2,169,577	2,102,168	2,148,143	2,096,471
	Principal cities	673,425	609,720	583,786	498,519
	Suburbs	1,496,152	1,492,448	1,564,357	1,701,161
	Race/ethnicity (%)				
	Non-Hispanic white	80	79	75	73
	Black	17	18	19	19
	Latino	2	2	3	4
	Asian/Pacific Islander (API)	1	1	1	2
	Other	0	0	2	1
	Percent foreign born	5.8	4.7	5.3	5.6
Income and poverty	Average annual earnings per job (2007 dollars) (place of work basis)	45,620	46,762	49,916	49,157
	Poverty rate (% persons)	9.7	11.8	10.8	12.7
	Principal cities	19.7	25.1	22.7	29.5
	Suburbs	5.2	6.3	6.3	8.8
	By percent federal poverty level				
	Below 100%	9.7	11.8	10.8	12.7
	Between 100% and 149%	6.2	6.6	6.9	7.4
	Between 150% and 199%	7.8	8.2	7.7	8.7
	Above 200%	76.3	73.4	74.7	71.2
	Poverty concentration				
	Percent of CBSA poor in high poverty tracts (poverty rate > 20%)	51	62	54	57
	Percent of CBSA poor in very high poverty tracts (poverty rate > 40%)	18	23	16	24
	80–20 household income ratio	4.3	4.4	4.3	4.8
	Income differentials (%)				
	Median Black household income relative to median white household income	64	53	56	51
	Median Latino household income relative to median white household income	67	66	65	57
	Median API household income relative to median white household income	111	118	108	114

Metropolitan characteristics	1980	1990	2000	2007
Educational attainment (population 25 years and older) (%)				
Less than high school	32	24	17	13
High school only	36	33	32	33
Some college	17	24	27	28
Bachelor's degree	11	12	15	16
Graduate or professional degree	5	7	9	10
Workers by industry (total employed population 16 years and older) (%)				
Agriculture and mining	1	1	1	1
Construction	4	4	5	5
Manufacturing	28	19	18	15
Transportation, warehousing, and utilities	6	6	5	5
Wholesale trade	5	5	4	4
Retail trade	16	16	16	17
Finance, insurance, and real estate	6	7	7	8
Professional services	5	7	8	8
Health services	8	10	10	12
Information	4	4	3	3
Education	7	8	8	9
Other services	7	8	9	10
Public administration	4	4	4	3
Public sector employment	12	12	11	11
Principal cities–suburbs job distribution				
Percent of jobs in principal cities	44	39	34	32
Percent of jobs in suburbs	56	61	66	68
Job growth over preceding decade (last 7 years for 2007) (%)				
All CBSA	–	2	7	–1
Principal cities	–	–9	–7	–5
Suburbs	–	11	15	1
Spatial segregation by income and race				
Poverty dissimilarity index	45.9	50.1	46.2	43.9
African American–white dissimilarity index	85.6	82.8	78.2	75.6
Latino–white dissimilarity index	58.2	58.8	58.5	56.3
All people of color–white dissimilarity index	76.7	73.4	67.1	63.6

Education and employment

Segregation

Overcoming decline and division

We have talked before about "ties that bind" – formal mechanisms of government or informal mechanisms of governance that create opportunities for regional leaders to interact, develop a common understanding, see that their fates are inter-related, and develop cohesive strategies to address their challenges. Cleveland leaders have tried over the years to develop such collaborative approaches but they are working against a legacy of segregation, fragmentation, and distrust. In what follows, we describe some of the efforts of different constituencies in the region – public, private, labor, community, and philanthropic – to develop cohesive and strategic responses to the region's challenges, highlighting both the challenges and areas of progress that were pointed out to us in the interview process.

Public sector

In contrast to most of our other cases, the Cleveland area has historically lacked a significant regional public sector body addressing broad metropolitan issues. The region's designated metropolitan planning organization (MPO) is known as the Northeast Ohio Areawide Coordinating Agency and it focuses quite narrowly on transportation and air and water quality management for the region.[38]

One attempt to overcome fragmentation is the Northeast Ohio First Suburbs Consortium that was founded in 1997; it now includes eighteen "mature, fully developed communities" in the Cleveland metropolitan area, has catalyzed similar consortiums in the Columbus, Cincinnati, and Dayton metro regions, and has been recognized as a national model for its efforts in aiding aging suburbs.[39] The group has heightened awareness about the adverse effects of sprawl on aging suburbs, such as declining infrastructure and aging housing stock, and it has been successful in developing innovative programs linking member suburbs with local banks and other loan sources to aid in the remodeling of low-income apartment buildings, the restoration of older and historic homes, and the mod-ernization of the existing housing stock. The organization has also worked to influence state policy by opposing the widening of major expressways that often bypass older communities to increase access to newly developed outlying areas (Puentes and Orfield 2002; Keating and Bier 2008). But it is telling that this is an organization of "first suburbs" rather than either all suburbs or inclusive of the central city of Cleveland.

There are other efforts to bring together public officials in the region, includ-ing the Northeast Ohio City Council Association and the Northeast Ohio Mayors and City Managers Association (MCMA). The latter has probably been the most significant, evolving from a small group of leaders meeting informally on a regu-lar basis to discuss issues that were affecting their communities and exchange strategies and best practices, to a formal group intentionally addressing issues together and seeking to avoid poaching businesses and opportunities from each other (Currin 2006). This association has played an important role in launching a Regional Prosperity Initiative (RPI). Begun in 2006 initially as simply an effort to study the potential benefits of regional tax revenue sharing (Orfield et al. 2008), it has grown into a broad collaborative effort to provide the structure for regionwide land use planning and new growth tax base sharing in a sixteen-county area of Northeast Ohio.

The barriers to making this vision a reality are substantial, and include the need to coordinate the activities of all the current regional MPOs in the sixteen-county region, work with sewer and water districts in the region to develop integrated planning systems, confirm formulas for new tax revenue sharing systems that are acceptable to affected jurisdictions, reconfigure state department districts to conform with the sixteen-county boundary of the RPI, and develop and pass appropriate state enabling legislation and financial incentives for implementation, among others.[40] The task will be facilitated with the awarding of a $4.5 million grant in 2010 from the Federal Sustainable Communities Initiative.[41] The grant is significant – as Brad Whitehead, president of the Fund of Our Economic Future says, "It's really the first time that the region has been able to come together to win a federal grant of this proportion and dimension" (Breckenridge 2010a). But overcoming the continued fragmentation of local governments – according to Hudson mayor William Currin, "in Northeast Ohio we have over 800 different forms of government" – will be a challenge.[42]

Private sector

The business community in Cleveland seems quite fractured as well. To some extent, this is the inevitable result of the loss of large-scale manufacturers in the area who used to anchor business leadership, along with the shift of capital to other parts of the country and a heavy de-concentration of jobs to the suburbs (Kaplan 1999). But as with the political bodies detailed above, the business sector has begun to realize the scale of the problem and has sought to address it with the formation of new organizations.

One of the most significant of these new organizations is the Greater Cleveland Partnership. The Partnership was founded in March of 2004, creating a single unified business entity out of a number of chambers of commerce and business associations, including Cleveland Tomorrow, the Greater Cleveland Growth Association, the Greater Cleveland Roundtable, the Northeast Ohio Technology Coalition, the Commission on Economic Inclusions, and the Council of Smaller Enterprises. It now has more than 15,000 members in the Northeast Ohio area. Although this is all hopeful, the Partnership tends to have a focus on physical projects or initiatives – the sort of downtown developments that have been the traditional focus of civic business leaders – rather than the emphasis that some regional business collaboratives have placed on promoting new driving sectors or industrial clusters, or addressing broader quality of life issues. On the other hand, GCP has been trying to move the business community in a more inclusive direction, especially in incorporating more racial diversity within its member-ship – and GCP suggests that, before businesses are accepted to join GCP, they should increase the minority membership on their boards.[43]

But addressing equity requires more than simply integrating minorities into business leadership – the challenge for the region is really the deeper poverty and lack of education affecting a large swath of the workforce. One way that GCP has played a role in these broader issues has been by playing an active role in the efforts being undertaken by the Fund for our Economic Future (described in depth below), although a rift with one of the major foundation sponsors of the initiative could present problems in the future. In any case, GCP leaders argue that their participation in the Fund – which is very much tied to the newer ideas of innovative clusters as a regional economic strategy – stems from their years of work on these issues, and that, in fact, the Fund's work is really a response to a network of people working on these issues that has been prompted by GCP's activities.

One way that GCP is involved directly in expanding educational opportuni-ties is through raising support for the construction of a new STEM (science, technology, engineering, and math)-focused high school located on a former GE Lighting facility in the city of East Cleveland. One of two new STEM-focused high schools in the Cleveland Metropolitan School District, the GE-located site is particular iconic since GE Lighting used to be the largest employer on the east side of Cleveland before it fell victim to de-industrialization, leading to massive lay-offs and a downward economic, political, and social spiral in the city of East Cleveland. The Greater Cleveland Partnership led the campaign to raise $4 mil-lion for the building renovation. The goal is for students in these schools to be paired with scientists or engineers who will serve as mentors, and for 11th and 12th graders to be able to take classes at Cleveland State University to advance their STEM education. As beneficial as this initiative may be for the students involved, the scale is small – each grade at each school will have enrollment capped at 100 (Starzyk 2009) – and GCP's overall engagement with K–12 educa-tion remains limited.

Another way that business leadership in the region has taken a coordinated strategic approach to the region's problems is through the creation of WIRE-Net in 1988. At a time of major plant closings and downsizing, WIRE-Net was founded to help manufacturing businesses and jobs stay in the community. Its focus has been on small firms (generally those with fewer than 100 employees), which provide about 60 percent of manufacturing jobs in the area. Much of its earlier work was on advocacy and building relationships between small business and public officials, but over the years it has expanded to include assistance in human resource management, training, and education, as well as real estate and expansion services and retention efforts (Indergaard 1997). The message articu-lated through WIRE-Net's efforts is that, although the city's manufacturing base has been diminishing steadily, it can still play an important role in the region's overall economic trajectory.[44] The focus is on homegrown small manufacturers, rather than trying to attract firms from other regions; hiring locally to benefit the region and preserve communities; and creating a pipeline of future workers by investing in local education (Cohen 1997).

The efforts to preserve manufacturing in the area seem to be having some impacts. One recent area of progress is the establishment of the Greater Lakes Wind Network, an industry-based organization of manufacturers, suppliers, and research organizations in the wind industry. Manufacturing the thousands of components that go into today's wind turbines in Cleveland makes sense: the region has a deep and strong history in manufacturing and, as such, may be able to achieve competitive advantage over other areas. The Cleveland area, and the Great Lakes region more generally, seems to be well positioned for growth in this rapidly expanding industry.[45]

WIRE-Net has also developed an innovative collaboration with the National Aeronautical and Space Administration (NASA) and the Cleveland Public School system to renovate Max Hayes High School, a school with a reputation for providing an extremely poor level of education. The partnership came about because members of the organization agreed that they had not been able to find skilled labor to fill exiting employment positions.[46] Additionally, in the beginning of 2008, after nearly a year of negotiations, the mayor was able to broker a deal with University Hospital to fund a $1 billion construction project that would include support to conduct an apprenticeship program with Max Hayes' students (Dubail 2008). Through this program, the students will learn about and participate in construction jobs and get paid real wages. In many ways, this type of endeavor represents the type of asset-based development that has a great deal of potential to bring about just growth as it may translate into economic growth in terms of companies having access to a viable workforce and social equity through the provision of real wages to participants.

Labor

With its historic manufacturing base, Cleveland has always been considered a labor town. Currently the Central Labor Council in Cleveland, known as the North Shore AFL-CIO Federation of Labor, counts 100,000 members as its base. However, its involvement in what might be termed more modern attempts to bring about greater levels of economic growth and social equity has been relatively weak (Dean and Reynolds 2009) and the focus has generally been on electoral politics.

Struggling to overcome a moribund leadership rooted in older manufacturing and building trade unions, a new leadership with stronger ties to public and service sector unions took over leadership of the Central Labor Council in 1996. Much of the work for the following decade focused on electoral campaigns and social service work through the United Labor Agency, a United Way affiliate. The CLC worked with a local Jobs with Justice coalition to persuade the Cleveland City Council to pass Ohio's first living wage law in 2000. However, the effects of the living wage law have been quite minimal, with modest pay raises for a small number of workers (Williams 2004). Also in 2000, the CLC played an important role in launching Policy Matters Ohio, a progressive research and policy institute modeled on similar non-profit, labor-linked organizations that have played a critical role in building cross-constituency alliances and broad regional coalitions in a number of other regions (Dean and Reynolds 2009; Pastor et al. 2009b). Policy Matters Ohio has been quite successful in producing timely reports, getting media attention, and establishing a reputation for high-quality research. However, despite the fact that Policy Matters is based in Cleveland and has a primarily Cleveland-based Board of Directors, its primary focus has been on state-level policy.

The current executive secretary of the CLC, Harriet Applegate, is the first woman to serve in this position in the council, and has been working to reposition the labor movement in the area in part by increasing levels of collaboration with other organizations and working in non-traditional ways. This includes getting more involved in economic development activities, reaching out to African Americans, and participating in regional leadership initiatives.[47] For example, Applegate served on the board of the Regional Energy Taskforce, which looks to bring together various stakeholders to discuss issues of sustainability, and has focused on linking employment opportunities for low-income communities with new green energy projects, particularly in wind power. Importantly, public and private entities are beginning to reach out and include labor in their efforts; although other leaders in the Cleveland area have stated that labor has not really played a role in the work of inclusion, they also note that labor is beginning to play a more active role in business growth and attraction and workforce talent.[48] Yet, overall, the work of the CLC in Cleveland is much less innovative and dynamic than in places like Los Angeles or San Jose (Eimer 2001; Luce 2001; Ness and Eimer 2001; Dean and Reynolds 2008).

Non-profit and community groups

The non-profit community sector in Cleveland has a long history. In the 1960s and 1970s, Cleveland had a vibrant network of neighborhood organizations that saw themselves as social movement organizations mobilizing for broad political and social change in the city. The Commission on Catholic Community Action (CCCA), for example, was an Alinsky-style organizing group that by 1974 had created at least ten neighborhood-based advocacy organizations, employed seventy-five full-time organizers, and had a budget of nearly $1 million (Krumholz and Forester 1990; Yin 1998). The strong tradition of neighborhood mobilization in Cleveland during the 1960s and 1970s was an important contributor to Carl Stokes being elected the first Black mayor of a major city in the country (in 1968) and to broad efforts at advocacy planning in the 1970s that have been an important theme within the entire planning profession ever since (Clavel 1986, 1994; Krumholz and Forester 1990).

Yet over time – mirroring parallel trends across the country – neighborhood organizations in Cleveland began to focus more on specific development initiatives, such as building affordable housing or renovating commercial storefronts.

These community development corporations in Cleveland have historically been some of the best in the nation. At the same time, their efforts have directed attention and resources toward geographically targeted locations in the inner city while neglecting the broader patterns of urban disinvestment and suburban sprawl. As beneficial as specific neighborhood development initiatives have been, they have not been able to overcome the larger regional forces that have undermined economic growth in the region and furthered social and economic divides (Rusk 1999). The focus on neighborhood development initiatives may also have been detrimental to social cohesion, especially in the context of limited resources – one interviewee described local community development corporations as being very turf-oriented and interested only in things that would benefit their particular service area.

Some of the non-profit policy work in the region contributes to a broader perspective on community issues. Policy Matters Ohio, for example, has conducted research on such issues as wage disparities, the diploma deficit, and spending on incarceration versus education – as well as the ways that these issues affect Black males. At the time of our interview, the organization had plans to pursue additional issues such as the foreclosure epidemic, increased spending on education, training, and infrastructure, and ways to induce economic growth and job creation through renewable energy.[49] Another non-profit policy organization that has recently appeared in Cleveland is PolicyBridge, an African-American think tank focused on issues in Cleveland's Black community, including workforce, economic development, housing, health, and wellness, and education.[50] The message promoted by PolicyBridge is actually pro-regional – but with warnings that such efforts to bridge city and suburb should not leave African Americans behind. In addition to conducting community forums at the prestigious Cleveland City Club, PolicyBridge has produced a number of reports that provide detailed analyses of the effects of such ills as low educational attainment, joblessness, poverty, and incarceration on Blacks and Black males in particular. By emphasizing the effects of their disconnection from the labor force, this research underscores the idea that the success of Black males is critical to the economic vitality and social equity of both local communities and the entire state.

The good research and analysis of groups such as PolicyBridge and Policy Matters are an important part of strengthening understanding of regional economic and social challenges, and building intellectual support for regional solutions to these problems. But intellectual content is not the same as social force, and these policy organizations themselves are not base-building organizations capable of bringing together diverse constituencies to implement change.

Philanthropy

Perhaps the most promising thing in Cleveland – and something that drew our attention as noted in the introduction to this chapter – has been a collaboration of philanthropic organizations that have united with the goal of strengthening the economic competitiveness of Northeast Ohio, through grant making, research, and civic engagement. The effort is called Fund for Our Economic Future and, since its founding in 2004, more than sixty foundations, individuals, companies, governments, and others have come together to raise more than $70 million for their coordinated efforts. The Fund is far more than simply a grant-making body, however, providing both high-quality research and building broad regional participation in the work of shaping the region's economic future. This innovative experiment has linked business experience with economic development and philanthropic know-how.

The geographical focus of the Fund encompasses sixteen counties – including five metropolitan areas – in the entire Northeast Ohio area, with Cleveland at its heart. From its creation, the Fund made transparency one of its top priorities. As one way of stirring commitment – and preventing smaller players from feeling overshadowed by the city of Cleveland and the Cleveland Foundation – any entity that could contribute at least $100,000 had an equal vote no matter how much was contributed.[51] This type of economic inclusion was emphasized by the Cleveland Foundation, which initially donated $10 million but wanted to ensure that smaller organizations would become involved and not feel intimidated by larger ones. Additionally, a core group (through collaboration with the Greater Cleveland Partnership) was developed to focus on minority inclusion, with the goal of assisting Black- and Latino-owned businesses through technical assistance, as well as contracts and other opportunities (from majority firms). Indeed the goal of racial and economic inclusion is one of the four central priorities of the Fund (the other three are business growth, talent development, and government efficiency and collaboration).

The Fund has already made a major contribution to regional equity by funding the creation of the Regional Dashboard of Economic Indicators. Published annually since 2006, the Dashboard offers a detailed analysis, comparing Northeast Ohio with metropolitan areas across the United States on a range of economic indicators. What makes this work particularly interesting is that, in addition to benchmarking Northeast Ohio's progress, it also specifically analyzes how a range of nine 'dashboard indicators' affect four different measures of economic growth: percentage change in per capita income, percentage change in employment, percentage change in gross metropolitan product, and percentage change in productivity.[52] Although all of the nine indicators are statistically associated with some measure of growth, the only indicator that is associated with all measures of growth is the racial inclusion and income equality measure (Austrian et al. 2009). The consistent link between growth and equity, including the early research conducted by Federal Reserve economists (Eberts et al. 2006), has helped lay the groundwork for both having philanthropists focus on growth (instead of just charity) and persuading business that caring about equity was not just a feel-good exercise, but in fact can contribute directly to economic growth.

In addition to its research and civic engagement, the Fund for Our Economic Future has provided more than $40 million in grants to targeted initiatives that are working on strengthening the region's economic competitiveness. The specific directions include growing the region's bioscience cluster, developing a regional venture capital fund, expanding advanced manufacturing and high-tech businesses, and promoting the growth of Black- and Hispanic-owned businesses. It has also funded broad regional initiatives affecting public sector activities, including the Regional Prosperity Initiative (the collaborative land use planning and regional revenue-sharing initiative described above) and a competitive grant program designed to encourage the region's local governments to collaborate in the delivery of services. In an innovative effort to help build support for government collaboration, grants through this later program are determined by a vote of the public. In the first round of this program in 2009, more than 13,000 Northeast Ohio residents voted for the three best government collaborations, which involved a total of twenty-one governmental entities whose collaborations reportedly resulted in an estimated saving of $1.8 million. In the 2010 round of funding, more than 17,500 Northeast Ohio residents voted for a consolidated land bank, a merged 911 safety dispatch system, and a joint Cleveland-First Suburbs initiative to expand the use of solar energy.

The work of the Fund has not been without some controversy. At the end of 2009, an apparently long-simmering dispute surfaced when the Cleveland Foundation decided to significantly cut back its participation to only $300,000 over the next three years, after committing $22 million over the previous six years (Breckenridge 2009, 2010b). Foundation leaders cited a change in the mission of the Fund, a broadening of the region beyond the scope of the Foundation's focus on Cleveland itself, and increased operating costs as reasons for reducing their involvement in the Fund. However, leaders of the Fund have pointed to the Foundation's desire to control more and collaborate less as reasons for reducing their role (*Plain Dealer* Editorial Board 2009; Larkin 2010). In interviews with community leaders, we also encountered concerns that the Fund is neglecting equity in its economic growth efforts, and that the efficient government initiative is feeding an anti-government perspective that will undermine government's ability to address key equity concerns in the region. The impressive collaborative glue keeping the fund together, and the substantial financial resources that have made it all real, may be at risk, threatened by all too familiar tensions between core and periphery perspectives in the region and control of limited resources.

Turning around a stuck region?

Cleveland was a hard case study for the research team – it is tough to start an interview by saying that you are studying how regions can achieve growth and equity and you came to Cleveland because it managed to strike out on both. Our presence was more welcomed, however, once we suggested that we were impressed by the current efforts to turn things around and that this was part of the reason we had come to "the Forest City."

But although the evidence of effort was there, the evidence of turnaround is still scant. The long experience of economic decline and social conflict in the Cleveland area has left a lasting legacy that makes it hard for the region to come together to reverse its fortunes. The high level of fragmentation in the region can be seen in many aspects – between majority and minority populations, the business community and the civil rights activists, the various and high number of council districts. There are even significant divides within the African-American community around the dynamics of the region, with some seeing regionalism as essential for reversing historical racial inequalities but others seeing the call for regionalism as an effort to dilute their influence and subvert racial justice concerns. These types of fragmentation and social divides are exactly the opposite of the kinds of broad communities and sharing of concerns and perspectives that we have pointed to in our more successful regions. It underscores the need for greater levels of dialogue between those working to collaborate in the name of regionalism.

The Fund for Our Economic Future is perhaps the most encouraging effort to bring equity and growth together explicitly, and it has been successful in linking public, private, and philanthropic constituencies together across the region. The First Suburbs Consortium has also been able to highlight the issues and needs of older inner-ring suburbs, PolicyBridge's research and activism have drawn attention to the specific needs of African Americans in the region, and WIRE-Net's innovative approaches to retraining the workforce offer great promise. More recent initiatives are equally hopeful, including collaborations between the region's educational institutions and the private sector to promote an "Eds and Meds" approach that might redirect resources to the historic urban core (Adams 2003; Bartik and Erickcek 2008). There are also innovative efforts afoot to take advantage of the historical industrial base of the region and transfer manufacturing skills to develop alternative energy sources while harnessing the wind power coming off of Lake Erie.

But Cleveland clearly remains faced with great challenges. Cleveland is deficient not just in jobs and wages but also in the broad-based collaborations that embrace a common regional fate. In this difficult terrain, seeds of strong regional collaborations have sprouted. With careful cultivation and sufficient fertilization, they may take deeper root – but it could take as long to get out of this decline as it has to get into it.

Slipping and a-sliding . . .

Sacramento, Denver, and Cleveland – what we earlier termed cases of slip back, bounce back and stuck back – offer some important but complicated lessons. Although we lift these up in more detail in the chapter that follows, synthesizing these along with our more successful cases, a few words here might be in order.

Our first observation has to do with a more nuanced understanding of the role of public sector employment. We see again in the case of Sacramento that large military base employment combined with stable state–government employment helped drive the region's beneficial development in the 1980s. But this dependence on military employment became a liability in the 1990s when Sacramento was disproportionately hit by base closures. More recently, Sacramento has struggled to recover from the Great Recession (which we discuss in more detail in Chapter 6), as the continued fiscal crisis in the state has resulted in continual declines in public sector employment in the region, which have outpaced the small job recovery in some private industries. Thus, although we still see public sector employment as an important stabilizing force in regional economies and an important component of linking growth with equity, it is not immune from economic shocks and needs to be complemented by a strong private sector as well.

Our second observation is that it is hard to break through a boom–bust cycle. Denver slipped in the 1980s, seemed to bounce back in the 1990s, then put in a middling performance on growth and a miserable performance on equity in the period from 2000 to 2007. Getting used to that rhythm may be addictive – the region is used to experiencing cycles and, although it did seem that some intentional action on the part of regional business elites helped to generate new investments in infrastructure, this did less to create a commitment to reducing inequality.

Our third observation is that another sort of path dependence is possible: Cleveland has been more or less stuck in place, with a legacy of fragmentation, separation, and de-industrialization proving very hard to overcome. A city sharply partitioned from its suburbs, race relations that have been tense, and a working population challenged to make the shift to a new economy have not constituted a recipe for success.

Our fourth observation is that new ways of thinking about the future can be generated. Even in Cleveland, the futility of past approaches has given way to a new and more collaborative strategy in the form of the Fund for Our Economic Future. In Sacramento, the damage wrought by military base closures and the disequalizing effects of providing back office operations for the Silicon Valley have generated a series of efforts to improve land use planning and generate a more sustainable economy. And Denver, although still struggling with boom and bust, shows that a region coming together can make some key infrastructure investments, including a new airport, a stadium, and an emerging light rail system that connects city and suburb.

At the same time, such new thinking will pay attention to issues of equity only if pro-equity constituencies are engaged and involved. Political realities have dictated that this will be the case in Cleveland – although some of these constituencies, particularly African Americans, have worried that their interests will be lost under the regional banner. In Denver, the relative lack of labor and community organizing has led equity to be less warmly embraced, while, in Sacramento, equity groups are busy playing catch-up, hoping to influence the regional policy train before the direction of the tracks is fully set.

5   What does it all mean?

Introduction

Travelers are often exhausted after a long trip – eager to rest, to settle back to daily routines, to find a bit of familiarity after the strangeness of the new. We did not travel to all of our cases back-to-back but we were exhausted nonetheless – dashing from Columbus to Jacksonville, from Kansas City to Nashville, from Cleveland to Denver, and finally back to Sacramento was quite a trek, not just on our bodies but also on our priors.

Analysts, after all, approach research with a set of prior beliefs that they often hold dear – in our case, that regions matter, that social movements are important, and that achieving equity is a bit like what Frederick Douglass said: if there is no struggle, there is no progress and power concedes nothing without a demand. But travel is all about that strangeness of the new – the lessons we had not anticipated and the characteristics that changed our own thinking about growth and equity.

We set ourselves up for such learning, of course, adopting a quantitative strategy to both select the cases and explore the determinants of "growth with equity" that was designed to keep us open to surprise. That work generated a more objective set of cases as well as unusual insights into the role of the middle class, the challenge of union presence (or at least that of older unions), and the dragging effect of immigration on equity. There were more familiar lessons, of course, including about the importance of equity to growth and the role of state employment, but the quantitative work also pointed to new insights, such as the potential effect of a new sort of regional consciousness (in the form of participation in regionalist organizations).

The case studies themselves have both echoed those findings and suggested a variety of factors, including the importance of consolidation along jurisdictional lines, the size of the public sector, the diversity of the industrial mix, the presence of a minority middle class, the role of universities, and – perhaps most to our surprise – the creation of diverse epistemic communities. Some of these factors were foreshadowed in the quantitative work while others, such as industrial diversity, seem to run counter to what the data suggest, an anomaly we take up below.

Moreover, these factors can actually be broken into two sorts: those that are essentially structural in nature – so they change slowly over time (if at all) – and those that are more amenable to change by direct civic action and policy development. On the structural side, for example, excessive reliance on an older industrial sector – say autos or metal working – can make it more difficult to generate continuing economic growth over time. The locational advantage of being a state capital, as is the case for four of our case studies (Denver, Columbus, Nashville, and Sacramento), is a permanent feature; other less fortunate regions cannot declare themselves capitals as well and thus attract public sector employment (although we might suggest it for especially bold and innovative activists).

But the fact that some things cannot change helps drive our attention to the measures that can change, such as the creation of community commitment, the promotion of smaller businesses, and the contribution of universities and community colleges to local economic development. It is important to understand the role of the constraint-style factors noted above – they indicate *which* regions might be best positioned for growth with equity – but it is especially critical to focus on those variables that are possible to change through focused attention and political will as they indicate *how* regions can move, from any starting point, onto a more sustainable path of both prosperity and inclusion.

Growth is affected by a series of factors, including the industrial base, past performance, and the rate of innovation. Equity is a matter of distributional (and political) choice but it too has a number of constraints, including the structure of the economy – which determines what is available to share – and both the history and ongoing nature of racial segregation and separation and how this affects the degree of social solidarity in a region. Putting together the constraints that are faced with the choices that can be made can offer a recipe for shared prosperity – and we draw upon our cases below to help sort out what ingredients are key.

The structural elements

Consolidation of political jurisdictions

One factor that clearly emerges in our case studies is the value of regional government. Nashville and Jacksonville were two of the earliest city–county mergers in the country, both merging in the 1960s. In both cases, the typical patterns of white flight and suburban/central city divides were much more muted, as the local city governments were essentially the closest thing to a true regional government of probably any metropolitan region in the country. Columbus also has a history of annexing surrounding communities as urbanization grew beyond city boundaries.

Kansas City may seem to be an exception, as it has a fragmented regional governance system that includes the complications of a bi-state metro, along with the more typical city and county fragmentation. This is perhaps mitigated by the large physical land area of the central city (Kansas City, Missouri is the thirteenth largest city by land area of cities in the United States with more than 100,000 people),[1] which contributes to principal cities in the region being able to still retain over half of all jobs in the region (see Table 3.1). Perhaps more importantly, voters in Wyandotte County and Kansas City, Kansas decided in

1997 to consolidate the city and county governments, one of only four successful voter-approved consolidations nationwide in the 1990s out of thirty referenda that were held in that decade, and the only one in the Midwest. Although Kansas City, Kansas is substantially smaller than its Missouri-based namesake, it faced many of the same challenges – central city population decline, growing African-American concentration, widening city–suburb income gaps, and declining tax base. The success of this initiative, and its apparent contribution to Wyandotte County landing a major new NASCAR raceway, has likely contributed to a greater appreciation for the values of collaboration across the region (Leland 2004). Finally, the Kansas City metro also has one of the most comprehensive MPOs in the country, one that engages in a wide range of issues beyond transportation. All these factors suggest the presence of a strong regional governance system, even in the absence of formal metropolitan government structures (Phares 2004).

Denver is perhaps the one case in which regional government did not emerge as an important theme in our interviews. But although the issue was not discussed by our respondents, it is the case that Denver has always been a combined city/county government, and it did annex neighboring land in the 1980s, although this was simply for the building of Stapleton Airport. Denver does have a remarkable centrality in Colorado State politics – metro Denver accounts for nearly 60 percent of the state's total population and about 60 percent of total jobs. But the relative lack of regional government may explain why there has been less will to tame the boom–bust cycle.

Sacramento also has a striking theme of governmental consolidation in the background. The city and county remain distinct but it is the only county in California that has tried – twice – to accomplish such a consolidation of government functions. Although referenda on city–county consolidation in 1974 and again in 1990 failed to pass with a majority of voters, they raised the issue of government consolidation and regional collaboration in the public sphere (Sparrow 2004). There was also a brief attempt to do tax-sharing across jurisdictions in the region in 2002, an effort that was struck down by the state legislature but the impulse for which says a great deal about the willingness to collaborate (PolicyLink 2002).

By contrast, the case study of Cleveland – a region marked by both inequity and economic stagnation – has all the characteristics of jurisdictional fragmentation that David Rusk (1993) contends should be bad for inclusion, and seem to be just as bad for growth. The central city, as in places like Detroit, is often viewed hostilely by the surrounding suburbs, racial disparities are marked, and municipalities have historically believed that they can wall themselves off from the sinking sound at the center of the region. They cannot, and the most recent efforts in the Cleveland metro have been all about replacing the lack of *government* structure with a new *governance* structure – collaboration through mayors' councils and new vehicles such as the Fund for Our Economic Future – that can make up for past history.

The benefits of economic diversity

As we have noted, economic diversity did not emerge as a winner in our regression analysis sweepstakes. This may be for several reasons, including the fact that "less diverse" regions may actually be hosting an industrial cluster or two that can drive fast growth, that such driving sectors can be filled with entrepreneurs deeply committed to the region (as in the Silicon Valley), and that diversity might be more about stability than fast growth *per se*. Moreover, measures of industrial diversity, including ours, have been the source of some controversy about what they really measure (Wagner 2000; Dissart 2003; Chandra 2005). Specifically, measures of economic diversity do not necessarily tell you about firm concentration within industry sectors, which also affects resilience to shocks. And certain situations with little diversity – say, a real concentration of university institutions – can actually lead to both stability in employment and the creation of a locally rooted or "homegrown" entrepreneurial class that helps a region weather the shocks that come its way.

As a result, it is folk wisdom – and probably right – that economic diversity matters. That is, although we may not be able to measure it as well as we might, business and civic leaders in our regions were generally worried about being over-reliant on one industry and praised the value of a diversified economic base. In Kansas City, for example, metropolitan leaders argued that growth had been steady, not spectacular, and had been rooted in a range of different industries: telecommunications, transportation and logistics, agriculture and food processing, linked biosciences for both agriculture-related production and health applications, creative industries (Hallmark Cards and related spin-offs), and architecture/engineering.[2]

Leaders in Jacksonville made a similar argument. Its manufacturing base is diverse, and thus the region was less affected by the de-industrialization that decimated some metros in the Midwest and elsewhere. Jacksonville is also less reliant on the tourism industry, and thus not subject to the seasonal and highly recession-dependent (as well as wage-disequalizing) nature of the hospitality industry.

Nashville is clearly more of a tourist spot – although the research crew conducting the site visit did not take the time to visit the Grand Ole Opry or other destinations (much to the approval of the university bureaucrats watching our expenses but also to the dismay of the rest of the research team who wanted a vicarious experience in the seat of country music). However, leaders here also talked about the importance of diversity in their regional economy, including the fact that they enjoyed a range of manufacturing enterprises (including many branch plant relocations from Northern states), healthcare (with benefits from the growth of healthcare and private hospitals), the music industry (and related creative industry spin-offs), and the education sector, with its concentration of universities.

Columbus leaders also tended to attribute some of their success to an industrial base that diversified before other regions in Ohio and other portions of the industrial Midwest. They did not suggest that this was entirely voluntary; partly because the region went through de-industrialization a bit earlier than others, it suffered early and wound up with a less concentrated set of industries. It is also one of the few places where the auto industry actually expanded in the Midwest; 1981 saw the arrival of a Honda plant right outside the city of Columbus. It is, as we noted, also host to the headquarters of several retail-oriented firms such as Limited, Express, and Victoria's Secret.

Denver is also illustrative of the pattern but in reverse. As will be recalled, this was a turnaround case – it did not fare well on growth and equity in the 1980s but came around in the 1990s. The tough first decade was attributed by most observers to an overreliance on oil and real estate, and hence susceptibility to a downturn in a few sectors. Denver claimed to have learned its lesson in the 1990s and civic leaders attempted to both forge a new and more productive infrastructure and try to attract and retain a more diversified industrial base. On the other hand, the 2000s brought a growth slowdown and poor performance on equity measures – perhaps more economic diversity could have provided a better cushion against the boom–bust cycle.

As a state capital, Sacramento has had the benefit of a stable base of public sector employment (at least until California's dramatic fiscal crisis in recent years). Although this is a slip-back case, in which the 1990s did not match the relative performance of the 1980s, Sacramento did try to diversify its economic base in that decade. This was not an entirely voluntary strategy: the closure of three military bases forced Sacramento to try to lure new businesses, including high-tech enterprises, which literally located in vacated bases, as well as call centers and other activities.

Finally, Cleveland shows the challenges of heavy reliance on a narrow set of industries when diversification is not successful. In its heyday, Cleveland was second only to Detroit in the percentage of the workforce employed in manufacturing, and even within manufacturing it was heavily concentrated in a few sectors – the auto industry, steel, and consumer durables – that were most heavily impacted by de-industrialization in the 1980s and 1990s. The region's efforts to diversify and develop new sectors have been constrained by the industrial legacy of shuttered plants and brownfields, out-migration of younger, more educated workers, and the regional fragmentation and social conflict that we discussed.

The role of the public sector

One factor associated with both growth and equity is the size of the public sector. A larger public sector may provide a sort of automatic stabilizer to the metro economy, allowing it to withstand shocks to the private sector base. It is also the case that public sector employment has been important for the advancement of white ethnics in the past and African Americans in the recent past, with the latter partly because the civil service standards allow Blacks to bypass the invidious effects of social networks as well as discriminatory practices in private hiring (Moss and Tilly 2001). Finally, not only does the sector itself help to produce a middle class but also its employment standards, when the sector is large, may influence private sector standards in the broader regional economy.

Four of our case study regions – Columbus, Denver, Nashville, and Sacramento – are state capitals, and thus have a significant share of public sector employment. Jacksonville also has a strong presence of federal employment in the form of the four navy bases and their ancillary operations. This has the same effect as the state sector employment in the other regions – an economic stabilizer and pathway to opportunity for some historically disadvantaged groups. In Jacksonville, respondents suggested that the significant Navy presence also had the interesting side effect of contributing to the high concentration of call centers in the region, as the disproportionate employment of men in the navy installations created relatively large numbers of 'naval wives' who were a prime workforce for this sector.

As noted above, metro regions cannot just declare themselves capitals – although, in large states such as California, perhaps secession into separate parts might be attractive! What the pattern suggests, however, is a parallel to the economic diversity – just as it makes sense to have a set of industries such that no particular individual shock can take you off course, it makes sense to have a base of employment less susceptible to shocks at all. The public sector generally fits that description and it also has a hiring structure that makes it more amenable to progress in both fairness in hiring and the creation of a minority middle class.

The importance of higher education

Universities are often talked about as being important "anchor" institutions within central cities, and an important driver of economic growth, particularly through research and diffusion into industry (Maurrasse 2007; McGahey and Vey 2008). Educational institutions also provide a stable source of decent employment, and are arguably counter-cyclical, as applications to higher education tend to go up in an economic downturn. But it goes well beyond universities to include the community college systems that often train the regional workforce and insure both competitiveness and individual mobility.

The importance of universities to the regional economy was specifically cited as a central issue in Nashville. Known as the "Athens of the South" (Athens, we might note, does not similarly call itself the "Nashville of the East"), the region has at least twenty-one universities (including Vanderbilt), six community colleges, and eleven vocational and technical schools. This includes three historically Black colleges and universities (HCBUs): Fisk University, Tennessee State University, and Meharry Medical College. Interestingly, community colleges have a relatively small role as seen in their small numbers; there is only one community college in Davidson County, the core county in the region, although there are also three technology centers that play a somewhat similar role.

Columbus meanwhile boasts Ohio State, a top-tier university with a strong research profile and a large cultural footprint as well, partly due to a stellar football team. Ohio State has several branches in smaller areas but Columbus is the central and key campus. Ohio State is also a significant employer, coming in right behind the public sector in terms of jobs within the metro area. The university presence may also have something to do with both attracting and retaining a Black middle class, as universities are often more open to talent and can also create a more culturally welcoming presence. This has indirect effects to the extent that a minority middle class has an important influence on the political economy of an area, a point we take up below.

Of course, universities are no panacea. Cleveland has Case Western as well as Cleveland State University. The latter is the more locally engaged of the two but it is less a positive influence on the region economically (both directly in terms of employment and indirectly in terms of innovation). Meanwhile, Case Western has a potentially bigger economic footprint but its conscious attempt to be a national university makes it seem less connected to the region's political economy and to solving the region's problems. Meanwhile, the Cleveland Clinic, essential to the "Eds and Meds" strategy of the city, is unusual in that it is not connected to the university institutions (although there is a joint medical school with Case Western Reserve that came about in 2004 and this may bode well for the future).

We would stress, however, that the focus on universities in innovation and development can miss an equally important part of the intersection of education and the economy: the community college system. In Kansas City and Jacksonville, community colleges, not universities, were seen as critically important to the regional economy. Neither city has a strong tier one research university. Kansas City does have a campus of the University of Missouri, but the closest major research university is the University of Kansas in Lawrence. Jacksonville has the University of North Florida, but the closest major research university is the University of Florida in Gainesville. The community colleges in both places, however, have played important roles in shaping regional growth dynamics.

Kansas City, for example, has truly exemplary examples of community colleges involved in workforce development initiatives, including substantial partnerships with private sector employers and substantial public sector training. In Jacksonville, the FCCJ (Florida Community College at Jacksonville) has the fourth largest community college-based workforce development program in the country.

Denver is also somewhat bereft of a major university presence: the flagship campus for the state system lies north in Boulder and there are no top-tier private universities. The region, however, boasts a community college system that is instrumental to addressing what is termed the "Colorado Paradox": the fact that the region boasts both a high share of college graduates and a high share of college dropouts. The reason, most observers believe, is that the graduates are attracted by the weather and the location while the dropouts are homegrown. Addressing this middle sector is the task of the community college system, as well as workforce efforts such as the region's Workforce Innovation in Regional Economic Development (WIRED) initiative. The general assessment is that the community college system is very good (although the challenge they are seeking to address is also quite large).

Sacramento has both a state university and a nearby campus of the University of California (in Davis). The latter has long been involved in extension work for agriculture and so has acquired a habit of directly interfacing with economic development efforts and opportunities. The Davis campus has also taken a lead on environmental issues, helping to position itself and the region for potential opportunities in the new green economy. Finally, the region has a very high-quality set of community college systems, including the Los Rios community college district with over 90,000 students.

Our regression analysis told us something we all know: education plays an important role in both generating growth and leveling the playing field to bring about more equitable outcomes. But what the case studies offer goes beyond this abstraction: to make education pay off for a region, it is important to have educational systems that see their own futures as really tied to that of the metropolitan area they inhabit. That seems to be the case with the first-tier universities in Columbus and Nashville (and not so much in Cleveland) and with the community college systems in Kansas City and Jacksonville. Denver lacks a flagship university while Sacramento enjoys a mix: a nearby first-tier research institution, a state university, and top-line community colleges.

Making a minority middle class

When you go out to do qualitative work, you never quite know what you will find. The model you have in your head of how the world works is often challenged by how practitioners actually practice: the regressions do not show a big role for economic diversity but the business leaders know it is important; economic theory says that markets can always recover equilibrium but some regions just seem stuck; all the models say that housing prices cannot fall and market derivatives are safe – and you know the rest of that story . . .

One of the biggest surprises in our regional interviews was the emphasis of respondents in Nashville, Columbus, and Kansas City on the important role of having a significant Black middle class. In Nashville, this emerged in discussions about the importance of the three HBCUs in the region, and the role they played in raising educational levels for the region's African-American population. In Kansas City, it emerged in discussions about the role of African-American leadership in promoting community development corporations from an early stage. In Columbus, respondents stressed that a large Black middle class had emerged through access to public sector employment and played a role in keeping the doors open for others.

The arguments about why this made a difference centered on three issues. First, and most directly, improved economic opportunities for African Americans helped raise income levels for a sector of the population that is all too often over-represented amongst the poor. Second, this middle-class presence was associated with more Black-owned businesses that were also more likely to provide employment opportunities for other African Americans (even if just through the impact of social networks on hiring practices). Third, it resulted in more African

Americans being represented in leadership positions throughout the region. These leaders, it was thought, were in both political and economic areas but the key thing was that they had both an interest in growth (typical of the middle class) but also an historic (and often ongoing) experience of exclusion and thus a commitment to equity.

This may also result in a sort of virtuous circle for growth and equity – and for the Black middle class itself. In a 2007 survey conducted by *Black Enterprise* magazine, Nashville was ranked as the number five metro in the country for Black families and entrepreneurs while Columbus was rated as the ninth and Jacksonville was ranked as the tenth.[3] Columbus was considered the best place for Black families to live according to an earlier Black Entertainment Television survey, with Nashville and Jacksonville sharing the number ten slot (see Table 3.3 and the discussion in that chapter).[4]

Cleveland also has a sizeable Black population but it is one heavily tilted to the poorer side of the income spectrum, a fact that might generate more interest in redistribution than in growth *per se*; in the same BET poll, Cleveland was ranked fifteenth in the list of twenty. Denver has a small Black population but a sizeable Latino population and also one with a prominent middle class. Prominent enough to produce Federico Peña as the mayor during the years 1983–1991, arguably the period in which the elements of the bounce back in the 1990s were engineered.

Finally, Sacramento's substantial Black middle class has been underpinned by public sector employment, including up until the 1990s in the region's military bases and defense industries. Base closures severely hurt portions of the African-American community, particularly in the historic Del Paso Heights neighborhood of north Sacramento, which was disproportionately hurt by the loss of 11,000 civilian jobs in the nearby McClellan Air Force Base. But the overall regional impact of this decline in middle-class jobs for African Americans has been moderated by the substantial in-migration of Latino and Asian (as well as increasingly Russian and Eastern European) immigrants. The city was the most diverse and integrated city in the country according to analysis of 2000 census data from the Harvard Civil Rights Project (Stodghill and Bower 2002). Sacramento's relatively integrated neighborhoods facilitate immigrant integration by helping to reduce isolation in ethnic enclaves and to broaden immigrants' social networks, thus further strengthening opportunities for immigrants to move into the middle class (Datel and Dingemans 2008).

The quantitative analysis offered an interesting twist on the role of the minority middle class, suggesting that the Black middle class might be more critical to promoting equity and the Latino middle class to promoting growth. Although this did not appear as strongly in the cases, this was partly because our metro areas generally did not have as strong a Latino presence. It is worth exploring if there are differences in the impact of Black and Latino middle-class households, but the basic argument here is that having a substantial proportion of middle-class residents of a minority, typically disproportionately poor, racial group will result in less "policy distance" between the poor of the region and regional leadership making decisions. This is a structural feature, to be sure, but it is not entirely immutable. Keeping the policy closeness is the task of organizers, movement builders, and civic leaders, and keeping and building a minority middle class might just be the gift that keeps giving, at least in terms of growth with equity.

Changing your fortunes

The factors examined above can all be thought of as structural – characteristics of the region that are either essentially unchangeable (e.g. do you have a state capital?) or that change only very slowly (e.g. broad patterns of industry employment or size of the minority middle class). But to paraphrase Karl Marx – something that does not happen as frequently in the academic world as it used to – whereas analysts generally seek to interpret the world, the point is to change it.

Our case studies lifted up a variety of areas in which such intentional change is possible. By this, we do not mean so much specific policies as broader strokes that have to do with the creation of a regional environment that can promote equity and growth. These elements range from the seemingly ephemeral – creating a "diverse epistemic community" – to the remarkably concrete – such as adopting an orientation to public transit opportunities. We turn to these below, partly because these are the activities whereby a region's leadership can take the cards it has been dealt and transform their fortunes.

Diverse epistemic communities

Generating a commitment to both growth and equity in a region necessarily involves a wide diversity of people and interests. Of course, when divergent constituencies come together to determine strategies for regional development, it frequently results in conflict not collaboration. At the root of the conflict are often differences not just in ideology or political position, but in more fundamental chasms in understandings of how change is made, what processes are important, and who should be involved. In essence, the conflict is rooted in people having different information and valuing differing knowledge in shaping their positions.

By taking this view, we do not mean to underrate the importance of ideology or partisanship. Business leaders are often deeply committed to an economic world view in which labor unions slow growth, regulation is an impediment, and fairness is an afterthought to be taken up in one's charitable spare time. In contrast, community and labor leaders may be steeped in a framework in which the economy is a site of exploitation, protection against insecurity is essential, and economic growth is someone else's concerns. It all gets worse when political entrepreneurs jump into the stew, seeking to advance their own partisan interests by fueling divisions in the pursuit of short-term gain – and this is something done by activists on both sides of the aisle.

We argued in the introduction that both of these underlying economic world views are wrong. In a game both of us have played with business leaders in leadership training sessions, we demonstrate that traders who propose fairer deals tend to make more deals and hence make more money.[5] Strikingly, business leaders already know that this is the case and many incorporate this into the way they treat their own employees or suppliers. But not the way they approach regional, state, or even federal public policy. Community leaders, meanwhile, are also often used to the role of challenging business. But most know, particularly in the wake of the Great Recession that began to wrack the nation in 2008, that generating growth, even if they know little about how to do it, is key to achieving their goals.

How do we get groups to break through, both in terms of their thinking and in terms of their relationships? How do we get various actors to go beyond the deal making that is at least one useful mode of "getting to yes," to a more fundamental "getting to we"? How do we move beyond transactions to transformations?

What was striking in a number of our case study regions was that some process or organization had helped bring people from widely different constituencies together in a way that helped them overcome differing perspectives and knowledge bases. This did not mean that conflict disappeared – our case study regions still exhibit many examples of conflicting priorities, viewpoints, and strategies. But regional leaders seemed to have an appreciation for, and acceptance of, a wide range of diverse perspectives, and a sense that, although they may not necessarily agree with those other viewpoints, those viewpoints are based on valid knowledge, and the future of the region in some way involves accommodating the diversity of priorities and perspectives. In essence, these processes had helped regional leaders develop a sense of regional common destiny.

Although we realize that the term is perhaps hopelessly academic, we can think of no better description of this process except as the construction of a diverse epistemic community. Haas (1992: 3) describes an epistemic community as a group of people who have:

> (1) a shared set of normative and principled beliefs, which provide a value-based rationale for the social action of community members; (2) shared causal beliefs, which are derived from their analysis of practices leading or contributing to a central set of problems in their domain and which then serve as the basis for elucidating the multiple linkages between possible policy actions and desired outcomes; (3) shared notions of validity – that is, intersubjective, internally defined criteria for weighing and validating knowledge in the domain of their expertise; and (4) a common policy enterprise – that is, a set of common practices associated with a set of problems to which their professional competence is directed, presumably out of the conviction that human welfare will be enhanced as a consequence

An epistemic community is essentially a group of people who share some common style of thinking, connected by some constellation of beliefs, values, and techniques that bind people into a collective endeavor.

How do epistemic communities form? Haas argues that the major dynamics are centered on uncertainty, interpretation, and institutionalization. Conditions

of uncertainty exist when actors must make decisions without adequate information or knowledge about the context of their decisions, or when they are unable
to accurately predict the outcomes of different courses of action. This can lead
them to seek out other sources of information and knowledge. Because outcomes
depend on the actions of multiple different actors, and choices will be shaped
by others' choices, there is also a process of collective interpretation of these
new forms of information and knowledge, including efforts to further estimate
possible consequences of different actions.

These processes of interaction are often institutionalized when the need for
collective interpretation and knowledge generation results in the need for repeated
interactions over extended periods of time. One variant of the model suggests
that hybrid groupings wind up pulling together both experts and lay people,
reducing the privileged position of one and incorporating the real-world insights
of the other (Irwin and Michael 2003; Chilvers 2008). Ultimately, the generation
of epistemic communities helps people to develop a common language and cog-
nitive frames that allow them to communicate effectively and share knowledge
(Hakanson 2005). Finally, it is important to recognize that, although the notion
of epistemic communities is linked with some kind of common policy enterprise,
these enterprises are not limited to formal legislative or policy processes. As
Adler and Haas (1992: 374) put it: "the policy ideas of epistemic communities
generally evolve independently, rather than under the direct influence of government sources of authority."

The processes by which such epistemic communities are formed in any
region, how they develop their policy agendas, and how they articulate with
governmental structures are complex. Furthermore, the specific outcomes of
such epistemic communities will undoubtedly be shaped by the character and
diversity of perspectives of people involved in these processes. Fully understanding such processes would require substantially more in-depth research than we
were able to conduct in this project. But we did find some intriguing evidence of
diverse epistemic community formation in the activities of particular organizations and policy processes in several of our regions.

In Nashville, for example, Leadership Nashville deliberately selects participants who represent the diversity of races, religions, ages, political persuasions,
and geographic location of residents of the Nashville region. Over a year-long
process, it brings leaders from these various constituencies together to talk about
a wide range of issues and processes shaping the region. The goal is not to solve
these problems, but simply to build channels of communication between various
leaders and to develop a common understanding of issues facing the region. Each
year a new set of leaders is selected, but interaction with previous groups occurs
both through the activities organized for each year's cohort, as well as through
collective alumni events.

At the time we visited, Leadership Nashville had been operating for thirty-
three years and more than 1,200 people had gone through the program, with more
than 80 percent of participants still living in Nashville. Leadership Nashville
makes a point of not taking stands on public issues, and so the organization itself

does not serve as a forum for developing specific solutions to regional problems. However, the discussions that occur during the program, and between participants and alumni, create new policy ideas that may be realized through other venues. Furthermore, alumni interact with each other in multiple other regional forums and organizations, and their experience in Leadership Nashville undoubtedly helps facilitate communication and knowledge sharing in those other forums as well.

The Jacksonville Community Council (JCCI) has played a prominent role in building cross-constituency communities as well. Since 1975, it has brought together diverse constituencies to address a broad range of issues – everything from teenage pregnancy to mass transit to air quality to racial relations to incentives for economic development.[6] Again, JCCI has a very deliberate process for selecting a diverse group of people to be part of its "study committees." The groups meet weekly for six to nine months to gain a deeper understanding of the issue under consideration, and recommend solutions. The process is driven by consensus, thus requiring detailed discussions to help reconcile differing interpretations of information, and finding solutions that, if not equally supported by all participants, are at least acceptable to all involved. Again, this process occurs outside of formal policy channels or governmental authority, by citizen representatives, not elected officials.

In Kansas City we did not uncover any similar organization that played this explicit role of building communication and conceptual understandings across multiple constituencies. In fact, several key informants described an undue influence on regional policy making of a few key private sector leaders. However, labor unions were accepted political players in regional development processes and, at the time of our visit, the African-American woman president of the Greater Kansas City Central Labor Council (CLC), Bridgette Williams, had just been appointed to the Board of Directors of the Greater Kansas City Chamber of Commerce. But in the absence of a JCCI- or Leadership Nashville-type organization, the Mid-America Regional Council (MARC) may play an important role in building a collaborative regional epistemic community, a role not always played by a metropolitan planning organization.

As we have noted, in 2000, MARC initiated a regional indicators project – very similar to the type of indicators work that JCCI has done as well – and this was followed quickly by a prominent Citistates report and Brookings study on the region (Brookings Institution 2002; Johnson and Peirce 2002). All of these publications, and the processes they involved, help develop a common understanding of the problems and future fate of Kansas City as being rooted in regional dynamics and regional solutions. The Citistates report seemed to be an especially influential process. In their research on the region, the Citistates team interviewed hundreds of Kansas City leaders and residents, from a wide range of constituencies. Many of those interviewed would have been aware of the influence that Citistates reports had had in other regions, and the results of the analysis were eagerly anticipated. The fact that the report was originally published in the newspaper – as most Citistates reports are – ensured that the findings were shared in a broad community of civic leaders, not just within certain academic or policy circles. The fact that the timing of this report coincided with new efforts at collaborative planning and governance processes within MARC suggested to us that some forms of regional epistemic communities were likely to have been formed in Kansas City as well.

In Denver, we also did not find formal mechanisms for creating shared leadership but we did find a common awareness of the importance of the region and a willingness to build regional connections, as evidenced by agreements to tax and spend in order to tie together the region with a light rail system. This is actually fairly remarkable for a state more typically committed to limiting both government and taxes. We also saw the increasing acceptance of the importance of including explicit equity strategies into the growth discussion, as indicated by the Cherokee-Gates community benefits agreement and the Economic Prosperity Taskforce (Read 2006).[7] Still, it is easy to conclude that the shared understandings were not as wide and deep as in other case studies and this is consistent with the slippage in the equity measures in the 2000–2007 period.

Columbus did not seem to have the sort of leadership program we profile here – but it did have the forced consciousness brought to bear by annexation and we noted a sense of collaboration amongst actors. Sacramento also lacked the sort of leadership program seen in a few of our cases; the closest analog is an American Leadership Forum program, which has been quite successful at building cross-sectoral understanding in the Silicon Valley but which has a high participation fee and is more exclusive in its membership and selection processes. Sacramento, however, has an analog to the role of MARC – an award-winning blueprint planning process launched by the Sacramento Council of Governments (SACOG) in 2002 that did help to create a more common sense of the region's issues, challenges, and opportunities.

Cleveland, on the other hand, is a place where the statistics are dismal but hope is increasingly high. The Fund for Our Economic Future came together in 2003 (and more formally in 2004) as a group of philanthropies who realized that fundamental to their shared charitable missions was the need to restore economic competitiveness in Northeast Ohio (a region they call Cleveland Plus). Two of the Fund's early actions included sponsorship of the Cleveland Federal Reserve Study, which determined that segregation and inequality were among the region's Achilles heels, as well as an eighteen-month outreach process that tried to build consciousness about the region and about the need to blend efficiency and equity. This eventually led to an action plan, "Advance Northeast Ohio," that included racial and economic inclusion as one of only four strategic priorities, with a focus on promoting minority-owned enterprises.[8]

We admit that pointing to the power of a new collaborative regional understanding or "diverse epistemic community" might seem like a hopefully untestable hypothesis (though we are considering future research projects – and would accept future funding – to do just that). But we would suggest that this story not only resonated in our case study work (well, maybe not the exact word "epistemic" but the general idea of shared understandings across diverse constituencies), but also showed up to some extent in our quantitative analysis when we saw the statistically significant effect of having participated in regionalist meetings.

Building such common ground might be particularly important in locations where the jurisdictional ties do not bind – leaders in this case need persuasion not legislation to see their common fate.

In our book (co-authored with Martha Matsuoka), *This Could Be the Start of Something Big: How Social Movements for Regional Equity are Reshaping Metropolitan America* (Pastor et al. 2009b), we argued that one critical element in the regional equity movement has been the development of long-term leadership-building and relationship-building organizations. Such efforts have forged a common understanding of issues and allies in the struggle for regional equity – and it is no different when we face the even more complex task of achieving growth with equity and spreading an understanding of that beyond the "usual suspects."

Can labor play a role?

As noted earlier, our quantitative work suggested that unionization rates were negatively associated with growth and did not bear a significant relationship to our measure of equity. We were curious about this – particularly as we have both been big supporters of the labor movement and particularly interested in the new labor organizing that has mobilized immigrants, pursued living wage legislation, and taken an explicitly regional approach to building both coalitions and power (Dean and Reynolds 2009).

Our case studies, however, did not really counter the early empirical observation. Overall unionization rates in our metropolitan areas were mostly below national averages. For example, in a ranking of 242 primary metropolitan statistical areas (PMSAs/MSAs) based on the percentage of the total workforce unionized in 1999 (the last year of the quantitative analysis that determined our "growth with equity" cuts), only two of our regions (Sacramento and Cleveland) ranked in the top half or had a higher than the national percentage of their labor force unionized. One of these, Cleveland, was suffering from sclerotic growth and relatively high levels of inequity while the other, Sacramento, had its numbers mostly driven by public sector unionism.[9]

In Kansas City, unions were accepted as legitimate actors in regional decision-making processes; the head of the Central Labor Council was on the Board of Directors of the Greater Kansas City Chamber of Commerce. In Nashville, the State Labor Federation has significant visibility and played a role, but mostly on state policy rather than regional issues. In Jacksonville, although unions were present, all of our non-labor informants told us that they had little political influence, and our interviews with labor leaders gave little indication of this being false.

Only in Denver is there some sign of substantial labor innovations (although Cleveland's Central Labor Council is showing nascent interest in going the way of the new and more regionalist labor movement). The Front Range Economic Strategy Center (FRESC) emerged out of the Denver Area Labor Federation in 2002 and is attempting to play a substantial role in engaging in and shaping economic growth in the region. It has been one of the national pioneers in pursuing community benefit agreements for major development initiatives, and working to ensure that public dollars are being leveraged to create quality jobs and improve communities.

Does this mean that labor is not important for achieving growth with equity? Several elements call for a more nuanced interpretation. First, unionization levels have been highest in older manufacturing industries, and regions that have had a high concentration of these industries generally have had lower growth rates over the 1980s and 1990s. Thus, the lack of union presence in our case studies is partly due to an industrial sector affect. Second, the presence of labor cannot be discounted if only because, as with the notion of a minority middle class, it is important to have a constituency that has an active interest in both growth and fairness.

Third, and perhaps most important, is the issue of timing. Recall that we selected regions based on their performance in the 1980s and 1990s. But it is the tail years of that second decade that brought the sort of regional reworking in the labor movement detailed in Dean and Reynolds (2009) and elsewhere (Kriesky 1998; Ness and Eimer 2001). Basically, the AFL-CIO sought to develop and support a new approach for Central Labor Councils, one that would put CLCs at the heart of regional politics, workforce development systems, and planning (Mort 1998). The new approach certainly did not take hold everywhere – and it actually seems that places where the old labor movement was strong (like Cleveland and Detroit) were not always places where the new labor movement most easily took root (like Los Angeles, the Silicon Valley, and later, Denver).

In these places, the CLCs set up separate institutions (such as the Los Angeles Alliance for a New Economy, Working Partnerships in San Jose, and FRESC) that were not strictly (although they were largely) identified with labor, and so facilitated new alliances with community organizations and leaders. These organizations, moreover, were quite focused on creating their own epistemic communities, replete with theories of the "new economy," "high road" economics, and other frames that seemed to bring together the imperatives of growth and equity.

So it is not clear that our traditional measurements of union density really capture this element – although one goal of all these CLCs was to increase unionization at a regional level. So our metric may be missing what is most important and we heartily acknowledge that. Still, it is striking that labor's presence was weak in many of the areas we examined – and strongest in places such as Cleveland that are doing badly. We think that this pattern speaks to the fact that labor may need to become flexible in its approach to suit the times, a topic we take up in the closing chapter.

Transit anyone?

Finally, we want to take up a relative absence in our case studies: the role of public transit. As anyone who is involved in urban development processes knows, transit-oriented development (TOD) has become a substantial focus of many progressive efforts to remake the metropolitan landscape. Often seen as central to "Smart Growth" and "New Urbanism" initiatives, TOD involves the creation of compact, walkable communities centered on train, light rail, or other forms of mass transit systems. Although a primary motivation behind TOD is environmental, including the reduction of greenhouse gas emissions, TOD is also often seen to have a variety of social and economic benefits as well as opening new opportunities for more equitable development.[10]

Yet in our in-depth case studies, we were struck by the lack of substantial transit systems, much less inspiring transit-oriented development. Of course, part of this was driven by the constraints of our case selection: Boston and Portland, both of which could have been studied, were dropped mostly because they had been examined so many times already. Still, in all of our regions, the percentage of the population using public transportation to get to work is below the national average, and in most cases as low as one-quarter of the national average (see Table 5.1). Denver currently has the highest level of public transit use, only slightly below the national average. Cleveland has the next highest public transit use of the cases, double that of Columbus, the sister Ohio case that scored far better on our growth and equity measures.

Most of the regions we studied depend entirely on a bus transit system. The only case study regions with a substantial light rail or train transit system are Denver and Sacramento, which do have some interesting examples of transit-oriented development. But the Denver system basically includes only two spur lines from downtown to neighborhoods in the southern suburbs. The situation is similar for Sacramento, which also has two lines that serve downtown but which do not amount to a major mover of people in the region.

Kansas City has struggled for years with an under-funded transit system, exacerbated in part by challenges of building a bi-state consensus on the importance of a regional transit system. In 2002, the Mid-America Regional Council played a lead role in creating Smart Moves, a regional vision for expanded and enhanced regional transit services. The initiative proposed a primarily bus-based system that would "increase transit service in the region to the level comparable with transit service available in peer cities."[11] Progress, however, has been slow, and voters in November 2008 defeated an effort to create a twelve-mile north–south light rail transit corridor that would have linked the metro region's most concentrated employment and residential areas, as well as many of the region's anchor institutions and cultural attractions. Another light rail ballot proposal that included plans for a twenty-seven-mile system was passed by voters in November 2006 – but this was the seventh ballot attempt in nine years, was opposed by almost all of the region's political establishment, and was later rescinded by the City Council.[12]

Jacksonville's transit system is predominantly bus based, with a downtown trolley and skyway service that expands mobility within the downtown area, and a new summertime-only beach trolley serving Jacksonville's beach communities. With only 1.1 percent of workers using public transport, it is clear that

Table 5.1 Commuting to work patterns, U.S. and selected metro regions

	United States	Cleveland	Columbus	Denver	Jacksonville	Kansas City	Nashville	Sacramento
Workers 16 years and over	100.0%	100.0%	100.0%	100.0%	100.0%	100.0%	100.0%	100.0%
Car, truck, or van – drove alone	75.9%	81.5%	82.9%	75.7%	80.9%	83.0%	81.8%	75.3%
Car, truck, or van – carpooled	10.5%	7.9%	8.2%	9.8%	11.0%	9.1%	10.3%	12.2%
Public transportation (excluding taxicab)	5.0%	4.0%	1.6%	4.7%	1.1%	1.3%	1.0%	2.6%
Walked	2.9%	2.2%	2.0%	2.3%	1.6%	1.4%	1.3%	2.1%
Other means	1.7%	1.1%	1.1%	1.9%	1.9%	1.3%	1.3%	2.7%
Worked at home	4.0%	3.2%	4.1%	5.7%	3.6%	3.9%	4.3%	5.1%

Source: U.S. Census, American Community Survey 2005–2009 (http://www.census.gov/acs/www/).

Note: All city figures are for the corresponding metropolitan statistical area.

the transportation system has a minimal impact on opportunities in the region. In Nashville, the percentage is even less – only 1.0 percent of workers use public transit to get to work.

This pattern hardly argues for a prominent role of mass transit systems in a "growth with equity" regime. At the same time, we are also aware of studies that demonstrate how high a transportation cost is born by low-income people in our car-dependent cities, and how valuable more compact developments and greater transit access can be in reducing household expenditures on transportation costs. The Center for Transit Oriented Development, for example, found that, although the average American household spends 19 percent of household expenditures on transportation, households in transit-rich neighborhoods spend only 9 percent, while those in auto-dependent suburbs spend on average 25 percent.[13] Moreover, transportation spending can be a key part of promoting job growth for those who are less skilled and less advantaged.

Still, the analysis here suggests that there are factors that matter more to promoting equitable growth, such as employment structures, housing markets, and democratic political processes. So although we are also proponents of public transit – and recognize the frequent dependence of low-income people on a functioning mass transit system – the lack of association with more equitable growth suggests that equity is not an automatic outcome of a transit-oriented approach.

New approaches

The analytical research presented above has followed a straightforward and logical path: we used quantitative analysis to identify regions where growth and equity seemed to go together, developed a set of profiles to narrow down our interest, selected seven regional case studies and explored them in detail, and then drew key lessons for policy-makers and civic leaders interested in pursuing prosperity and inclusion. All good, to be sure, and even better that such an approach is explicitly designed to surface some "unusual suspects" – regions that are not frequently thought of as pace setters in regional development initiatives – as well as some structural and more contingent factors and processes that help shape growth and equity.

But although this is a logical sequence of research, it can also lead us to miss some important innovations. After all, we based our case selection on performance in the 1980s and the 1990s – but it is largely since the late 1990s that a movement for regional equity has emerged. And throughout the first decade of the twenty-first century, we have seen a number of policies emerge that may have great promise for better linking prosperity and inclusion and are worth mentioning here.

Some of these new policies have come from a transformed labor movement. Although in the past, unions have often been seen as being narrowly focused on workplace issues – issues that are particularly relevant to their own members and potential future members – increasingly local unions and Central Labor Councils are playing a leading role in building broad-based progressive coalitions that bridge multiple issues. In our case study of the Denver region, for example, the labor-affiliated FRESC has strategically bridged a set of comprehensive community issues around government accountability, private development, affordable housing, the environment, and employment. And the work in Denver is mirrored by organizations similar to FRESC in other localities throughout the country: in places such as Los Angeles with the Los Angeles Alliance for a New Economy; Pittsburgh's Unions and Neighborhoods Invested in Transforming Economic Development (Pittsburgh UNITED); and Milwaukee's Good Jobs and Livable Neighborhoods Coalition.

These organizations and others have been influential in not only changing labor's own role in regional economies, but also shaping a broader economic discourse and forging new models for accountable development. One of the strongest tools they have brought to bear in this effort have been community benefits agreements (CBAs) related to major development initiatives.

Community benefits agreements are legally enforceable contracts, signed by community groups and a developer, that lay out a range of community benefits that the developer agrees to provide as part of a development project (Gross et al. 2005). CBAs are usually the end product of researching, organizing, coalition building, and negotiating in which the developer signs a CBA in return for local community support during the permitting process (Lin et al. 2008). Los Angeles has been a pioneer in such CBAs, with the nation's first CBA negotiated in 1999 with the help of councilwoman Jackie Goldberg and the Los Angeles Alliance for a New Economy (LAANE) for a development at Hollywood and Highland (Saito 2007). The template was set for future CBAs covering the expansion of a downtown sports complex called the Staples Center and the expansion of the Los Angeles International Airport, and the model has since been replicated across the United States (Parks and Warren 2009).

CBAs are a good practice for development but they are more than that: they tend to reframe discussions around economic growth to include the implications for equity even as they engage communities in the development process. And we would stress one aspect not always noted by observers: much as they force developers to think about the community, they force community members and advocates to understand and support strategies for economic growth. They are, in short, as important for the understanding they promote as the benefits they deliver (Annie E. Casey Foundation 2007; Baxamusa 2008).

Another new set of approaches has emerged from the workforce development world. Good quality jobs are, of course, one of the critical markers we used to determine growth and equity – but the benefits of public sector workforce development programs for disadvantaged job seekers has traditionally been modest (Grubb 1995). Part of the reason, experts have argued, was the relative isolation of these programs from employers and their lack of connection to good jobs with clear paths of mobility (Osterman 1999). In the framework of Benner, Leete, and Pastor (2007), the system focused on "meeting" the market (bringing together employers and employees), to some degree "molding" the market (facilitating the development of supply-side human capital), but not really on "making" the market (helping to generate demand and improve job quality in industries).

A new class of programs has been focused on taking on this broader task, particularly in the 2000s, trying to link both sides of the labor market and transform employment conditions as well. These *"workforce intermediaries"* are "deeply connected or 'embedded' in low-income communities *and* in networks of employers, workforce providers, and community organizations" (Giloth 2004: 6, emphasis added). Embodying a wide range of non-profit, public sector, labor-based, and even for-profit initiatives, these organizations (at least in their best practices) meet the needs of both employers and job seekers, go beyond simply job matching to provide a range of additional support services, are able to integrate multiple funding streams and revenue sources, become sources of innovations and ideas about what workers, firms, and communities need in order to prosper, and are far more than simply stand-alone training providers (Kazis 1998; Benner 2003; PEERS 2003; Wolf-Powers 2003; Benner et al. 2007).

The attempts to move workforce development away from its history as an anti-poverty strategy and toward an approach that aims to promote economic development as much as expand economic opportunity has been difficult and uneven across the country. Bureaucratic inertia, programmatic silos, conflicting organizational cultures and agendas, and political conflict, along with the inherent difficulties of developing effective training and economic development programs in a rapidly changing, technologically dynamic and volatile economy, are just a few of the factors inhibiting effective reform. Yet there are signs that effective transformations are increasingly taking root around the country.

In Pennsylvania, for example, comprehensive workforce development reform legislation was passed in 2005/2006. This included $20 million in direct support for industry partnerships (a type of workforce intermediary), including funding for incumbent worker training as well as organizational support to build the capacity of these sector partnerships. The state also directed all training funds toward high priority occupations and sectors that were identified through a detailed analysis of employment and economic growth patterns. By June 2009, the state had seventy-seven active industry partnerships in eleven broad industry sectors, which involved about 6,300 companies and over 75,000 employees from these companies that had participated in training, with most focused on particular regional labor markets.[14] Outcomes of this program were substantial. According to state figures, workers who were trained experienced a nearly 7 percent wage increase; 84 percent of surveyed businesses reported significant productivity gains and a 69 percent employee retention rate increase; 83 percent reported improved efficiency as a result of training; and 64 percent reported that the training opportunities allowed them to use new technology in the workplace.[15]

Washington State is another state that has made substantial progress in reforming its workforce development system. Oversight of the system is handled by the Washington State Workforce Training and Education Coordinating

Board (WTECB), which has developed substantial accountability and detailed data-driven performance monitoring and management. This includes biennial independent evaluations providing detailed outcomes data on a range of skills, wage, and productivity indicators for participants in the system, which document substantial benefits for both individuals and the broader economy.[16] The state has a clearly articulated strategic plan for workforce development that is required by law to be updated every two years and which plays an important role in building coordination across the multiple agencies involved in the system. Industry skills panels in major sectors play an important role in focusing resources of business, labor, education, and the state on identifying and closing worker skills gaps in specific industries and clusters.

Our point here is that this too is an emerging area of work in which growth and equity, prosperity and inclusion, are being consciously linked. Far from being a program to simply help disadvantaged workers gain a toehold in the labor market, the new efforts are seeing the training of such disadvantaged workers as a way to grow regional and state economies.

That same linkage can be seen in community colleges – which have become an important site of innovations that are linking economic growth and social equity. The role and responsibilities of community colleges are complex and multi-faceted – they are institutions that are accountable to a wide range of stakeholders: students, their communities, local governments, higher-level post-secondary institutions, and employers and businesses. Starting in the 1970s, community colleges expanded beyond their role of providing academic education, increasingly becoming the gateway for students to access occupational and professional programs (Cohen and Brawer 2002). This transformation resulted in the community college broadening its role as a transfer and degree-granting institution to include a workforce development component.

Today, community colleges play a central role in integrating diverse populations into the workforce to boost regional economies and to promote regional equity. In most community colleges, students vary from recent high school graduates preparing to transfer to four-year universities to laid-off, low-income adults returning for additional job training and skills certification, or what some refer to as a "second chance" to obtain a college degree.

Throughout the country there are examples of how community colleges have creatively responded to the needs of their region and students, some of which have been considered in our case studies. In a study of community college practices, the Workforce Strategy Center (WSC) highlights the State of Washington's Puget Sound Partnership as a prime example of how community colleges coordinated with social service agencies to work on Washington's Career Pathway Initiatives. Together, the partners developed career pathways for their region's fast-growth and high-wage industries. Each community college then built relationships with employers to develop employment strategies for graduates, and together formulated a short training program, internship, or paid work experience, and a pathway for future training opportunities to lay the foundation for continuing education (WSC 2002).

The general point of the Workforce Strategy Center is that strategic partnerships are one of the key components of successful community college strategies – particularly regional partnerships based on a shared regional pathway vision, a network of partnerships, regional integration of resources, and a focus on critical industries or sectors. In this view, equity and growth are part and parcel of a holistic approach to solving the problems of employers and workers.

Shaping the future

Case study approaches are always frustrating: the inductive method means that you are discerning patterns and building hypotheses from a messy reality filled with changing variables, shifting contexts, and, worse of all, social agents that may not behave as you predict and are constantly trying to change the landscape even as you seek to theorize its firm shape. We sought to tame this empirical beast with a bit of quantitative work early on, developing and testing hypotheses that could then be explored in the field. We were, of course, still surprised by some of what we found and we have tried to draw from this constantly transforming milieu key lessons about the policies and politics that can marry prosperity and inclusion.

We have suggested that there are a series of structural factors that tend to contribute to a region having a higher likelihood of achieving growth with equity. For example, jurisdictional ties, including city–county consolidation or the power of annexation, seem to force a sense of common fate – or at least ensure that the usual escape of economic activity and the middle class to far-flung suburbs is less likely. The importance of having a diversified economic base does not emerge in our quantitative estimates, as seems to be the case in much of the statistical work – but go talk to people in the regions and they will stress that your measures must be wrong because diversity allows you to weather economic storms in any particular sector. Public employment is also a bit of a buffer to a downturn and may provide an avenue to create a minority middle class in the face of discrimination in private sector hiring (and the equally problematic but less intentional consequences of hiring based on closed social networks).

That middle class itself is important: having a constituency that has clear interests in growing the economy but also some interest in making it fairer may be critical to keeping equity and growth tied together in local conversations and regional goal setting. There are causality issues here, of course, as a sizable minority middle class may itself be the product of more equitable processes. Still, it is striking that Nashville, Jacksonville, and Columbus are highly ranked as locations for Black professionals, that Sacramento was rated by the Harvard Civil Rights project as the most integrated city in 2002, and that our "stuck-back" case, Cleveland, is known as a highly segregated and racially tense metropolitan area.

We also find an important role for higher education. We note that some universities are more regionally rooted than others. The trick is to have one that has national ambitions and a national reputation but is committed to being a part of the region that hosts it. Less celebrated but equally critical is the community college system as this generates the workforce to sustain the region – and it may be especially important in places, such as Denver, where the highly educated can be imported in the absence of a local prominent university producing its own professional elite.

Although we pay some attention to the structural factors that induce growth with equity, we are more interested in what advocates can do to steer their region from a path of poor outcomes to a path of good outcomes. Part of that is affecting the structure: as we note, improving race relations is important, improving the community college system generates workforce pay-offs, and linking up to university-based innovation is helpful. And if you cannot get ties that bind through explicit political boundaries, you may just need to get them through creating what we term a "diverse epistemic community."

We realize that the term is vague – and "let's get epistemic" is unlikely to make it onto either a protest placard or a mission statement – but the concept is essential. It is not about agreeing about every single policy that should or should not be implemented in a region – it is about creating a shared vision, a shared discourse, and a shared destiny. It is about building the leadership so that people know each other well, and can work through uncertainty. And it is crucially about creating a framework in which key social actors truly believe that there are ways that growth and equity can go together.

Leadership to that end can come from anywhere. Leadership Nashville played such a role in our case studies, as did the Jacksonville Community Council. We argue that the Fund for Our Economic Future is potentially poised to play the same role in Cleveland – and it is a role distinct from that of the Greater Cleveland Partnership, which, although broad in its scope, inclusive in its language, and probably more important in its presence, is not perceived as really fully buying into the notion that inclusion really will spur growth.

It is also one of the reasons why we believe that, although labor did not come up as an important player in our case studies, it may be a key actor in other locations and situations. As we have noted, labor has been transformed in recent years and we think that the set of organizations reflected in the Partnership for Working Families – a family of think tanks associated with Central Labor Councils but with a broader and more regionally oriented vision that we review in the next chapter – is trying to craft exactly the new frame that is needed: a progressive vision in which equity is central, growth is important, and the two are mutually reinforcing.

The importance of such a framework cannot be overstated. If you are locked in an ideology of competing interests and constant conflict, it is not surprising if you find and perpetuate that. If you look for ways to achieve growth with equity, you may just find and agree on a strategy that works. We would label both that process and that outcome "just growth."

6   Just growth

Introduction

Our research on economic prosperity and social inclusion in metropolitan America has revealed a complex range of strategies across a diverse set of regions. There is clearly no "silver bullet" solution, no simple practice that can be adopted everywhere that will automatically lead to beneficial economic and social outcomes. Economies and regions are complicated and multi-faceted – and so is the task of tying together growth and equity.

At the same time, we are great believers in the need for academics to adopt the discipline of not just rigorous research but also parsimonious, simple, and decisive speech. President Harry Truman, after all, is reported to have been exasperated when his economists kept saying, "on one hand this, on the other that" – he finally requested that his staff bring him a one-armed economist. That said – and perhaps wanting to avoid a perilous fate – we would suggest that, despite the complexity, our research points to three simple conclusions.

First, to achieve regional equity, you need some kind of ties that bind people together. This can happen through formal mechanisms, such as happens through inclusive regional political boundaries, but it can also happen through other mechanisms, such as a large minority middle class, which can build solidarity across class and race lines as well as geographic barriers. These structures and mechanism are an important part of the process of building a sense of common destiny across diverse constituencies in a region.

Second, growth can emerge from a variety of different economic sectors, but to achieve sustained growth that is resilient in the face of broad economic cycles and shocks requires a diverse, responsive, and stable employment base. Education, healthcare, and especially public sector employment seem to be important sectors for cushioning regional economies from volatile market changes. Equity proponents should, we suggest, pay more attention to those factors that contribute to both economic expansion and fairer distribution.

Third, to achieve both growth and equity, you also need leadership. The leadership can come from virtually anywhere – our case study regions have important regional leadership from private, public, labor, and non-profit sectors – but in all cases these regional leadership initiatives have been sustained over long periods of time, have focused on building a shared understanding of a region's current problems, and have allowed for some degree of cross-sectoral collaboration on solutions.

We began the research that led to these broad conclusions back in early 2007. Although we did not anticipate what was to come – the worst recession since the Great Depression and the election of the first African-American president of the United States – we were convinced that our findings on how certain metropolitan areas were blending prosperity and inclusion might be useful not just for urban development initiatives, but also for national economic policies.

In some sense, the timing could not have been better; in some sense, it could not have been worse. Clearly, we need a new economic model that can go beyond dealing with the wreckage of the current crisis and create a more sustainable and equitable path for the future. At the same time, the anxieties of tough times have produced a turn to conservatism in the United States and elsewhere, and ideas that "we are all in it together" sometimes fall on deaf ears.

But we are indeed in it together. Because of this, "just growth" means more than a set of outcomes that land you in the "good" quadrant of an equity–growth matrix; it also means inclusion in the decision making that sets the conditions for prosperity. It is process as much as outcome, it is community building as much as business building, it is democratic practice as much as it is economic policy.

This may seem either a bit too broad or a bit too ephemeral, but it is actually the "epistemic" glue that we found so crucial in several of our case studies. We have a highly polarized nation in which fragmentation by race, class, and geography has eroded a sense of common good, in which broadcast news has given way to "narrow-cast" cable, in which partisans would rather wreck the whole system than yield the advantage of a good policy victory to the other side. It is, in short, a lot different from the Jacksonville Community Council – and America is the worse for it.

We do not think there was an idyllic earlier era – American social history is fraught with conflicts in which people have struggled for their rights and American economic history is also replete with examples of well-meaning redistributionist approaches that hobbled overall growth. But our metropolitan regions have become laboratories for a different approach in which face-to-face conversations yield agreements, in which prosperity and inclusion are not seen as opposed, and in which conflicts and collaborations are managed with equal grace. As a nation, we can both learn from those experiments and help them grow.

In this final chapter, we explore the potential for building a stronger national commitment to just growth, to a vision in which economic prosperity and social inclusion are seen as intimately connected. We examine this potential along three different dimensions. First, we explore how it is that positive lessons from some regions could bubble up and over to other regions – what are and should be the mechanisms for peer learning that can share lessons from deliberate attempts to ensure inclusion in economic growth trajectories? Second, we ask how it is that the federal government might be more supportive of equitable growth, shifting from its historic promotion of sprawl to something that might bring more economic, environmental, and social sustainability. Third, we go a bit beyond the evidence in our case studies – risky, we know, but also imperative at such a critical conjuncture in our history – to speculate on the broader implications for developing economic theory and policy that can better recognize and support the link between equity and growth.

This last task – finding and articulating these fundamental connections between prosperity and inclusion – is a key part of the challenge ahead. We certainly need processes that can bring people to a common understanding, but we as a nation also need an economic story that makes sense of the growth and equity connection. We have generally been taught on an economy-wide scale that too much attention to fairness will shrink the economic pie. But ask successful businesses how they get ahead and the answer generally revolves around treating both their customers and their employees right. Successful regions also seem to be able to make the same connection – and we need to lift up these lessons so they become more central to our national discourse.

How did we do?

Before exploring these broader national implications of our work, it is worth pausing for a moment to consider another empirical question: Did our categorizations hold up in recent years – and, in particular, how did our case study metro regions fare in the Great Recession? After all, our primary data analysis for case selection and model testing focused on the 1980s and 1990s. We did update our data after we hit the field in 2008 and the first half of 2009 to consider what had happened between 2000 and 2007 – finding out that most of our characterizations had held up but also that Denver had cycled back into poor performance on equity, Sacramento had recovered to some degree, and Columbus – so hopeful in the context of the Midwest – had remained steady on the economic measures but slipped significantly (along with the rest of Ohio) on the equity measures.

What about regional resiliency in the face of the dramatic economic downturn that began in 2007–2008? To what extent do the historical patterns of growth and equity we identified in our regions help explain their more recent fortunes? To what extent were regions that have integrated economic prosperity and social inclusion also able to weather our recent historic crisis? Were the relationships and institutions that helped underpin these experiences of growth and equity better able to handle the shocks of the national economic crisis than those of other regions?

To examine this briefly, we take a page from the Brookings Institution and its "MetroMonitor" – a system of tracking the recession and recovery in the nation's 100 largest metro areas (Wial and Shearer 2011). Although this tracking system also looks at change in housing price, gross regional product, and unemployment rate, we focused on the measurement of employment growth, which most closely matches one of our growth indicators. We then added to the data series our own measure of change in percent below poverty, one of our key equity indicators.[1] The employment series – taken directly from Brookings – is the (seasonally adjusted) percentage change in employment from each metropolitan area's peak employment quarter to the most recent quarter available, in the case of these data the fourth quarter of 2010.[2] The median for the sample from peak to last observation was three years; because we were going for a parallel length of time on the equity side, we calculated the change in the poverty rate over the most recent three years for which we had data.[3]

We then ranked the top 100 metro regions, including our case study seven, in terms of the employment growth and poverty reduction measures. However, whereas the Brookings rankings (which include the aforementioned other variables and do not include equity measures) are conducted nationally, we benchmarked each metropolitan area, as in our initial rankings, against the performance of its respective census region. Thus, a "good" performance in this period could mean that employment fell and poverty increased, just not as much as others in that census region. We also followed the Brookings procedure to come up with a single ranking – in this case, we averaged the growth and equity scores and then re-ranked those averages within the various census regions.

The results are quite interesting – and very consistent with our earlier categorization of the metros. Of our "growth with equity" regions, Columbus, for example, is right about the median for the Midwest for the combined score, doing slightly better on employment than poverty. Kansas City is one of the best Midwest performers for the combined score, with a ranking on growth just below the top tercile and an equity score that is near the top. Nashville is just out of the top tercile but well above the median on the combined score, with the performance on poverty better than the performance on growth.

Jacksonville seems to be an exception to the rule that our earlier categorizations more or less persisted in the recent past: it is twenty-eighth out of the thirty-seven metropolitan areas in the South. However, that seems to be a function of being in Florida: it is the best performer on the combined score of the eight Florida metros, all of which occupy the bottom rungs for the South, doing second best in terms of employment growth and above median in terms of changes in poverty.

Meanwhile, Denver's role as the wild cycler seems secure: on our combined measure it was near the top in the West on both growth and equity (recall that it performed middling on growth and miserably on equity in the 2000–2007 period). Despite its recent hopeful regional planning efforts, Sacramento slipped back again, landing in the lowest quarter of metros in that census division on both the growth and equity measures (probably because it was hard hit by the housing crisis; in California, only Modesto and Riverside-San Bernardino did worse on these measures). Finally, Cleveland, which was tied for last in its census division when we did a similar ranking for the top 100 using the historical growth and equity indices, kicked up a few positions in the most recent data. This reflects both its "stuck-back" status and the glimmers of hope that may be emerging from the new regionalist efforts in that area.

These patterns of growth and equity during the Great Recession and not-so-great recovery for our seven case study regions are mostly consistent with the patterns we profiled over the previous three decades. This gives us some confidence that the structural characteristics we saw as fundamental to explaining growth and equity, and the more political economy factors involving significant minority middle classes and regional leadership efforts, may be deep-rooted. Of course, the challenge facing America is whether or not lessons from these regional patterns might be diffused across the country to other regions and filtered up to national-level economic policy processes. It is to those dimensions that we now turn.

Scaling across regions

The infamous slogan of the casino capital of the United States is that "what happens in Las Vegas, stays in Las Vegas." This sort of makes sense, given the quiet nod in the accompanying ads to gambling, marital affairs, and excessive drinking – but when it comes to the more benign and often more helpful work of regional leaders, figuring out how to learn across regions is critical.

Several national intermediaries are already playing an important and helpful role in helping develop and disseminate best practice learning across regions, with somewhat different emphases. The two most prominent of these are the Brookings Institution's Metropolitan Policy Program, which has put out a series of influential reports, often focused on the competitiveness agenda, and Oakland-based PolicyLink, which has hosted a series of Regional Equity Summits that have allowed for sharing of strategies on how best to promote the equity side of the equation. Both pay some attention to the other's expertise – Brookings consistently discusses issues of racial segregation and income gaps while PolicyLink refers to "equitable development" and not just equity – but there is a bit of a gap on both sides that could use a bridge.

There are bubble-up efforts to network regions in their learnings about growth and equity, including the work of the Partnership for Working Families (PWF).[4] PWF was founded in 2002 by four labor-linked organizations in California that had prominently promoted community benefits agreements and other strategies for producing more accountable and beneficial economic development strategies. By 2009, the Partnership had grown to include seventeen organizations in eleven states. The Partnership organizations aim to influence land use and economic development decisions in their regions, frequently using as points of leverage government procurement, regulation, incentives, employment, contracting, and construction to improve the quality of existing jobs and attract better-quality new jobs and sustainable industries. Specific local strategies include living wage policies, minimum development standards, community impact reports on development initiatives, and prevailing wage, worker retention, and local hiring provisions.

By the end of 2008, the network had built on this strong history of local programs to develop a powerful and comprehensive set of recommendations for federal urban policy. Entitled "A New Urban Agenda for America," the recommendations included specific proposals to improve job quality and expand job opportunities in a range of industries, including construction trades, green jobs such as building retrofitting and new energy sectors, transportation and logistics, and fast-growing sectors such as retail, hospitality, and healthcare.[5] A national conference in DC in May 2009 on Advancing the New Urban Agenda drew nearly 400 people from across the country to discuss strategies for implementing these economic strategies.

Lessons from workforce development reform efforts, which directly link growth and equity, are also bubbling across regions and states, often with the support of philanthropy. The National Fund for Workforce Solutions (NFWS), for example, is a national funding partnership, led by the Ford Foundation and the Annie E. Casey Foundation, but including financial investments from seven other funding sources, including the U.S. Department of Labor.[6] The national fund provides one-to-four matching funds for at least twenty-two regional funding collaboratives in at least eighteen states and the District of Columbia that bring together local foundations and some private sector investment.

These regional funding collaboratives in turn invest in local workforce partnerships that are pursuing a "dual customer approach," serving businesses looking for qualified workers and job seekers and workers looking to advance their careers, hence concretely blending growth and equity concerns.[7] It is still too early to see demonstrable outcomes from this initiative for workers or regional economies, and its effectiveness is undoubtedly limited by the fact that the effort was launched in a recessionary period in which an abundance of unemployed workers made placing disadvantaged workers tough. Nonetheless, by the end of its second year of operation in 2009, it had posted impressive indicators of success: the number of funders supporting the collaboratives grew from 183 in 2008 to 256 in 2009; the number of workforce partnerships had increased from thirty-seven in 2008 to sixty-three in 2009; the number of participants served by these partnerships grew from 6,306 in 2008 to 18,036 in 2009, with the total number receiving some kind of degree or credential increasing from 679 to 9,735 and the total number of job seekers securing jobs as a result of their participation rising from 893 in 2008 to 4,058 in 2009; and the number of employers receiving services grew from 504 in 2008 to 998 in 2009. There was growing qualitative evidence that employer engagement in the more mature partnerships was strengthening, with signs of changing employment practices (Baran et al. 2010).

More importantly and fundamentally, the NFWS represents an effort to migrate change across regions, creating a just-in-time learning system so that collaboratives can share strategies for changing workforce systems and employer practices (such as pre-payment of tuition for incumbent workers to return to school, employer funding for basic skills training, and greater flexibility in work schedules for incumbent workers attending classes).

Another arena for sharing lessons across regions involves leadership development. This is particularly important as it helps construct the kinds of shared understandings that we have thought so crucial, both within regions and across regions. Groups such as Leadership Nashville, Denver's Economic Prosperity Taskforce and Metro Mayors Caucus, and the Jacksonville Community Council Inc. played a key role in developing common understandings of challenges facing the region, and a common language, or even commonly accepted solutions, for addressing those challenges. In these cases, the organizations make an explicit goal of being non-partisan, and typically focus on generating new ideas and discussion across constituencies.

Efforts to build cross-regional leadership networks along similar lines have emerged from multiple different constituencies. For example, starting in 2008, the American Chamber of Commerce Executives (ACCE) ran a year-long program for personnel of local chambers of commerce, funded by the Ford Foundation, that helped create a sense of what regional sustainable development might look like, including issues of inclusion and equity.[8] The fellowship program provides hands-on training, peer learning, and examination of effective regional strategies around the country, and over its first three years of operation created a network of at least 125 key regional business leaders from across the country who are exploring links between growth and equity in their work.[9] PolicyLink's regional equity summits play the same sort of learning role – albeit in mass fashion – for those more interested in distributional issues. We would stress the important role of directing specific attention to building a strong constituency for equity; without this, the ability of such cross-constituency community building is somewhat limited. The challenge is also imparting in those equity-oriented constituencies a sense of economic dynamics and possibilities.

Another interesting leadership development initiative focuses on building political will and power for implementing strategies that simultaneously promote growth and equity. Called Building Partnerships USA (BPUSA), this effort was founded in 2005 by two California-based organizations, Working Partnerships USA (WPUSA) in San Jose and SCOPE in Los Angeles.[10] It was based on work in San Jose in which WPUSA developed a Civic Leadership Institute (CLI) – an intensive workshop program designed to help local leaders build relationships across diverse constituencies, develop a common vision and vocabulary for regional economic growth, and enhance leadership skills for base building, political advocacy, and policy change. One key component of the CLI approach was to specifically target key constituencies that hadn't frequently worked together, including not just the traditional labor, community, and faith-based social justice communities, but also private sector leaders, particularly those in small businesses and ethnic chambers of commerce whose interests may be less represented in the more dominant private sector leadership circles in the region, and public sector leadership. One thing that distinguished this approach from other coalition-building efforts is that the effort to build cross-constituency collaboration was not rooted in specific campaigns or policy agendas. As BPUSA co-founder Amy Dean says, "You don't build relationships in the midst of a fight; you have to create deliberate space to understand each other's interests" (Pastor et al. 2009b: 172–3). BPUSA has helped expand this model, working with Central Labor Council leadership to develop similar leadership institutes in Boston, New Haven, Denver, Atlanta, Milwaukee, and Hartford – but the key point here is the need to generate new communities of understanding through conscious leadership-building programs across multiple constituencies.

How national policy can help

Whereas the dynamics and experiments we have discussed have been at the metropolitan level, to ultimately have a substantial impact on a national scale they also have to be integrated with national policy efforts. Achieving this will involve reversing much of the role of national policy, which has been a substantial force in pushing the landscape of regional inequity and social inequality against which these efforts are working – think, for example, how the National Housing Act of 1934 resulted in disproportionately insuring reasonable mortgages to middle-class families in new suburban areas, and the Federal Aid Highway Act of 1956 built highways that further induced such sprawling development. Although state and local government have certainly had a hand at building regional exclusion, the point here is that sprawl and regional inequality were partially the results of government policy and not just the free market – and so policy could be part of the solution.

There are a range of policy advocacy groups, rooted in a perspective that links growth and equity at a regional scale, that are seeking to have influence on national policy. The Brookings Metropolitan Policy Program, for example, is a decidedly non-partisan effort trying to shift national policy in a way that supports metropolitan development. It has brought together business, labor, and civic leaders in multiple regions to see their common interests in regional prosperity, and then emphasized the need for policies that would recognize the centrality of metropolitan economies to strengthening the American economy. The director of that program, Bruce Katz, has been a special advisor to U.S. Department of Housing and Urban Development (HUD) Secretary Shaun Donovan, and the White House's Office for Urban Affairs has taken a decidedly regionalist approach, with President Obama's pre-election speech to the U.S. Conference of Mayors recognizing the need for a regional strategy for growing local economies.[11]

It is not just Brookings, of course. Other organizations such as PolicyLink, Smart Growth America, Partnership for Working Families, and Green for All have been trying to infuse the national agenda with a framework that stresses equity as well as growth, inclusion as well as prosperity. Some of these groups noted that the stress on "shovel-ready" projects in the American Recovery and Reinvestment Act (ARRA) tended to disadvantage efforts such as transit-oriented development, alternative transit modes in low-income communities, or "fix it first" infrastructure spending in older areas that might take longer to generate but could better target poverty (Fox and Rice 2009). Just growth, it seems, might just take more time.

Looking forward to longer-term policy, a critical area is transportation spending. In the last major round of reworking federal transportation dollars, the 2005 adoption of the Safe, Accountable, Flexible, and Efficient Transportation Equity Act – A Legacy for Users (SAFETEA-LU), community organizers were able to win a provision allowing for local hiring programs; one of the two Senate champions of that provision was an Illinois freshman named Barack Obama.

But this simply opened up the possibility for local groups to apply pressure rather than mandating local hiring and apprenticeship programs as part of the usual requirements. The next round of multi-year funding was supposed to be approved in 2009 but a plethora of other legislative priorities, including the ARRA and healthcare reform, have meant that the bill design and decision keep being pushed back.

Transportation policy is important not simply for reversing patterns of highway-induced sprawl, but also for even more direct influences on equity and growth. Policies in transit and other arenas of public investment can actually be effective in encouraging more equity for each growth-inducing dollar. Although our case studies did not find much of a role for transit-oriented development, a recent study found that spending through the 2009 stimulus program on public transportation created nearly twice as many jobs per dollar as money spent on highway maintenance and construction (CNT et al. 2010) – and public transportation also helps low-income individuals make it more effectively to work and around their regions (as well as freeing money to increase consumer spending on other items; Litman 2006, 2009). Prioritizing "fix it first" strategies for road infrastructure – investing in repairing what is broken before adding new infrastructure – would also be a useful way of helping older cities and suburbs.

Housing issues are also critical to growth and equity – business needs housing affordability to attract and retain workers, and this is obviously a central issue for many equity-oriented planners and community advocates. One recent encouraging innovation is the creation of the National Housing Trust Fund as part of the Housing and Economic Recovery Act of 2008, the first legislation since the HOME program in 1990 that dedicates funds to extremely low-income households.[12] This much-needed infusion of resources for affordable rental housing has the potential to reduce hardship and expand opportunities for low-income families, but not if all the funds are used to build or preserve housing in high-poverty and distressed neighborhoods. Instead, rental support must be targeted in opportunity-rich neighborhoods where affordable rental options are scarce, and in gentrifying neighborhoods where lower-income renters are being squeezed out.

Incentives could change such that Low Income Housing Tax Credits (LIHTC) do not further concentrate affordable housing and hence poverty,[13] HUD grants could fund working with local planning agencies to update zoning, enable TODs, and promote integrated and inclusionary housing, and regional business leaders could, as with Chicago Metro 2020 and the Silicon Valley Leadership Group, take a key role on insisting that jurisdictions provide an opening for developers of workforce housing.

A final – and probably politically difficult – change in the housing arena would be reform of the mortgage interest tax deduction, one of the largest sources of federal tax revenue loss. The Congressional Research Services estimated this program alone accounted for $72 billion in lost federal revenue in 2005. When combined with the exclusion of capital gains on the sales of homes, and the state and local real estate tax deduction, this represents over $100 billion a year in lost revenue, compared with the total appropriations for HUD in that year of $31.5 million (Jackson 2005).[14] The beneficiaries of this program are dispropor-tionately wealthy Americans, and most economists agree that the program has little if any impact on overall homeownership rates (Glaeser and Shapiro 2003; Brown 2009). Other targeted homeownership subsidies, such as down-payment assistance programs, could be much more effective at increasing homeownership amongst lower-income families and would be less expensive than the mortgage interest tax deduction (Herbert and Tsen 2007) – and this would free money for more job-inducing strategies.

Any reform of the mortgage interest tax deduction would have to be balanced against any overall impacts on the construction industry, which as we saw in our regression and logistic analyses was positively associated with equitable growth. This drives us in the direction of jobs policies – with the challenge being not simply to promote more job creation but to promote *better* job creation and to expand access to those better jobs for disadvantaged populations. The growing trend within the Department of Labor to prioritize sectoral workforce develop-ment efforts is positive in this regard; in the best cases, these efforts are linked with economic development initiatives, which can provide valuable technologi-cal, marketing, and financial assistance to firms, along with the creation of effec-tive intermediaries that assist low-income job seekers in gaining the skills, job placement, mentoring, and social support services they need to take advantage of new and good job opportunities (Glover and King 2010).

A fully effective jobs policy, however, needs to include more than just grow-ing good jobs, and helping more people get access to those jobs. The third leg of the stool that is all too often missing is raising the wages and working conditions in existing low-wage jobs. The need for this third leg is underscored by new research documenting the growth of the working poor, rather than simply the unemployed, and the ways that social policies typically miss the needs of this important population (Zuberi 2006; Pastor and Scoggins 2007). Policies such as living wage requirements, community benefits agreements, employment standards, and workers rights (including the Employee Free Choice Act) are all mechanisms that can effectively improve wages in existing low-wage jobs (Luce 2004; Logan 2009).

Much of what will make these changes happen revolves around improving the governance systems in our metropolitan areas that are so important for deter-mining conditions of economic growth and inclusion. Metropolitan planning organizations (MPOs) are the most widespread form of regional government, yet they are limited in their utility because they are restricted in most cases to steer-ing transportation spending and have little ability to actually control (or even significantly influence) local land use and economic decisions. Furthermore, MPOs are constrained by their formal structures, which are typically based on a "one jurisdiction, one vote" system that tends to give a disproportionate voice to smaller suburbs (Nelson et al. 2004; Sanchez 2005). Although some MPOs, such as MARC in the Kansas City area, step up to be broader and more representative in terms of their concerns and initiatives, it is hard to make equity central when your voting rules work directly against that. If federal authorities really do want to promote more integrated regional land use and transportation planning efforts, they may have to be part of reform efforts for more democratic accountability on the part of MPOs (Rubin 2009).

Governance goes well beyond *government* to incorporate the multiple formal and informal processes, both within government institutions and beyond, that shape public sector decision-making processes (Peters and Pierre 1998; Phares 2004). One of the key findings from our case study research was the importance of some process or organization bringing together people from widely different constituencies in a way that helped overcome widely differing perspectives and knowledge bases. This finding about achieving collaborative *governance* at a regional scale has direct correlation to federal policy: at that level, too, there is a need to move away from programmatic silos, integrate approaches across multiple agencies, and better integrate government efforts with local community and private sector initiatives.

One significant effort toward this goal from the Obama administration is the Federal Partnership for Sustainable Communities, an infrastructure-focused partnership designed to link together housing, transportation, and environmental programs. The Environmental Protection Agency (EPA), HUD, and Department of Transportation specifically wanted to apply the program to metropolitan areas in "developing truly integrated transportation, land use, and economic development plans to serve projected growth over the next several decades" while supporting MPOs to "to devise their own innovations for coping with congestion and greenhouse gas emissions across transportation, housing, land use, economic development, and energy policies" (Puentes 2009). In the first round of funding in FY2010, $98 million was allocated for a Regional Grant Competition. The agencies received more than 1,300 expressions of interest and 225 completed applications, with both the number of participants and the total request of $444 million in funding indicating widespread interest in these broader, integrative approaches. The Partnership ended up funding forty-five of these proposals for comprehensive Regional Planning Grants, and another forty-two for somewhat more limited Sustainable Community Challenge grants.[15]

Several features of the initial program design are especially attractive. The first is that it embraces comprehensive livability principles, including the provision of more transportation options, the promotion of affordable housing, the enhancement of economic competitiveness, support to existing communities, the coordination of policies, and a value for communities and neighborhoods.[16] But the second and most important is the possibility (with the devil in the details) of creating financial incentives for interjurisdictional cooperation about sustainable development. The worry, of course, is not only the details but the fact that this is an entirely new way of doing business, local resistance may be high, and some of the seemingly best ideas can wind up furthering inequality (think, for example, of the unintended concentration effects of the LIHTC). But still this sets the structural stage for thinking and working together that we have emphasized.

What all this means for economic policy and theory

In the context of a deep recession, economic policy is the subject of heated national debate. And in the context of a seeming meltdown of the world as we knew it – remember the story that house prices always rise, markets always correct, and growth will inevitably trickle down – economic theory itself is up for grabs.

On the policy side, the evidence from our research – particularly the important role in our case studies of stable public employment and the critical role of construction employment in our just growth regressions – supports those who have argued at the moment for large-scale public investments to create jobs. The Economic Policy Institute, for example, leaned against the political wind in late 2009 to propose a five-point American Jobs Plan that included $150 billion in fiscal relief for state and local governments; $30 billion for maintaining and repairing public schools and at least $50 billion for transportation spending, with an emphasis on transit; and $40 billion per year for public service jobs, primarily in cleaning up abandoned and vacant lots and renovating and maintaining parks, playgrounds and other public spaces, as well as critical social services and early education programs.[17] These proposals would lead to substantial expansion in both public sector and construction-related jobs, the two industry sectors that show up in our research as the most strongly correlated with both economic growth and social equity.

Another strategic investment that is broadly supported by our research, with certain caveats, is investments in "green jobs." Although there remains conceptual confusion about what exactly constitutes a "green job," most definitions share a core focus on three significant subsectors: renewable energy generation and production, including manufacturing of wind turbines, solar systems, and other related jobs; energy efficiencies in all aspects of building construction and retrofitting; and transportation jobs related to a shift to more energy-efficient vehicles and expansion of transit systems (Chapple 2008). The Pew Center on the States found that, between 1998 and 2007, employment in "clean energy jobs" grew two and a half times faster than jobs overall, and employed three times as many people as were employed in biotechnology, a sector with significant public policy and government and private sector investment. Green businesses, particularly those in energy generation and building construction and retrofitting, are also very locally rooted, less likely to be shipped overseas to low-cost locations, and therefore more amenable to pressures to improve the quality of employment.[18]

Of course, the numbers of such jobs is actually quite small, with the Pew Study suggesting that "clean economy jobs" amount to approximately 0.6 percent of all jobs in the country, a figure echoed by research on the green economy in California (Chapple and Hudson 2010). Yet if the transition to a clean energy economy is understood in relation to *green skills* required in *many* jobs, rather than simply green jobs, the scale is much larger. For example, the installation of residential solar electricity or water heating systems requires certain new skills, but these skills are as likely, if not more likely, to be held by people in traditional carpenter, plumber, and electrician occupations as by specialized solar system installers. Likewise, as electricity utilities shift toward more renewable energy sources in their portfolios, many existing utility workers will need re-skilling. In essence, the *green skills* need is much larger than the *green jobs* count.

In any case, this is a growth sector of the economy and it is open to equity entreaties, partly because promoting the sector requires early public policy incentives and therefore lobbying by community advocates. Fortunately, there are now many examples of innovative training programs and targeted employment programs that blend equity with the growth of the green economy. One recent example is a diverse group of partners who have come together in New Jersey to promote a Weatherization Training Consortium. With assistance from the Black Ministers Council of New Jersey, this program targets unemployed and underemployed in urban centers, provides training in both job readiness skills and weatherization vocational training, and then works with the Laborers Local Union 55 to help place people in unionized contractors to provide decent employment.[19]

In another example, the Los Angeles Apollo Alliance played a key role in getting the City of Los Angeles to adopt an ordinance promoting energy and water efficiency retrofitting for all city buildings, linked with a Green Retrofit training program to help connect residents of low-income communities to the new jobs created.[20] Los Angeles' broader Green LA Initiative envisions the city becoming a leader in municipal programs that fight greenhouse gas emissions. This includes substantial green skill training programs and promotion of green jobs through, in part, specific policies that expand the city's efforts to buy environmentally sustainable products and encourage local green manufacturing.[21] At a national level, the advocacy organization Green for All tracks similar efforts all across the country to focus on getting disadvantaged communities into green jobs.[22]

Although there are numerous concrete policy manifestations, an underlying issue is more philosophical but no less important: what all this means for economic theory. We understand that much of what we have written here goes against the grain of traditional theory: the ideas that equity can promote growth, that the norms created by epistemic communities can regulate individual understandings and behavior, and that certain social actors, such as the minority middle class, are critical to blending growth and equity, do not fit neatly into a landscape of utility functions, profit maximization, and Pareto-optimal outcomes.

But nobody actually lives in that landscape – and old theory may not be a good road map to what's ahead in the real world. In one exciting development, George Akerlof and Rachel Kranton have argued for a fundamentally different view of "economic man" – that is, a model in which individuals not only maximize their individual well-being (the traditional view) but also seek to construct identities and adhere to norms consistent with those identities (Akerlof and Kranton 2010). As noted in Chapter 1, Akerlof and Kranton specifically suggest that organizations in which identity counts can utilize a flatter wage structure as some of the motivation is intrinsic, such as sense of purpose; this may allow us to explain why epistemic communities matter – they create identity and norms of understanding and practice, and therefore allow regions to both succeed economically with a flatter or more equal distribution of income, and value that as an outcome.

Such work in the economics profession reflects a valuable effort to incorporate into formal economic analysis a set of ideas that has also been developed since the early 1990s through more qualitative methods by economic geographers (Crang 1997; Schoenberger 1997; Storper 1997). Other fields are also helping to change the way economists think. In their new book, *The Spirit Level: Why Greater Equality Makes Societies Stronger*, health researchers Richard Wilkinson and Kate Pickett utilize both international and state (within the United States) comparisons to show that inequality – and not just poverty – is responsible for poor health and a variety of suboptimal social outcomes (Pickett and Wilkinson 2009).

None of this fits very well into standard theory – the Akerlof and Kranton addition of identity to utility maximization seems a bit clunky, the geographers frequently lack the quantitative specifications that the economics profession usually desires, and the empirical analysis by Wilkinson and Pickett seems just a bit too simple – and understandable – to be truly convincing to the high priests of the economics profession. But it must also be said that this is a profession (of which one of us is a member) that ought to be chagrined by its failure to predict the most serious crisis in modern times, by the muddled directions it has generally offered since, and by the apologia it has constructed for selfish – and truly bad – behavior in its models and its policy prescriptions.

It is time to try something new. It will be a bit confusing and a lot messy, just as it was when John Maynard Keynes was trying to explain the collapse of capitalism in the 1930s with a "general theory" that really did little more than actually take the world as it was. It will require the constant interaction of qualitative and quantitative work – as we have tried to do in this book – and an understanding that both are needed. But we have much to gain by making the effort – and much to offer if we can provide a better economic guidepost to achieving just growth.

The politics of just growth

In our 2009 volume, *This Could Be the Start of Something Big: How Social Movements for Regional Equity are Reshaping Metropolitan America* (Pastor et al. 2009b), we argued that getting to what we call here "just growth" will require more than good research, smart ideas, and innovative policies. We suggested instead a three-dimensional approach to achieving change: demonstration projects that show us what is possible, policy changes that make the possible standard operating procedure, and a power-building and political strategy to make policy reform happen.

What will it take to go national with a program linking prosperity and inclusion? Certainly we will need to design and promote better policies, and so the organizations, policies, and other programs we have discussed will play an important role. But we want to return here to a point we have stressed throughout our analysis: the need to build civic capacity and engagement.

After all, one of our fundamental findings in our case studies is the notion of an "epistemic community" in which facts are accepted, values are shared, and destinies are intertwined amongst a broad and diverse set of constituencies. This is, we would argue, not just a feature of the cases we happened to choose and study. Consider Chicago, where Metropolis 2020 has brought together business leaders to insist that affordable workforce housing be available through the region, promising that this will factor into business location decisions. Think about the Bay Area where community organizers, non-profits, and foundation leaders have come together for the Great Communities Collaborative, an effort to generate transit-oriented development all over the region and affordable housing in the suburbs – and they are actively working with both developers and the local MPO to make their visions real.

This shared understanding of our national dilemma has been sorely missing. We are a country that has been highly fragmented and deeply divided by current politics. The last presidential campaign seemed to suggest an underlying urge for a common national story. At the same time, the victory triggered a sharp reaction, one that has elements of pulling up the drawbridges to protect current privilege and maintain the disconnection that helped sink us into a national economic morass.

At no time is the message that just growth is both desirable and possible more needed. If we want to make sure that federal policies live up to the promise of both promoting economic growth and helping those most in need, the sorts of coalitions of "unusual partners" that have been emerging at the regional level need to be replicated and scaled up to federal decision making.

It will not be easy. Achieving just growth, after all, is as much a struggle of ideas as it is a battle of policies, as much the embrace of shared fate as it is the reflection of econometric findings. Getting there will require that business leaders fully and deeply realize that regions wracked by poverty and inequality will not grow. It will require that community leaders realize that asking for a fair share of economic opportunity works best when accompanied by a coherent plan to grow the pie. And it will require the patient investment of time and energy by civic, business, and community leaders to build that common understanding.

It will require the equally patient work of researchers who can enter with few priors, new questions, and a willingness to understand the alchemy of change that animates successful regions. More studies and more statistics are needed – providing full employment for at least one sector of our population – but also on the table is an evolution of theory to understand when both prosperity and inclusion come together and how best to make the happy concurrence a more frequent outcome in America's metropolitan communities.

Appendix

Interviewees with title at time of interview and organizations

Cleveland

Harriet Applegate, Executive Secretary
North Shore AFL-CIO Federation of Labor
Jenelle Dame, Lead Community Organizer
James Jones, Director of Foreclosure Prevention
Samantha Pierce, Staff Director
Empowering & Strengthening Ohio's People (ESOP)
Amy Hanauer, Founder and Executive Director
Zach Schiller, Research Director
Policy Matters Ohio
Ned Hill, Dean
Maxine Goodman Levin College of Urban Affairs, Cleveland State University
Robert Kleidman, Associate Professor
Department of Sociology, Cleveland State University
Norm Krumholz, Professor
Levin College of Urban Affairs, Cleveland State University
Christine Mayer, Vice Chair
Brad Whitehead, President
Fund for Our Economic Future
Randy McShepard
Policy Bridge, RPM International, Inc.
Joseph Roman, CEO
Greater Cleveland Partnership
Honorable Jay Westbrook, Council Member
Cleveland City Council

Columbus

Rev. John Aeschbury, Lead Organizer
B.R.E.A.D. Organization, Building Responsibility, Equality, and Dignity
Dave Alstadt, Senior Research Associate
Bobbie Garber, Executive Director
Community Research Partners

Lavea Brachman, Executive Director
Gene Krebs, Senior Director of Government Affairs and Policy
Greater Ohio Policy Center
Cheryl Hay, Administrator, Business and Industry
Dr. Michael Snider, Interim Provost
Columbus State Community College
Chester Jourdan, Jr., Executive Director
Mid-Ohio Regional Planning Commission (MORPC)
Christy Rogers, Senior Researcher
The Kirwan Institute for the Study of Race and Ethnicity, Ohio State University
Mike Wilkos, Senior Impact Director
Building Neighborhoods Initiative, United Way of Central Ohio

Denver

Terri Bailey, Senior Research Officer
Matt Barry, Research Officer
The Piton Foundation
Elaine DeLott Baker, Director
Center for Workforce Initiatives, Community College of Denver
Lisa Durán, Executive Director
Rights for All People
Ledy Garcia-Eckstein, Executive Director
Vic Smith, Controller, Denver Metro Chamber of Commerce
The Metro Denver Economic Development Corporation (MDEDC/WIRED)
Paula Gomez Farrell, Director
Bobbie Smith, Manager of Operations
Elizabeth Abeyta, Business Development Associate
Division of Business Development, Denver Office of Economic Development
Carol Hedges, Senior Policy Analyst
Colorado Fiscal Policy Center
Irene Ibarra, President and CEO
The Colorado Trust
Peter Kenney, Principal and Co-founder
Civic Results
Jim Kirchheimer, Senior Director of Economic Development
Downtown Denver Partnership
Mike Kromrey, Executive Director
Metro Organizations for People
Karen Lado, Vice President
Enterprise Community Partners
Leslie Moody, Executive Director
Partnership for Working Families
Carmen Rhodes, Executive Director
Robin Kniech, Program Director and Staff Attorney
The Front Range Economic Strategy Center, FRESC

Tony Robinson, Associate Professor
Department of Political Science, University of Colorado, Denver
Mike Roque, Director
Office of Strategic Partnership
Jaime Van Leeuwen, Executive Director
Denver's Road Home

Jacksonville

Andy Bell, President
North Florida Central Labor Council, AFL-CIO
Rena Coughlin, President and CEO
Nonprofit Center of Northeast Florida
Lad Daniels, President
First Coast Manufacturer's Association
Bruce Ferguson, President and CEO
Candace L. Moody, Vice President of Communications
Bryan Stone, President Policy and Programs
WorkSource
Skip Kramer, President
Ben Warner, Deputy Director
Jacksonville Community Council, Inc., JCCI
Henry Luke, Consultant
Luke Planning, Inc.
Rob Sievert-Wagner, Lead Organizer
Interchurch Coalition for Action, Reconciliation and Empowerment (ICARE)
Jim Simpson, Associate Vice President, Workforce Development
Florida Community Colleges at Jacksonville, FCCJ
Cleve Warren, President and CEO
Essential Capital, formerly Jacksonville Economic Development Corporation

Kansas City

Damion Daniel, Community Organizer
Communities Creating Opportunity
Lara Granich, Director
St. Louis Area Jobs with Justice
Garry Kemp, Executive Vice President
Greater Kansas City Building & Construction Trades Council
Frank Lenk, Director of Research Services
Mid-America Regional Council
Pete Levi, President
Greater Kansas City Chamber of Commerce
Mary Lim-Lampe, Organizer
Metro Organization for Racial and Economic Equity (MORE2)

Bob Litan, Vice President for Research and Policy
Kauffman Foundation
Laura Loyacono, Regional Director
Project Lead the Way, Metropolitan Community College of Kansas City
Pat McDonald, Director of Community Investment
Greater Kansas City Community Foundation
Clyde McQueen, President and CEO
Full Employment Council
Gary Sage, Executive Director
Economic and Resource Development, Business and Technology Campus, Metropolitan Community College of Kansas City
Jewel Scott, Executive Director
Civic Council of Greater Kansas City
Bridgette Williams, President
Greater Kansas City AFL-CIO

Nashville

Phil Armor, Deputy Executive Director and Director of Regional Planning
Greater Nashville Regional Council
Lewis O. Beck, Jr., President
Nashville and Middle Tennessee Central Labor Council AFL-CIO
Bill Canak, Professor
Sociology and Anthropology, Middle Tennessee State University
Won Choi, Executive Director
Ray Sellis, Former Director
Tying Nashville Together
Chris Cotton, Research Coordinator
Garret Harper, Director of Research
Nashville Area Chamber of Commerce
Nancy Eisenbrandt, Chair
Paul Haynes, Executive Director
Nashville Career Advancement Center, Local Workforce Investment Board
Lindsay Jerry Lee, President
Tennessee AFL-CIO
Bridget Jones, Executive Director
Cumberland Region Tomorrow
Megan Macaraeg, Director
Middle Tennessee Jobs with Justice
Janet Miller, Chief Economic Development and Marketing Officer
Chamber of Commerce's P2010
Paul Ney, Director
Charlie Williams, Deputy Director
Mayor's Office of Economic and Community Development
Phil Orr, Sr., Vice President, Community Investments

United Way of Metropolitan Nashville
Ralph Schulz, President and CEO
Nashville Area Chamber of Commerce
Karen Stevenson, Dean
Business, Applied Arts & Technologies, Nashville State Community College
Lani Wilkeson Rossman, Vice President
The Community Foundation of Middle Tennessee
Jerry Williams, Executive Director
Leadership Nashville

Sacramento

Barbara Hayes, President and CEO
Sacramento Area Trade & Commerce Organization
Bill Kennedy, Executive Director
Legal Services of Northern California
Kathy Kossick, Executive Director
Sacramento Employment and Training Agency
Bill Mueller, Executive Director
Valley Vision

Other key informants in Sacramento who were interviewed for other research projects on closely related topics include:
Elaine Abelaye, Executive Director
Mae Lee, Former Executive Director
Asian Resources, Inc.
Bill Camp, Executive Secretary
Sacramento Central Labor Council
Richard Dana, Executive Director
Mutual Assistance Network of Del Paso Heights
Larry Ferlazzo, Former Organizer
Sacramento Valley Organizing Committee
Pat Fong Kushida, President and CEO
Sacramento Asian Pacific Chamber of Commerce
Shamus Roller, Executive Director
Sacramento Housing Alliance
Constance Slider, Program Director
Coalition on Regional Equity

Notes

1 Inequality and its discontents

1 Rajan offers a related explanation, suggesting that politicians responded to the growing inequality by expanding credit for housing (see Rajan 2010).
2 The discussion here is of work on equity and growth in U.S. regions. This actually builds on a longer tradition that has looked at the relationship between distribution and growth in developing countries; for an overview, see Thorbecke and Charumilind (2002).
3 According to the Brookings Institution: "Metropolitan areas are home to 83% of the U.S. population, 85% of the nation's jobs, and 92% of all college graduates. They are our hubs of research and innovation, our centers of human capital, and our gateways of trade and immigration. They are, in short, the drivers of our economy, and American competitiveness depends on their vitality" (http://www.brookings.edu/metro/About-Us.aspx, accessed August 25, 2011).
4 In explaining the finding, Savitch et al. (1993: 347) argue that "[t]he blight of the inner city casts a long shadow. Companies will not grow or thrive in, or move to, a declining environment."
5 Timing may matter in another way: it is easy to think of equity and growth as being a U-shaped relationship in which too much inequality dampens growth but so does too much equality – particularly if it is accomplished through heavy-handed means that kill incentives. It is possible, in short, that we are on the declining side of the (upside down) U – and so marginal improvements in inclusion actually drive you to higher output. In this case, one still needs to have an explanation for why you have a positive equity–growth relationship on any part of the curve.
6 See also Pickett and Wilkinson (2009).
7 See Orfield and Luce (2010) for a recent and in-depth coverage of the Twin Cities, and Seltzer (2008) for a good summary of the Portland experience.
8 The basic approach is very similar to the nested analysis strategy – combining large n statistical analysis with small n case study approaches – recommended in Lieberman (2005).
9 Another reason why diversity may not show up in the statistical picture but does show up in the field: the impact that industrial concentration can have on regional organizing by a local business class. For example, in Charlotte, North Carolina, the Bank of America (or better put, its former manifestation as Nations Bank) has been important for regionalist efforts, and high-technology firms have played a significant role in the efforts of Joint Venture: Silicon Valley Network, a leading regional public–private collaborative in the San Jose metro. Although not "single sector" efforts, they add a coherence and common interest to the political work of the business class. We should note, however, that the examples above tend to be from sectors with a broader and longer-term vision of the economy; having a single sector such as auto dominate

regional business has done little for Detroit's sustainability. Given this complexity, it is perhaps unsurprising that a single measure might neither capture the whole picture nor turn up as significant in regression analysis.

2 Measuring what we mean

1 The database referred to here is known as the Building Resilient Regions (BRR) data-base, a project of the Building Resilient Regions network, funded by the John D. and Catherine T. MacArthur Foundation (Pastor et al. forthcoming).

2 By the time we completed the book, the U.S. census had released a 2005–2009 sum-mary file of the American Community Survey that went down to the tract level. This allowed us to reconstruct some of the variables that were possible to generate only from the tract data in the decennial census (partly given our effort to have geographi-cally consistent shapes of time), with the middle year in that set of summary files being 2007.

3 To calculate this variable we employed a technique known as Pareto interpolation. Interpolation was necessary both because the summary files of the various decen-nial censuses used do not report household income percentile values (aside from the median – the 50th percentile), and because all metro area-level information from the summary files had to be "added up" from the census tracts in order to obtain geographic consistency over time. Specifically, categorical household income information (i.e. the number of households in each income bracket) was summed up across tracts for each metro area, approximating the distribution of household income, and allowing the identification of the income bracket containing the 80th and 20th income percentiles. Households within the bracket were then assumed to follow a Pareto distribution with respect to income, allowing for the interpolation of the 80th and 20th household income percentile. The 1980 data had fewer and broader brackets, making an 80–20 ratio much more accurate than a 90–10 ratio for that year, offering another reason to choose those distributional comparison points through the subsequent years.

4 See http://www.census.gov/population/www/metroareas/files/00–32997.pdf for a defi-nition of principal cities (accessed August 25, 2011).

5 We do this because, as noted above, one of the important features of the database we use is its geographic consistency over time. Essentially, the database is built taking the geography of Core Based Statistical Areas (CBSAs) from December 2003, and reconstructing census tract-level data from the decennial censuses to match the more contemporary definition of metropolitan and micropolitan statistical areas purveyed by the Office of Management and Budget. In the new vintage of metro-area definitions, what were previously known as "central cities" were replaced with what are referred to as "principal cities." The latter definition tends to include additional cities that did not meet the central city criteria under the previous metro-area definitions. Although there are plans for the next iteration of the BRR database to generate data for a set of cities that are more aligned with the central cities of the past, these data were not available for this project. We do not use the city–suburb poverty differential in the actual case selection.

6 After narrowing down for theoretical reasons, we then conducted tests for representa-tion and stability. These suggested that focusing on these four indicators as representa-tive of all ten did not distort the overall rankings profiles or result in unstable relative rankings.

7 One way to understand the way in which these six categories were constructed is to consider simply the four variables and three time periods that were used; this approach is less intuitive but also lets us spell out what we meant by "consistently" good or bad (which turns out to be less stringent than "perfectly" good or bad). During each time period, the change in each variable for a region is considered "good" if it was at least as good as the middle (median) region within the census region, and "bad" if it

was not. In terms of the two equity measures, of course, downward movements are considered good (e.g. a decline in poverty), whereas increases are considered good for the two growth measures. Given this setup, "twenty-year bad" metros did bad in all four changes for the overall twenty-year period, and "twenty-year good" metros did good in all four changes in the twenty-year period; "consistently good" metros were those that did good in seven out of the eight changes that were observed for the 1980s and 1990s (four in each time period) and "consistently bad" metros did bad in seven out of the eight changes that were observed in the 1980s and 1990s; "bounce-back" metros did bad in at least three of the four changes in the 1980s and good in all four changes in the 1990s or bad in all four changes in the 1980s and good in at least three of the four changes in the 1990s; "slip-back" metros did good in at least three of the four changes in the 1980s and bad in all four changes in the 1990s or good in all four changes in the 1980s and bad in at least three of the four changes in the 1990s.

8   This is exactly the sort of detailed and painstaking work for which God invented graduate students – and we were lucky that He sent our way Rosa Ramirez of UC Davis.

9   See http://www.metrooutlook.org/ (accessed August 25, 2011).

10 See http://www.jcci.org/ (accessed August 25, 2011).

11 Among the various measures not included in Tables 2.3 and 2.4 because they lacked a strong and consistent relationship to the equity and growth indices is a measure of "jurisdictional complexity" that was developed by Chapple and Lester (2010) and provided to us in the course of constructing the database. Figured as the number of incorporated and census-designated places (CDPs) per 10,000 people in a metro area, the measure (along with various transformations of it) was found to be only marginally significant in the negative direction with the growth index and strikingly insignificant with the equity index. Although we believe that political fragmentation is, in theory and in practice, a hindrance to growth and equity coming together – a pattern suggested by the role of annexation and regional leadership programs in the case studies profiled later in this book – this measure of jurisdictional complexity falls short in the statistical side of our study. There are several reasons why this could be the case: perhaps this is because it treats unincorporated population centers (CDPs) as independent jurisdictions when in reality they fall under the same county government. Perhaps it is because it does not fully account for how much of an area's population falls under one jurisdiction (consider that a region with one large municipality and four minor hamlets would get the same score as a region with five equal-size and rivalrous municipalities). Perhaps it is because the population denominator can produce misleading comparisons (consider that a smaller mid-size region with a single government could get the same score as a region with five times the population and five times the governments). A more robust and pure measure of political fragmentation – the derivation of which remains both unclear and challenging – might yield statistically significant results but we did not pursue this further in the quantitative portion of this volume.

12 Part of the reason for the negative association with growth may have to do with the way in which this measure was derived: it is a measure of the evenness of employment across the fourteen major industries according to the two-digit North American Industrial Classification System (NAICS). It would likely be important to go below these two-digit codes to get at excessive concentration in any particular subcategory of, say, manufacturing.

13 Trendle (2006) provides a good review of the literature, both noting the mixed results and stressing that the argument about diversification is more that it is good for regional economic stability than it is for economic growth. Trendle himself provides some evidence for a positive effect on stability, making creative use of modern techniques to deal with spatial relationships in data to capture spill-over effects from neighbors – suggesting another reason why at least benchmarking against census regions can be important. For an effort which found that diversity was associated with lower unemployment but only weakly with per capita income, see Izraeli and Murphy (2003); for an early and frequently cited effort which found a weak relationship with unemployment and that

diversity actually reduced per capita income (with the logic being that more specialized industries promoted more income), see Attaran (1986).

14 The remaining workforce and housing measures that were found to be significant in the initial correlations – the percentage of the population who are working age and the measures of education – seem to have surrendered their significance to more telling measures that were included in the multivariate model from the employment and industrial composition category.

15 We should note that, although data were available for the variables in this model for all 192 CBSAs, we restricted the sample to the same set of 175 observations that were included in the growth model for the sake of consistency; the results are very similar if we include all 192 CBSAs.

16 Note that, although the table is organized by the category of the response variable being predicted (nearly high-performing and really high-performing region), the columns beneath each category correspond to the two different model specifications (in terms of the independent variables included) for which results are reported. Thus, the first and third columns are from the one regression, while the second and fourth columns are from the other, which explains why each couplet has the same model fit and other information reported in the last three rows of the table.

3 Getting it right

1 These included the Gamaliel Network (http://www.gamaliel.org/), the Industrial Areas Foundation (http://www.industrialareasfoundation.org/), the PICO network (http://www.piconetwork.org/), and the Direct Action and Research Training Center network (http://www.thedartcenter.org/) (accessed August 25, 2011).

2 For more on JwJ, a network of community-based labor organizing, see http://www.jwj.org/ (accessed August 25, 2011).

3 For more on Partnership for Working Families, a network of groups focused on community benefits agreements and regional equity organizing, see http://www.communitybenefits.org/ (accessed August 25, 2011).

4 The interviews for our Sacramento case study include only four interviews specifically for this research project, but also interviews with key informants on closely related topics of regional growth and equity since 1999. These include detailed analysis of regional opportunities and a broad evaluation of the seven-year California Works for Better Health Initiative (Pastor et al. 2008; Pastor et al. 2009c,d), and analysis of youth employment opportunities as part of a two-year study of youth pathways to opportunity in the region (Benner et al. 2010; Benner et al. 2010). Furthermore, both authors have been researching economic and political dynamics in the Sacramento region since the mid-1990s, and intensively since 2007 when one of us (Benner) moved to the region.

5 For the Kansas City metropolitan area map and subsequent metro area maps, primary cities, other major cities, and other cities are defined as follows. "Primary cities" include the largest principal city within a metro region and, in some cases, other principal cities that meet certain population criteria. For the most part, we applied the Brookings Institution's "primary cities" definition to 2000 U.S. census population data (Brookings Institution 2010). The one exception is the Kansas City metro area in which Brookings includes Kansas City, Kansas as a primary city on the grounds that it shares the same name as the city listed in the official name of the metro area; however, this is a city that is even smaller than Overland Park, which is not considered a primary city, and our reading is that the metro name refers to only the biggest of the two Kansas Cities. "Other major cities" are smaller principal cities not considered primary. "Other cities" are cities that are neither principal nor primary. The metropolitan area refers to the "Core Based Statistical Area" as defined by the U.S. Census Bureau; we use 2003 CBSA definitions and corresponding U.S. Census TIGER/Line® shapefiles. All other, non-CBSA shapefiles are 2000 U.S. Census TIGER/Line®.

6 Unless otherwise noted below, all metro areas and their corresponding principal cities in the tables presented before each case study are defined according to the U.S. Office of Management and Budget's December 2003 definitions of CBSAs, and all data are from the aforementioned Building Resilient Regions (BRR) database. However, because the BRR database reports slightly different data for city population (because it works from a tract-level summing and tracts can cross jurisdictional lines), we substitute in the tables actual population data for principal cities, using the geography at the time of reporting. Principal city population information for 1980, 1990, and 2000 is from http://www.city-population.de (accessed August 25, 2011), which uses official census data when available and otherwise draws on local government and other sources. The 2007 principal city population is from the U.S. Census Bureau's 2007 American Community Survey 1-Year Estimates. For three principal cities (Woodland in the Sacramento metro area, and Elyria and Mentor in the Cleveland metro area) the 2007 estimates were unavailable so 2008 American Community Survey 3-Year Estimates (representing 2006–2008 averages) were used instead. Suburban population is defined as the difference between total CBSA population and that of all principal cities combined. As there are no data beyond 2000 in the BRR database, all 2007 measures are from other sources as follows. Race/ethnicity is from the U.S. Census Bureau's 2007 American Community Survey 1-Year Estimates, made available by the Missouri Census Data Center (MCDC) at http://mcdc.missouri.edu/ (accessed August 25, 2011). Poverty is also from the 2007 American Community Survey 1-Year Estimates, but accessed via American Factfinder. Spatial measures, including poverty concentration and spatial segregation by income and race, are based on the U.S. Census Bureau's 2009 American Community Survey 5-Year Estimates using 2000 census tracts as the underlying geography; thus, the data actually represent 2005–2009 averages. The 80–20 household income ratio is based on the authors' tabulations of data from the 2007 American Community Survey Public Use Microdata (PUMS) file from the Integrated Public Use Microdata Series (IPUMS) by Ruggles et al. (2010). Income differentials and educational attainment are from the 2007 American Community Survey 1-Year Estimates (MCDC). Data on average annual earnings per job and public sector employment are from the Regional Economic Information System (REIS) from the U.S. Bureau of Economic Analysis (BEA). Educational attainment information for 1980 only is based on the author's tabulations of the data from IPUMS. The microdata were used because they allowed for the estimation of the number of people with a graduate or professional degree (those who had completed six or more years of college). It should be noted that the geographic boundaries of the metropolitan areas identified in the 1980 microdata often do not match those found under the Office of Management and Budget's December 2003 definitions, which are used for all other calculations. However, after comparing the microdata estimates of educational attainment distribution for the categories that were available in the BRR database for 1980, the numbers were extremely close and so we decided to use the microdata in the interests of providing more detail. Finally, data for all years on workers by industry are based on the authors' tabulations of microdata from IPUMS, and data on the principal city and suburban job distribution for 1980, 1990, and 2000 are from the State of the Cities Data Systems (SOCDS) from the U.S. Department of Housing and Urban Development (HUD); 2007 data are from the U.S. Census Bureau's Local Employment Dynamics (LED) program. Job growth is calculated from these same sources.

7 In 1950, with a city population of 456,622, 12.2 percent of the city's population was African American. Fifty years later, the city's population was roughly the same – 441,545 people – but the African-American population had risen to 31.2 percent of the city's population (U.S. census, cited in Gotham 2002: p17).

8 See http://www.kceconomy.com/MajorEmployers.asp (accessed May 4, 2011).

9 See Mid-America Regional Council (2005).

10 See http://corporate.hallmark.com/Company (accessed August 25, 2011).

11 See http://www.nndb.com/company/093/000122724/ (accessed August 25, 2011).

12 See http://www.cerner.com (accessed August 25, 2011).

13 See http://www.kclifesciences.org/ (accessed August 25, 2011).

14 Interview with Jewel Scott, Executive Director, Civic Council of Greater Kansas City, July 2, 2008, conducted by C. Benner and R. Ramirez.

15 The figure is for the twenty-five largest metros in 1990, the original set used in the calculations maintained for metro areas over time by the Foundation Center (see http://www.foundationcenter.org/findfunders/statistics/listing01.html, accessed August 25, 2011); the actual twenty-five has changed over time as some metros have gained and others lost populations but the Foundation Center keeps the same group for the sake of a consistent series.

16 See http://foundationcenter.org/findfunders/topfunders/top25assets.html (accessed August 25, 2011).

17 When completed in 1986, this thirty-eight-story building was the tallest building in Missouri, and was seen by business and public sector leaders as a major anchor for downtown revitalization.

18 See http://www.lisc.org/kansascity/BEU.htm (accessed May 4, 2011).

19 CCO trains community leaders, identifies common concerns, researches possible solutions, and leverages their power to collaborate with the key decision-makers to implement solutions.

20 Interview with Bridgette Williams, June 4, 2009, conducted by C. Benner and R. Ramirez.

21 MARC's Board of Directors consists of thirty-three locally elected leaders representing nine counties and 120 cities in the region.

22 Mid-America Regional Council, Departments webpage, available at http://www.marc.org/departments.htm (accessed August 25, 2011).

23 Metro Outlook Live, Grand Summary and Conclusion, available at http://www.metrooutlook.org/conclusions.asp (accessed August 25, 2011).

24 The indicators in Metro Outlook 2.0 are attractiveness of place, social cohesion, strategic decision-making capacity, institutional performance, human capacity, economic competitiveness, efficient use of resources. See http://www.metrooutlook.org (accessed August 25, 2011).

25 See http://www.marc.org/regionalsnapshot.pdf (accessed August 25, 2011).

26 A study of authorities in the region found that "cities are most likely involved with MARC in . . . 9-1-1 services, public transit, aging services, public health, child care, parks/trails, purchasing, emergency medical services, emergency preparedness, stormwater, solid waste disposal, and solid waste collection . . . [and to a lesser extent] in airports, economic development, sewage collection and treatment, contractor licensing, fire, tourism, and land use planning, and . . . not [at all] with police, jails, recreation programs, or zoos" (Wood 2005: 9–10).

27 Interview with Clyde McQueen, President and CEO of the Full Employment Council, July 1, 2008, conducted by C. Benner and R. Ramirez.

28 Interview with Gary Sage, Executive Director of Economic and Resource Development, Business and Technology, Metropolitan Community College, July 2, 2008, conducted by C. Benner and R. Ramirez.

29 See http://www.thepowerpartners.com/images/projectprepare.pdf (accessed May 4, 2011).

30 Interview, January 30, 2009, conducted by C. Benner and R. Ramirez.

31 Nashville Area Chamber of Commerce, Corporate Headquarters, available at http://www.nashvillechamber.com/Homepage/Relocation/RelocateBusiness/TargetIndustries/CorporateHeadquarters.aspx (accessed March 20, 2011).

32 See http://www.nashvillechamber.com/Homepage/Relocation/RelocateBusiness/TargetIndustries/AdvancedManufacturing.aspx (accessed March 20, 2011).

33 The twenty universities and colleges are found in the mid-Tennessee area, most of which are within the Nashville CBSA.

34 See Carole Bucy (1995).

35 The time was right – politically. Prior to consolidation, Mayor Ben West ran an administration that was seen as the epitome of mismanagement and patronage politics, and led some to call his politics "the South's version of old style politics in Chicago" (interview with Lewis Beck, president of the Nashville and Middle Tennessee AFL-CIO Central Labor Council, January 28, 2009, conducted by C. Benner and R. Ramirez). The consolidation created a greater sense of ownership and hope, and higher expectations for the future of Nashville.

36 Interview with Janet Miller, Chief Economic Development and Marketing Officer, Nashville Chamber of Commerce, January 28, 2009, conducted by C. Benner and R. Ramirez.

37 Interview, January 29, 2009, conducted by C. Benner and R. Ramirez.

38 See http://www.fisk.edu/AboutFisk/HistoryOfFisk.aspx (accessed March 20, 2011).

39 See http://www.mmc.edu/ (accessed August 25, 2011).

40 See http://www.tnstate.edu/interior.asp?mid=398&ptid=1 (accessed March 20, 2011).

41 The cities were selected by a process that involved an online survey that had respondents rank their cities according to their level of satisfaction with over twenty quality of life factors; this led to the nomination of 300 cities, which was narrowed to the top thirteen and then combined with statistical analysis of census and other data. See http://www.blackenterprise.com/2007/05/01/top-10-cities-for-african-americans-2007/ (accessed August 25, 2011). The ranking supposedly considers median household income, percent of business ownership, percent of college graduates, and homeownership rates among others factors (Brown 2007). However, the data are not well cited in the report – and often do not square perfectly with any existing data, including on metro populations, and so we reconstructed the data for Table 3.3 directly from the 2007 American Community Survey.

42 One example is Tying Nashville Together (TNT), an affiliate of the Industrial Areas Foundation (IAF), that began in 1989 when Forrest Harris, a National Baptist pastor and Vanderbilt University faculty member, invited IAF organizer Gerald Taylor to begin preliminary discussions with Nashville clergy. At its peak in the late 1990s, TNT could turn out more than 2,500 people to community meetings and political events. Interview with Won Choi, Organizer, and Ray Sellis, Board Member, TNT, January 30, 2009, conducted by C. Benner and R. Ramirez.

43 Interview with Janet Miller, Chief Economic Development and Marketing Officer, Nashville Chamber of Commerce, January 28, 2009, conducted by C. Benner and R. Ramirez.

44 See http://www.nashvillechamber.com/Homepage/AboutUs/ChamberInitiatives/PublicBenefitFoundation.aspx (accessed August 25, 2011).

45 See http://thedavidsongroup.org (accessed May 4, 2011).

46 Leadership Nashville reports that 84 percent of its alumni are still in the Nashville or middle Tennessee region. See http://www.leadershipnashville.org/about/overview (accessed April 23, 2011).

47 The middle class is measured as a proportion of all families in metro areas making between 80 and 150 percent of the metro area's median income. See Muro et al. (2008).

48 See http://www.nefrpc.org/about.htm (accessed August 25, 2011).

49 See the official website of the City of Jacksonville, Florida, Biography of Mayor, at http://news.jacksonville.com/specials/peyton/ (accessed August 25, 2011).

50 Before 2030, the non-white population will likely exceed 50 percent of Duval County's population (City of Jacksonville 2007).

51 See http://www.expandinjax.com/About/Regional_Overview/Duval_Co.aspx (accessed April 23, 2011).

52 The bases include the Naval Air Station in Jacksonville, Naval Station Mayport, Blount Island (Marine Corps) Command, and the Kings Bay Naval Submarine Base just over the Georgia border.

53 Cornerstone Regional Development Partnership, ExpandJax: Workforce Profile – Highly Motivated Highly Skilled. See http://www.expandinjax.com/WorkForce/Work_Profile.aspx (accessed March 20, 2011).

54 Another important feature of the region's economy is that it has a community-owned utility company. Jacksonville Electric Authority (JEA) is the largest community-owned municipal electric utility in Florida, and the eighth largest in the United States. Lower electricity prices is a feature typical of publicly owned utilities (Savitch and Kantor 2004) and, in keeping with this, customers of JEA have lower electric rates than most of the rest of Florida, helping to fuel economic growth by reducing business costs.

55 Interview with Charles 'Skip' Kramer, President of the Jacksonville Community Council, July 23, 2008, conducted by C. Benner and R. Ramirez.

56 Interview with Charles 'Skip' Kramer, President of the Jacksonville Community Council, July 23, 2008, conducted by C. Benner and R. Ramirez.

57 There are a range of other examples where JCCI's work has had impact in the region. An early study of local government finance led to putting the city's pension fund on a sounder financial footing. Another report focused on affordable housing and led to the passage of a fair housing ordinance by the City Council. A more recent study of how to attract and retain talent to the region has led to the creation of the Healthcare and Bioscience Council, which hopes to help attract more companies in the bioscience industry to the area, develop a public education pipeline for bioscience, and develop more high-wage jobs.

58 JCCI's regional indicators project documents conditions in nine broad areas of the regional society: education, economy, natural environment, social environment, arts and culture, health, government, transportation, and public safety. For more, see JCCI's Community Indicator Project, available at http://www.jcci.org/jcciwebsite/pages/indicators.html (accessed May 4, 2011).

59 Interview with Jerry Mallot, Executive Vice President, Jacksonville Chamber of Commerce, July 21, 2008, conducted by C. Benner and R. Ramirez.

60 Interview with Jerry Mallot, Executive Vice President, Jacksonville Chamber of Commerce, July 21, 2008, conducted by C. Benner and R. Ramirez.

61 See http://jacksonville.com/tu-online/stories/070408/met_299825057.shtml (accessed May 4, 2011).

62 Under the racial opportunity and harmony focus, specific goals included "eradicate structural and institutional racism by committing to eliminate the racial/ethnic gaps in education, employment and income, neighborhoods and housing, health access and outcomes, justice and the legal system, and the political process and civic engagement" (City of Jacksonville 2007: 31).

63 Based on interviews with Henri Luke (Blueprint facilitator), Skip Kramer and Ben Warner (JCCI), Jerry Mallot (Jacksonville Chamber of Commerce), July 28–30, 2008, conducted by C. Benner and R. Ramirez.

64 Interview with Jerry Mallot, Executive Vice President, Jacksonville Chamber of Commerce, July 21, 2008, conducted by C. Benner and R. Ramirez.

65 Interview with Jim Simpson, Associate Vice President for Workforce Development at FCCJ, July 23, 2008, conducted by C. Benner and R. Ramirez.

66 See http://www.careeracademies.net/ (accessed March 20, 2011).

67 In 1920, Cleveland was reportedly the fifth largest city in the United States, with three times as many people as Columbus. By 2000, with their fortunes reversed, Columbus had climbed to be the fifteenth largest city in the country, while Cleveland had slipped to thirty-third (Tobar and Fields 2001).

68 According to Columbus mayor Michael Coleman, speaking at the Brookings Institution-sponsored event "Restoring Prosperity: The State Role in Revitalizing Ohio's Core Communities," September 10, 2008. See http://www.brookings.edu/events/2008/0910_restoring_prosperity.aspx (accessed April 24, 2011).

69 Interview with Christy Rogers, Research Associate, Kirwan Institute for the Study of Race and Ethnicity at Ohio State University, September 9, 2008, conducted by M. Pastor, R. Ortiz, and N. Sessoms.
70 See Powell (2004).
71 See http://econdev.columbus.gov/growth_cluster/technology.aspx (accessed March 20, 2011).
72 Interview with Chester Jourdan, Executive Director of the Mid-Ohio Regional Planning Commission, September 11, 2008,conducted by R. Ortiz and N. Sessoms.
73 See http://kirwaninstitute.org/ (accessed August 25, 2011).
74 See http://uso.edu/aboutUs/index.php (accessed August 25, 2011).
75 See http://uso.edu/opportunities/ohioskillsbank/index.php (accessed August 25, 2011).
76 Interview with Mike Snider and Cheryl Hay, Provost and Administrator at Columbus State Community College, September 11, 2008, conducted by N. Sessoms.
77 Interview with Mike Snider and Cheryl Hay, Provost and Administrator at Columbus State Community College, September 11, 2008, conducted by N. Sessoms.
78 Calculations by authors. For a discussion of the driving forces behind the surge in poverty in Ohio, see Community Research Partners (2008, 2010).
79 See http://www.morpc.org/transportation/freight/freight.asp and http://www.morpc.org/pdf/Projects_with_Significance_for_Freight.pdf (accessed April 24, 2011).
80 See http://communityresearchpartners.org/14651.cfm for links to all three reports (accessed March 20, 2011).
81 See http://columbus2020.org/ (accessed August 25, 2011).
82 See Hirsch, Barry and Davis Macpherson, Metropolitan Area: Union Membership, Coverage, Density and Employment by Metropolitan Area and Sector, 1986–2010, Union Membership and Coverage Database from the CPS (http://unionstats.com/, accessed August 25, 2011).
83 Interview with Bobbie Garber and Dave Alstadt, Executive Director and Project Manager, Community Research Partners, September 11, 2008, conducted by R. Ortiz and N. Sessoms.
84 "Restoring Prosperity" initiative, the Greater Ohio Policy Center, available at http://www.greaterohio.org/initiatives/restoring-prosperity (accessed March 29, 2011).
85 Interview with Mike Wilkos, Senior Impact Director, Building Neighborhoods Initiative, United Way of Central Ohio, September 12, 2008, conducted by N. Sessoms.

4 Slipping, reversing, stuck

1 Kevin Johnson, presentation, May 12, 2010, at UC Davis event "E3: Economic Prosperity, Energy and the Environment"; see http://www.dateline.ucdavis.edu/dl_detail.lasso?id=12719 (accessed August 25, 2011).
2 Detailed statistics from the California Employment Development Department, Labor Market Information Division, see http://www.labormarketinfo.edd.ca.gov/ (accessed August 25, 2011).
3 Interview with Kathy Kossick, Executive Director, Sacramento Employment and Training Agency, March 17, 2011, conducted by C. Benner.
4 According to the California State Military Museum; see http://www.militarymuseum.org/Beale.html (accessed August 25, 2011).
5 That said, Sacramento was not quite as prominent as the large defense contractors and high-tech firms of Silicon Valley. For example, Santa Clara County (the heart of Silicon Valley) approached nearly $5 billion per year in prime contracts in the 1980s (Leslie 2000) and Los Angeles and San Diego were also major recipients.
6 Interviews with Bill Mueller, Executive Director, Valley Vision, March 18, 2011, and Barbara Hayes, president and CEO, SACTO, March 17, 2011, conducted by C. Benner.
7 See Hirsch, Barry and Davis Macpherson, Metropolitan Area: Union Membership, Coverage, Density and Employment by Metropolitan Area and Sector, 1986–2010,

Union Membership and Coverage Database from the CPS (http://unionstats.com/, accessed August 25, 2011).

8 The growth in high-tech jobs is often cited as contributing to inequality, but this generally occurs in the context of job polarization with the simultaneous growth of both high-tech and low-wage service sector jobs and the disappearance of mid-skill jobs (Massey and Hirst 1998; Milkman and Dwyer 2002).

9 Five out of seventeen bases in the first round of closures were in Sacramento: George Air Force Base near Victorville in Southern California, Hamilton Air Force Base near Novato, Mather Air Force Base near Sacramento, Norton Air Force Base near San Bernardino, and the Presidio in San Francisco.

10 Sacramento Business Journal Book of Lists, 1999, see http://www.bizjournals.com/ sacramento/research/bol-marketing/ (accessed August 25, 2011).

11 Number of residents certified eligible for MediCal divided by the total population. Data sources are State of California, Department of Health Services: Medical Care Statistics Section and State of California, Department of Finances, Population of California Counties May 1998. See http://www.dhcs.ca.gov/dataandstats/statistics/ Pages/mcsshomepage.aspx and http://www.dof.ca.gov/research/demographic/reports/ view.php (accessed August 25, 2011).

12 Number of TANF recipients divided by total population. Data sources are State of California Department of Social Services, Statistical Services Bureau, and State of California, Department of Finances, Population of California Counties May 1998. See http://www.cdss.ca.gov/research/default.htm and http://www.dof.ca.gov/research/ demographic/reports/view.php (accessed August 25, 2011).

13 Interviews with Kathy Kossick, Executive Director, Sacramento Employment and Training Agency, and Barbara Hayes, president and CEO, SACTO, March 17, 2011, conducted by C. Benner. Unfortunately, by 1999, after being bought out by NEC, Packard Bell rapidly lost market share and the parent company racked up more than $1 billion in losses. NEC announced in November 1999 that they were discontinuing the Packard Bell label in the United States and would entirely close down their Sacramento Army Depot operations, laying off the remaining people working there.

14 See http://seta.net/employer/workforce-resources/ (accessed August 25, 2011).

15 Interview with Kathy Kossick, Executive Director, SETA, March 17, 2011, conducted by C. Benner.

16 Interview with Barbara Hayes, President and CEO, SACTO, March 17, 2011, conducted by C. Benner.

17 In 2009, the total union membership rate in the Sacramento–Arden-Arcade–Roseville MSA was 23.5 percent (http://www.unionstats.com, accessed August 25, 2011).

18 The median home price in the four-county Sacramento MSA dropped from a high of $375,900 in 2005 to $177,800 by the fourth quarter of 2010, according to the National Association of Realtors (http://www.realtor.org/research/research/metroprice, accessed August 25, 2011).

19 The suburbanization of employment is masked a bit in Table 4.1 because we are using the principal city definitions of 2003 and these include areas that would have been considered suburban in earlier decades; recall that one of the strengths (and potential weaknesses) of the BRR database underlying our work is that the geographic shapes are consistent moving backward through time.

20 Interview with Carol Hedges, Senior Fiscal Analyst of the Colorado Fiscal Policy Institute, October 20, 2008, conducted by R. Ortiz and J. Tran.

21 Interview with Mike Roque, Director of Denver's Office of Strategic Partnerships, October 20, 2008, conducted by R. Ortiz and J. Tran.

22 Interview with Peter Kenney, Principal of Civic Results, October 10, 2008, conducted by R. Ortiz and M. Pastor.

23 The figures are from our calculations using the 2007 American Community Survey.

24 Interview with Terri Bailey, Senior Research Officer at the Piton Foundation, October 28, 2008, conducted by R. Ortiz and J. Tran.

25 Interview with Carol Hedges, Senior Fiscal Analyst of Colorado Fiscal Policy Institute, October 20, 2008, conducted by R. Ortiz and J. Tran.

26 Several of our interviewees were members of the taskforce, including representatives from the Office of Economic Development, FRESC, and the Downtown Denver Partnership.

27 Interview with Lisa Durban, Executive Director of Rights for All People, October 20, 2008, conducted by R. Ortiz and J. Tran.

28 See http://www.fresc.org/article.php?id=59 (accessed August 25, 2011).

29 Interview with Elaine Baker, Director of Workforce Initiatives at Community College of Denver, February 27, 2009, conducted by R. Ortiz.

30 MOP's organizing covers approximately 60 percent of the state.

31 Interview with Karen Lado, Director, Enterprise Community Partners Denver office, October 28, 2008, conducted by R. Ortiz and J. Tran.

32 See http://www.ohiohistorycentral.org/ (accessed August 25, 2011).

33 Historic Data, Northern Ohio Data & Information Service, Maxine Goodman Levin College of Urban Affairs, Cleveland State University, see http://urban.csuohio.edu/nodis/historic.html (accessed March 22, 2011). Data for 2007 are from the American Community Survey; note that the totals are different from the values in Table 4.3 because that includes the population of other principal cities.

34 Interview with Joe Roman, Executive Director of the Greater Cleveland Partnership, September 8, 2008, conducted by M. Pastor and R. Ortiz.

35 American Communities Project, University of Albany Lewis Mumford Center and Brown University Initiative in Spatial Structures in the Social Sciences, see http://www.s4.brown.edu/cen2000/WholePop/WPsort/sort_d1.html (accessed August 25, 2011).

36 Interview with Jay Westbrook, Cleveland Councilman, Ward 18, September 8, 2008, conducted by M. Pastor and R. Ortiz.

37 See Brookings Institution, State of Metropolitan American, http://www.brookings.edu/metro/stateofmetroamerica.aspx (accessed August 25, 2011).

38 See http://www.noaca.org/ (accessed August 25, 2011).

39 See http://www.firstsuburbs.org/neohio/index.htm (accessed August 25, 2011).

40 See http://www.neo-rpi.org/site.cfm/About-RPI/Strategic-Direction.cfm (accessed August 25, 2011).

41 A joint funding initiative of the U.S. Departments of Transportation and Housing and Urban Development, and the Environmental Protection Agency.

42 See Kate Gluck (2010).

43 Interview with Joe Roman, Executive Director, Greater Cleveland Partnership, September 8, 2008, conducted by M. Pastor and R. Ortiz.

44 Interview with Jay Westbrook, Cleveland Councilman, Ward 18, September 8, 2008, conducted by M. Pastor and R. Ortiz.

45 See http://www.glwn.org/ (accessed August 25, 2011).

46 Interview with Jay Westbrook, Cleveland Councilman, Ward 18, September 8, 2008, conducted by M. Pastor and R. Ortiz.

47 Interview with Harriet Applegate, Executive Secretary, North Shore AFL-CIO Federation of Labor, September 8, 2008, conducted by R. Ortiz and M. Pastor.

48 Interview with Brad Whitehead, president and Christine Mayer, vice chair, Fund for Our Economic Future, September 8, 2008, conducted by R. Ortiz and M. Pastor.

49 Interview with Amy Hanauer, Research Director, and Zach Schiller, Research Director, Policy Matters Ohio, September 9, 2008, conducted by M. Pastor and R. Ortiz.

50 See http://www.policy-bridge.org/ (accessed August 25, 2011).

51 Interview with Brad Whitehead, president and Christine Mayer, vice chair, Fund for Our Economic Future, September 8, 2008, conducted by R. Ortiz and M. Pastor.

52 The nine broad indicators are skilled workforce and research and development, legacy of place, urban assimilation, racial inclusion and income equality, locational amenities, technology commercialization, urban/metro structure, individual entrepreneurship, and business dynamics.

5 What does it all mean?

1 See http://www.census.gov/statab/ccdb/cit1010r.txt (accessed August 25, 2011).
2 According to the Kansas City Economic Development Corporation, four of the top fifty architecture and engineering firms in the country are in Kansas City. See http://edckc. com/why-kansas-city-missouri/target-industries/engineering-creative/ (accessed May 6, 2011).
3 See http://www.blackenterprise.com/2007/05/01/top-10-cities-for-african-ameri-cans-2007/ (accessed August 25, 2011).
4 The results came from a remarkably rigorous survey by Black Entertainment Television (BET), discussed here: http://bet.mediaroom.com/index.php?s=43&item=304 (accessed August 25, 2011). As remarkable as the statistic itself is the way in which the mayor of Columbus is quoted by BET boasting about Columbus' number one ranking by saying, "we've got it going on," his way of apparently trying to attract an even larger cohort of middle-class African Americans.
5 See Nowak et al. (2000) for a description of the "ultimatum game" and an argument for why fairness tends to dominate over the unfair outcomes that would be predicted if people truly acted as independent, rational utility maximizers. Interestingly, Jensen et al. (2007) conducted an innovative version of the ultimatum game with chimpanzees and found them to more closely approximate the rational maximizers of traditional economic theory!
6 A full list of more than thirty years of reports and studies conducted through JCCIs broad consultative process is available at http://www.jcci.org/jcciwebsite/pages/stud-ies.html (accessed August 25, 2011).
7 Unfortunately, the Cherokee-Gates project fell victim to the financial crisis but our point here is not whether the project was carried out but whether the framework of including an equity component in the prosperity strategy was making its way into standard operating procedure in Denver (Read 2006).
8 See http://www.theplus.us/advance.aspx (accessed August 25, 2011).
9 While the national percentage in 1999 was a 13.9 percent membership rate, our case studies had the following: Sacramento ranked thirty-ninth with 21.6 percent member-ship, although this was mostly due to public sector unions with Sacramento ranking ninety-fourth for private sector unionization, with no other case having such a large disparity between rank for private and public sector unionism; Cleveland, 101st with 15.0 percent membership; Columbus, 127th with 12.9 percent; Kansas City, 129th with 12.4 percent; Denver, 139th with 11.0 percent; Jacksonville, 191st with 6.4 percent; and Nashville, 203rd with 5.8 percent. Data from the CPS, as reported at http://union-stats.com/ (accessed August 25, 2011).
10 For eight interesting examples of community-led transit-oriented development initia-tives, see Grady and Leroy (2006).
11 See http://www.kcsmartmoves.org/pdf/smartmoves_update_report.pdf (accessed August 25, 2011).
12 See http://www.lightrailnow.org/news/n_lrt_2006–11b.htm#KC_20061110 and http://www.lightrailnow.org/news/n_lrt_2008–10a.htm (accessed August 25, 2011).
13 See http://www.cnt.org/repository/CTOD_5YearBro_Final_LoRez.pdf (accessed August 25, 2011).
14 See http://www.paworkforce.state.pa.us/about/cwp/view.asp?a=471&q=152120 (accessed August 25, 2011).

15 See http://www.lvwib.org/Portals/2/2009%20PDF%20Files/Job%20Ready%20 Update.pdf (accessed August 25, 2011).
16 See, for example, Hollenbeck and Hunag (2006).

6 Just growth

1 Note that to replicate our 80–20 income ratio requires building up the analysis from the census tract level. The data to carry out this analysis for the recession and recovery period were not yet available at the time of writing.
2 Although made available by Brookings, the underlying data for the calculations are from Moody's Analytics (http://www.moodysanalytics.com/, accessed August 25, 2011).
3 Because the American Community Survey for 2010 was not yet available, this meant the calculations were for the period 2006–2009; the results are not much different if we use 2007–2009 instead.
4 See http://www.communitybenefits.org/ (accessed August 25, 2011).
5 See http://www.communitybenefits.org/downloads/A%20New%20Urban%20 Agenda%20for%20America.pdf (accessed August 25, 2011).
6 See http://www.nfwsolutions.org/ (accessed August 25, 2011).
7 See http://www.nfwsolutions.org/workforce_partnership_model.html (accessed August 25, 2011).
8 ACCE has also taken over the Alliance for Regional Stewardship, a pioneer in building business understanding and networks around more sustainable and inclusive growth.
9 See http://www.acce.org/rsd/the-ford-foundation-fellowship-for-regional-sustainable-development-rsd/ (accessed August 25, 2011).
10 See http://building-partnerships.org/ (accessed August 25, 2011).
11 Senator Barack Obama, speech to the U.S. Conference of Mayors, Miami, June 21, 2008.
12 See http://www.communitychange.org/our-projects/htf/national-housing-trust-fund (accessed April 3, 2011).
13 This occurs both because of the qualified census tract requirement for the LIHTC and because the developer profit is higher where competing market rents are lower (Hollar and Usowski 2007; Lang 2009).
14 The origins of this provision in the tax code actually have nothing to do with home-ownership – it actually dates to 1894 and the very origins of federal income tax, when *all* interest was made deductible, and when the target was predominantly farmers and small proprietors for whom interest on loans was primarily a business expense (Lowenstein 2006; Ventry 2010).
15 See http://portal.hud.gov/hudportal/HUD?src=/program_offices/sustainable_housing_communities (accessed March 31, 2011).
16 See http://www.dot.gov/affairs/2009/dot8009.htm (accessed August 25, 2011).
17 See http://www.epi.org/index.php/american_jobs/american_jobs_plan (accessed August 25, 2011).
18 Recent research in California found that green businesses overall seem to have much strong ties to their local and state market areas than traditional business (Chapple and Hudson 2010).
19 See http://www.greenforall.org/resources/people-programs/NJ-consortium (accessed August 25, 2011).
20 See http://apolloalliance.org/state-local/los-angeles (accessed August 25, 2011)/.
21 See http://www.ci.la.ca.us/MAYOR/villaraigosaplan/EnergyandEnvironment/ LACITY_004467.htm (accessed August 25, 2011).
22 See http://www.greenforall.org/ (accessed August 25, 2011).

References

Adams, Carolyn (2003). "The meds and eds in urban economic development." *Journal of Urban Affairs* 25(5): 571–588.

Adler, Emanual and Peter Haas (1992). "Epistemic communities, world order and the creation of a reflective research program." *International Organization* 46(1): 367–390.

Akerlof, George A. and Rachel E. Kranton (2010). *Identity Economics: How Our Identities Shape Our Work, Wages, and Well-being.* Princeton, NJ: Princeton University Press.

Alesina, A. and D. Rodrik (1994). "Distributive politics and economic growth." *The Quarterly Journal of Economics* 109(2): 465–490.

Alesina, Alberto and Roberto Perotti (1996). "Income distribution, political instability, and investment." *European Economic Review* 40: 1203–1228.

Alex-Assensoh, Yvette M. (2004). "Taking the sanctuary to the streets: religion, race, and community development in Columbus, Ohio." *Annals of the American Academy of Political and Social Sciences* 594(1): 79–91.

Annie E. Casey Foundation (2007). "The Power, Practice and Promise of a Responsible Development Tool: Community Benefits Agreements." Part of a Monograph Series on Neighborhood Development. Baltimore: Annie E. Casey Foundation.

Arik, Murat (2010). "The Health Care Industry in the Nashville MSA: Its Scope and Impact on the Regional Economy." Nashville: Middle Tennessee State University Business and Economic Research Center.

Atkinson, Anthony B., Thomas Piketty and Emmanuel Saez (2011). "Top incomes in the long run of history." *Journal of Economic Literature* 49(1): 3–71.

Atlas, John (2010). *Seeds of Change: The Story of ACORN, America's Most Controversial Antipoverty Community Organizing Group.* Nashville: Vanderbilt University Press.

Attaran, Mohsen (1986). "Industrial diversity and economic performance in U.S. areas." *Annals of Regional Science* 20(2): 44–54.

Austrian, Ziona, Afia Yamoah and Candi Clouse (2009). "Regional Dashboard of Economic Indicators 2009: Comparative Performance of Leading, Midwest, and Northeast Ohio Metropolitan Areas." Cleveland: Center for Economic Development, Maxine Goodmand Levin College of Urban Affairs, Cleveland State University, prepared for the Fund for Our Economic Future.

Avella, Steven M. (2003). *Sacramento: The Indomitable City.* San Francisco: Arcadia.

Baran, Barbara, Stephen Michon, Suzanne Teegarden, Leanne Giordono and Kendra Lodewick (2010). "Implementing the National Fund for Workforce Solutions." Boston: National Fund for Workforce Solutions.

Bartik, Timothy J. and George Erickcek (2008). "Eds and meds and metropolitan economic development." In M. Austin Turner, H. Wial and H. Wolman (eds.), *Urban and Regional Policy and its Effects.* Washington, DC: Brookings Institution Press, pp. 21–59.

Bartley, Abel A. (2000). *Keeping the Faith: Race, Politics, and Social Development in Jacksonville, Florida, 1940–1970*. Westport, CT: Greenwood.

Baxamusa, Murtaza Hatim (2008). "Beyond the Limits to Planning for Equity: The Emergence of Community Benefits Agreements as Empowerment Models in Participatory Processes." Ph.D. Dissertation, Urban Planning and Development, University of Southern California, Los Angeles.

Benner, Chris (2003). "Labour flexibility and regional development: the role of labour market intermediaries." *Regional Studies* 37(6/7): 621–633.

Benner, Chris, Laura Leete and Manuel Pastor (2007). *Staircases or Treadmills? Labor Market Intermediaries and Economic Opportunity in a Changing Economy*. New York: Russell Sage Foundation Press.

Benner, Chris, Gideon Mazinga and Ganlin Huang (2010). "Race, Space and Youth Labor Market Opportunities in the Sacramento Region." Report to the Sierra Health Foundation and the California Endowment as part of the Healthy Youth Healthy Regions initiative. Davis: Center for Regional Change, UC Davis.

Benner, Chris, Gloria Rodriguez, Bidita Tithi and Cassie Hertzog (2010). "Costs of Drop-outs in the Sacramento Capital Region." Report to the Sierra Health Foundation and the California Endowment as part of the Healthy Youth Healthy Regions initiative. Davis: Center for Regional Change, UC Davis.

Berg, Andrew G. and Jonathan D. Ostry (2011). "Inequality and Unsustainable Growth: Two Sides of the Same Coin?" IMF Staff Discussion Note SDN/11/08. Washington, DC: International Monetary Fund.

Berube, Alan, William Frey, Alec Friedhoff, Emily Garr, Emilia Istrate, Elizabeth Kneebone, Robert Puentes, Audrey Singer, Adie Tomer, Howard Wial and Jill Wilson (2010). "State of Metropolitan America: On the Front Lines of Demographic Transformation." Washington, DC: Brookings Institution Metropolitan Policy Program.

Birdsall, N., D. Ross and R. Sabot (1995). "Inequality and growth reconsidered: lessons from East Asia." *The World Bank Economic Review* 9(3): 477.

Blanchflower, David and Andrew Oswald (1990). "The Wage Curve." National Bureau of Economic Research Working Paper Series. Cambridge, MA: Publisher.

Blount, Donald (1998). "Decade of change: '80s downturn spurred state to scale new peaks." Denver Post Online. Retrieved August 25, 2011, from http://extras.denverpost.com/snapshot/part1g.htm.

Booth, David A. (1963). *Metropolitics: The Nashville Consolidation*. East Lansing: Institute for Community Development and Services, Michigan State University.

Brechin, Gray (1999). *Imperial San Francisco: Urban Power, Earthly Ruin*. Berkeley: University of California Press.

Breckenridge, Tom (2009). "Cleveland Foundation slashes its contribution to the Fund for Our Economic Future." *The Plain Dealer*, December 17. Retrieved August 25, 2011, from http://www.cleveland.com/business/index.ssf/2009/12/cleveland_foundation_slashes_i.html.

Breckenridge, Tom (2010a). "Cleveland, Akron part of regional planning group that wins $4.25 million 'sustainable communities' grant." *The Plain Dealer*, October 15. Retrieved August 25, 2011, from http://blog.cleveland.com/metro/2010/10/cleveland_akron_part_of_region.html.

Breckenridge, Tom (2010b). "Why the Cleveland Foundation cut its contribution to the Fund for Our Economic Future." *The Plain Dealer*, January 31. Retrieved August 25, 2011, from http://www.cleveland.com/business/index.ssf/2010/01/why_the_cleveland_foundation_c_1.html.

Brookings Institution (2002). "Growth in the Heartland: Challenges and Opportunities for Missouri." Washington, DC: Brookings Institution.

Brookings Institution (2003a). "Kansas City in Focus: A Profile from the Census 2000." Washington, DC: Brookings Institution.

Brookings Institution (2003b). "Living Cities: The National Community Development Initiative. Columbus In Focus: A Profile from Census 2000." Washington, DC: Brookings Institution Center on Urban and Metropolitan Policy.

Brookings Institution (2010). "State of Metropolitan America: On the Front Lines of Demographic Transformation." Washington, DC: Brookings Institution.

Brown, Carolyn (2007). "Top 10 cities for African Americans 2007." *Black Enterprise*, May 1. Retrieved August 25, 2011, from http://www.blackenterprise.com/2007/05/01/top-10-cities-for-african-americans-2007/.

Brown, D. A. (2009). "Race, class, and the Obama tax plan." *Denver University Law Review* 86(3): 575–584.

Brundage, David (1994). *The Making of Western Labor Radicalism: Denver's Organized Workers, 1878-1905*. Urbana, IL: University of Illinois Press.

Bucy, Carole (1995). "Short History of Metropolitan Government for Nashville–Davidson County." Retrieved March 20, 2011, from http://www.library.nashville.org/research/res_nash_history_metrohistory.asp.

Chandra, Siddharth (2005). "Composition, similarity, and the measurement of economic homogeneity." *Journal of Regional Science* 45(3): 591–616.

Chapple, Karen (2008). "Defining the Green Economy: An Economic Development Primer." Berkeley, CA: Center for Community Innovation, UC Berkeley.

Chapple, Karen and Malo Hudson (2010). "Innovating the Green Economy in California Regions." Berkeley, CA: Center for Community Innovation, UC Berkeley.

Chapple, Karen and William T. Lester (2010). "The resilient regional labour market? The US case." *Cambridge Journal of Regions, Economy and Society* 3(1): 85–104.

Chilvers, Jason, (2008). "Environmental risk, uncertainty and participation: mapping an emergent epistemic community." *Environment & Planning A* 40: 2990–3008.

Christopherson, Susan, Harry Garretsen and Ron Martin (2008). "The world is not flat: putting globalization in its place." *Cambridge Journal of Regions, Economy and Society* 1(3): 343.

Cisneros, Henry (1993). *Interwoven Destinies: Cities and the Nation.* New York: W. W. Norton.

City of Jacksonville (2007). "Blueprint for Prosperity: Community Progress Report." Jacksonville, FL: City of Jacksonville.

Clavel, Pierre (1986). *The Progressive City: Planning and Participation, 1969–1984.* New Brunswick, NJ: Rutgers University Press.

Clavel, Pierre (1994). "The evolution of advocacy planning." *Journal of the American Planning Association* 60(2): 146–149.

Clayton, James L. (1962). "Defense spending: key to California's growth," *The Western Political Quarterly* 15(2): 280–293.

CNT, SGA and U.S. PIRG (2010). "What We Learned from the Stimulus." Washington, DC: Center for Neighborhood Technology, Smart Growth America, U.S. Public Interest Research Group.

Cohen, A. M. and F. B. Brawer (2002). *The American Community College.* San Francisco: Jossey-Bass.

Cohen, Warren (1997). "Jobs in the 'Hood: A Cleveland Group Keeps Employers from Fleeing to the Burbs." *U.S. News & World Report*, June 9.

Community Research Partners (2008). "The Real Bottom Line: The State of Poverty in Ohio 2008." Columbus, OH: Community Research Partners.

Community Research Partners (2010). "The State of Poverty in Ohio: Building a Foundation for Prosperity." Columbus, OH: Community Research Partners.

Cox, Kevin (2010). "The problem of metropolitan governance and the politics of scale." *Regional Studies* 44(2): 215–227.

Crang, P, (1997). "Cultural turns and the (re) constitution of economic geography." In R. Lee and J. Wills (eds.), *Geographies of Economies.* London: Arnold, pp. 3–15.

CREDP (2010). "Advanced Manufacturing Labor Market Analysis: Cecil Commerce Center Jacksonville, Florida." Jacksonville, FL: The Cornerstone Regional Economic Development Partnerships.

Crooks, James B. (2004). *Jacksonville: The Consolidation Story, from Civil Rights to the Jaguars.* Gainesville: University Press of Florida.

Crotty, J. (2009). "Structural causes of the global financial crisis: a critical assessment of the 'new financial architecture.' " *Cambridge Journal of Economics* 33(4): 563.

Currin, W. A. (2006). "NEO Mayers & City Managers Association." *NEO Municipal Leader* Spring: pp. 44–45.

Datel, Robin and Dennis Dingemans (2008). "Immigrant space and place in suburban Sacramento." In Audrey Singer, Susan W. Hardwick and Caroline Brettell (eds.), *Twenty-First Century Gateways: Immigrant Incorporation in Suburban America.* Washington, DC: Brookings Institution, pp. 171–199.

Dean, Amy and David Reynolds (2008). "Labor's new regional strategy: the rebirth of Central Labor Councils." *New Labor Forum* 17(1): 46–55.

Dean, Amy and David Reynolds (2009). *A New New Deal: How Regional Activism Will Reshape the American Labor Movement.* Ithaca, NY: ILR Press.

Delaney, Kevin J. and Rick Eckstein (2003). *Public Dollars, Private Stadiums: The Battle over Building Sports Stadiums.* Rutgers, NJ: Rutgers University Press.

Demyanyk, Y. and O. Van Hemert (2009). "Understanding the subprime mortgage crisis." *Review of Financial Studies* 24(6): 1848–1880.

Deninger, K. and L. Squire (1996). "Measuring income inequality: a new database." *The World Bank Economic Review* 10(3): 565–591.

Denton, James A. (1997). *Rocky Mountain Radical: Myron W. Reed, Christian Socialist.* Albuquerque: University of New Mexico Press.

Dissart, J. C. (2003). "Regional economic diversity and regional economic stability: research results and agenda." *International Regional Science Review* 26(4): 423.

Dixon, Marc (2004). "Status divisions and worker mobilization." *Sociological Spectrum: Mid-South Sociological Association* 24(3): 369–396.

Dubail, Jean (2008). "University hospitals and organized labor unveil novel agreement." *The Plain Dealer*, January 15. Retrieved August 25, 2011, from http://blog.cleveland.com/metro/2008/01/university_hospitals_and_organ.html.

Dynan, K. E. (2009). "Changing household financial opportunities and economic security." *Journal of Economic Perspectives* 23(4): 49–68.

Eberts, Randall, George Erickcek and Jack Kleinhenz (2006). "Dashboard Indicators for the Northeast Ohio Economy: Prepared for the Fund for Our Economic Future." Working Paper 06-05. Cleveland, OH: Federal Reserve Bank of Cleveland.

Eifler, Mark (2002). *Gold Rush Capitalists: Greed and Growth in Sacramento.* Albuquerque: University of New Mexico Press.

Eimer, Stuart (2001). "Fighting for justice beyond the contract: the Milwaukee County Labor Council and sustainable Milwaukee." In Immanuel Ness and Stuart Eimer (eds.),

Central Labor Councils and the Revival of American Unionism. Armonk, NY: M. E. Sharpe, pp. 102–117.

Fisher, Robert (2009). *The People Shall Rule: ACORN, Community Organizing, and the Struggle for Economic Justice.* Nashville: Vanderbilt University Press.

Fligstein, Neil and Adam Goldstein (2009). "The Anatomy of the Mortgage Securitization Crisis." Working Paper Series. Berkeley, CA: Institutefor Research on Labor and Employment, UC Berkeley.

Fox, Radhika and Solana Rice (2009). "An Engine of Opportunity: A User's Guide to Advocating for Transportation Equity in the 2009 Recovery Act." Oakland, CA: PolicyLink.

Freedman, Michael and Tim Ransdell (2005). "California Institute Special Report: California's Past Base Closure Experiences and the 2005 BRAC Round." Washington, DC: California Institute for Federal Policy Research.

Friedman, Thomas (2007). *The World is Flat: A Brief History of the Twenty-First Century.* New York: Picador.

George Jr., Hermon (2004). "Community development and the politics of deracialization: the case of Denver, Colorado, 1991–2003." *Annals of the American Academy of Political and Social Sciences* 594: 143–157.

Giloth, Robert (ed.) (2004). *Workforce Intermediaries for the 21st Century.* Philadelphia: Temple University Press.

Glaeser, E. L. and J. M. Shapiro (2003). "The benefits of the home mortgage interest deduction." *Tax Policy and the Economy* 17: 37–82.

Glover, Robert T. and Christopher T. King (2010). "Toward an effective U.S. labor-market policy." In Charles J. Whalen (ed.), *Human Resource Economics and Public Policy: Essays in Honor of Vernon M. Briggs Jr.* Kalamazoo, MI: W. E. Upjohn Institute for Employment Research, p. 215.

Gluck, Kate (2010). "Regionalism ideas explored by collaboration of Northeast Ohio officials" Cleveland.com, May 14, 2010. Retrieved August 25, 2011, from http://www.cleveland.com/sun/all/index.ssf/2010/05/regionalism_ideas_explored_by.html.

Gotham, Kevin Fox (2002). *Race, Real Estate, and Uneven Development: The Kansas City Experience, 1900–2000.* Albany, NY: SUNY Press.

Gottlieb, Paul D. (2000). "The effects of poverty on metropolitan area economic performance." In Wim Wiewel and Roz Greenstein (eds.), *Urban–Suburban Interdependence: New Directions for Research and Policy.* Cambridge, MA: Lincoln Institute for Land Policy, pp. 21–48.

Grady, Sarah and Greg Leroy (2006). "Making the Connection: Transit-Oriented Development and Jobs." Washington, DC: Good Jobs First.

Gross, Julian, Greg LeRoy and Madeline Janis (2005). "Community Benefits Agreements: Making Development Projects Accountable." Washington, DC: Good Jobs First.

Gross, Sylvia Maria (2008). "Proposed Ballot Measure Seeks to Ban Affirmative Action in Missouri." Kansas City. MI: KBIA.

Grubb, Norton (1995). "Evaluating Job Training Programs in the United States: Evidence and Explanations." Berkeley, CA: National Center for Research in Vocational Education.

Haas, Peter (1992). "Introduction: epistemic communities and international policy coordination." *International Organization* 46(1): 1–35.

Haas, P. M. (ed.) (1997). *Knowledge, Power, and International Policy Coordination.* Columbia: University of South Carolina Press.

Hakanson, Lars (2005). "Epistemic communities and cluster dynamics: on the role of knowledge in industrial districts." *Industy and Innovation* 12(4): 433–463.

Hawkins, Brett W. (1966). *Nashville Metro: The Politics of City–County Consolidation.* Nashville: Vanderbilt University Press.

Herbert, Christopher E. and Winnie Tsen (2007). "The potential of downpayment assistance for increasing homeownership among minority and low-income households." *Cityscape* 9(2): 153–184.

Hightower, Jim (1998). *There's Nothing in the Middle of the Road but Yellow Stripes and Dead Armadillos.* New York: Harper Paperbacks.

Hollar, Michael and Kurt Usowski (2007). "Low-income housing tax credit qualified census tracts." *Citiscape* 9(3).

Hollenbeck, Kevin and Wei-Jang Hunag (2006). "Net Impact and Benefit Cost Estimates of the Workforce Development System in Washington State." Kalamazoo, MI: Upjohn Institute.

Holliday, J. S. (1981). *The World Rushed In: The California Gold Rush Experience.* New York: Simon and Schuster.

Indergaard, Michael (1997). "Community-based restructuring? Institution building in the industrial Midwest." *Urban Affairs Review* 32(5): 662–682.

Irwin, Alan and Mike Michael (2003). *Science, Social Theory and Public Knowledge.* Milton Keynes: Open University Press.

Izraeli, Oded and Kevin J. Murphy (2003). "The effect of industrial diversity on state unemployment rate and per capita income." *Annals of Regional Science* 37(1): 1–14.

Jackson, Pamela A. (2005). "Fundamental Tax Reform: Options for the Mortgage Interest Deduction." Washingon, DC: Congressional Research Service.

JCCI (2000). "Improving Regional Cooperation in Northeast Florida." Jacksonville, FL: Jacksonville Community Council Inc.

JCCI (2002). "Beyond the Talk: Improving Race Relations." Jacksonville, FL: Jacksonville Community Council Inc.

JCCI (2006). "Attracting and Retaining Talent: People and Jobs for the 21st Century." Jacksonville, FL: Jacksonville Community Council Incorporated.

Jensen, Keith, Josep Call and Michael Tomasello (2007). "Chimpanzees are rational maximizers in an ultimatum game." *Science* 318(5847): 107.

Johansson, Ola (2007). "Ten people can't run this city anymore: neoliberalism and governance change in Nashville, Tennessee." *Southeastern Geographer* 47(2): 293–319.

Johnson, Curtis W. and Neal R. Peirce (2002). "Many communities, one region" (four-part series). *Kansas City Star*, January 6, 13, 20, 27.

Jonas, A. E. G. (1991). "Urban growth coalitions and urban development policy: postwar growth and the politics of annexation in metropolitan Columbus." *Urban Geography* 12(3): 197–225.

Kaldor, N. (1977). "Capitalism and industrial development: some lessons from Britain's experience." *Cambridge Journal of Economics* 1(2): 193–204.

Kaplan, David H. (1999). "The uneven distribution of employment opportunities: neighborhood and race in Cleveland, Ohio." *Journal of Urban Affairs* 21(2): 189–212.

Katz, Bruce (2007). "The Sticker Shock of Sprawl: Housing/Transportation Tradeoffs in Metro Kansas City." Speech given to the Kansas City Housing Matters Forum, April 12, 2007. Washington, DC: Brookings Institution.

Kazis, Richard (1998). "New Labor Market Intermediaries: What's Driving Them? Where Are They Headed?" Cambridge, MA: MIT Sloan School of Management.

Keating, A. D. (2005). "Review essay: planning in two Ohio cities: Cincinnati and Columbus." *Journal of Planning History* 4(2): 183.

Keating, W. Dennis and Thomas Bier (2008). "Greater Cleveland's first suburbs consortium: fighting sprawl and suburban decline." *Housing Policy Debate* 19(3): 457–477.

Keating, W. Dennis, Norman Krumholz and David C. Perry (1995). *Cleveland: A Metropolitan Reader.* Kent, OH: Kent State University Press.

Kneebone, Elizabeth (2009). "Job Sprawl Revisited: The Changing Geography of Metropolitan Employment." Metro Economy Series for the Metropolitan Policy Program at Brookings. Washington, DC: Brookings Institution.

Kriesky, Jill (ed.) (1998). *Working Together to Revitalize Labor in our Communities: Case Studies of Labor Education–Central Labor Body Collaboration.* Orono: University and College Labor Education Association, University of Maine.

Krumholz, Norman and John Forester (1990). *Making Equity Planning Work: Leadership in the Public Sector.* Philadelphia: Temple University Press.

Krumholz, Norman and Daniel E. Berry (2007). "The Cleveland experience: municipal-led economic and workforce initiaties during the 1990s." In Michael I. J. Bennett and Robert P. Giloth (eds.), *Economic Development in American Cities: The Pursuit of an Equity Agenda.* Albany, NY: State University of New York Press, pp. 133–158.

Kusmer, Kenneth L. (1978). *A Ghetto Takes Shape: Black Cleveland 1870–1930.* Chicago: University of Illinois Press.

Kuznets, S. (1955). "Economic growth and income inequality." *The American Economic Review* 45(1): 1–28.

Lamoreaux, Naomi and Margaret Levenstein (2008). "The Decline of an Innovative Region: Cleveland, Ohio, in the Twentieth Century." Unpublished paper prepared for the 2008 Annual Meeting of the Economic History Association, UCLA History Department, Los Angeles. Retrieved August 25, 2011, from http://www.econ.ucla.edu/people/papers/Lamoreaux/Lamoreaux472.pdf.

Lang, Bree Jones (2009). "The Low-Income Housing Tax Credit: Subsidizing Affordable Housing or Developer Profit?" APPAM Fall Research Conference. Washington, DC.

Larkin, Brent (2010). "By yanking support for Fund for Our Economic Future, Cleveland Foundation earns its criticism: Brent Larkin." Cleveland.com, January 31. Retrieved August 25, 2011, from http://www.cleveland.com/open/index.ssf/2010/01/by_yanking_support_for_fund_fo.html.

Ledebur, Larry C. and William R. Barnes (1993). "All In It Together: Cities, Suburbs and Local Economic Regions." Washington, DC: National League of Cities.

Leland, Suzanne M. (2004). "Reforming politics through reorganization: consolidation in Wyandotte/Kansas City, KS." In Suzanne M. Leland and Kurt Thurmaier (eds.), *Case Studies of City–County Consolidation: Reshaping the Local Government Landscape.* Armonk, NY: M. E. Sharpe, pp. 261–271.

Leonard, Stephen J. and Tom Noel (1991). *Mile High City, Denver: Mining Camp to Metropolis.* Denver: University Press of Colorado.

Leslie, Stuart (2000). "The biggest 'angel' of them all: the military and the making of Silicon Valley." In Martin Kenney (ed.), *Understanding Silicon Valley: The Anatomy of an Entrepreneurial Region.* Stanford, CA: Stanford University Press, pp. 48–70.

Lieberman, Evan (2005). "Nested analysis as a mixed-method strategy for comparative research." *American Political Science Review* 99(3): 435–452.

Lin, Jennifer, Kate O'Hara and Howard Greenwich (2008). "Building a Better Bay Area: Community Benefit Tools and Case Studies to Achieve Responsible Development." Oakland, CA: EBASE (East Bay Alliance for a New Economy).

Litman, T. (2006). "Evaluating Public Transit Benefits and Costs." Victoria, Canada: Transport Policy Institute.

Litman, T. (2009). "Rail Transit in America: A Comprehensive Evaluation of Benefits." Victoria, Canada: Transport Policy Institute.

Logan, John (ed.) (2009). *Academics on Employee Free Choice: Multidisciplinary Approaches to Labor Law Reform.* Berkeley, CA: UC Berkeley Labor Center.

Logan, John and Harvey Molotch (1987). *Urban Fortunes: The Political Economy of Place.* Berkeley: University of California Press.

Longfellow, Henry Wadsworth (1835). *Outre-mer: A Pilgrimage beyond the Sea, Volume 2.* New York: Harper & Brothers.

Lopez, Humberto and Luis Serven (2009). "Too Poor to Grow." World Bank Policy Research Working Paper Series. Washington, DC: World Bank.

Lotspeich, Katherine, Michael Fix, Jason Ost and Dan Perez-Lopez (2003). "A Profile of the Foreign-Born in the Nashville Economic Market." Washington, DC: Urban Institute.

Lowenstein, Roger (2006). "Who needs the mortgage-interest deduction." *The New York Times*, March 5. Retrieved August 25, 2011, from http://www.nytimes.com/2006/03/05/magazine/305deduction.1.html.

Luce, Stephanie (2001). "Building political power and community coalitions: the role of Central Labor Councils in the living-wage movement." In Immanuel Ness and Stuart Eimer (eds.), *Central Labor Councils and the Revival of American Unionism.* Armonk, NY: M. E. Sharpe, pp. 140–163.

Luce, Stephanie (2004). *Fighting for a Living Wage.* Ithaca, NY: ILR Press.

Luce, Stephanie and Mark Nelson (2004). "Starting down the road to power: the Denver area labor federation." *WorkingUSA* 8(2): 183–206.

McCormick, Kathleen (2006). "Regional thinking." *Urban Land* September: 88–98.

McGahey, Rick and Jennifer Vey (2008). *Retooling for Growth: Building a 21st Century Economy in America's Older Industrial Regions.* New York: American Assembly, Columbia University.

MARC (2001). "Metro Outlook: Measuring the Progress of Metropolitan Kansas City." Kansas City: Mid-America Regional Council.

Markusen, Ann, Peter A. Hall, Scott Campbell and Sabina Deitrick (1991). *The Rise of the Gunbelt: The Military Remapping of Industrial America.* Oxford: Oxford University Press.

Maskell, Peter and Anders Malmberg (1999). "The competitiveness of firms and regions: ubiquitification and the importance of localized learning." *European Urban and Regional Studies* 6(1): 9–25.

Massey, Douglas and Deborah Hirst (1998). "From escalator to hourglass: changes in the U.S. occupational wage structure 1949–1989." *Social Science Research* 27(1): 51–71.

Maurrasse, David (2007). "City Anchors: Leveraging Anchor Institutions for Urban Success." Chicago: CEOs for Cities.

Mayer, Heike (2007). "Biotech industry clusters in the United States: the case of Washington DC and Kansas City." *Geopraphische Rundschau International Edition* 3(1): 10–16.

Mid-America Regional Council (2005). "Regional Data Snapshot." Retrieved May 2009, from Metrodata Online: http://www.marc.org/metrodataline/reg_data_snapshot.htm.

Milkman, Ruth (2006). *The L.A. Story: Immigrant Workers and the Future of the U.S. Labor Movement.* New York: Russell Sage Foundation.

Milkman, Ruth and Rachel Dwyer (2002). "Growing apart: the 'new economy' and job polarization in California, 1992–2000." In Ruth Milkman (ed.), *The State of California Labor, 2002.* Berkeley, University of California Institute for Labor and Employment, pp. 3–36.

Montgomery, Christopher (2005). "Massive homes project rises from Denver's runways." *The Plain Dealer*, November 29. Retrieved August 25, 2011, from http://www.cleveland.com/forestcity/plaindealer/index.ssf?/forestcity/more/1133256922178001.html.

Morgan, K. (2007). "The learning region: institutions, innovation and regional renewal." *Regional Studies* 41: 147–159.

Mort, Jo-Ann (ed.) (1998). *Not Your Father's Union Movement: Inside the AFL-CIO.* New York, Verso Press.

Moss, Philip and Chris Tilly (2001). *Stories Employers Tell: Race, Skill, and Hiring in America.* New York: Russell Sage Foundation.

Muro, Mark, Bruce Katz, Sarah Rahman and David Warren (2008). "MetroPolicy: Shaping a New Federal Partnership for a Metropolitan Nation." Washington, DC: Brookings Institution.

Nashville Public Library (2011). "Nashville History." Retrieved March 21, 2011, from http://www.city-data.com/us-cities/The-South/Nashville-History.html.

Nashville's Agenda (2007). "Nashville's Agenda 2007: Conversation across the City Final Report." Nashville: Nashville's Agenda.

Nelson, Arthur C., Thomas W. Sanchez, James F. Wolf and Mary Beth Farquhar (2004). "Metropolitan planning organization voting structure and transit investment bias: preliminary analysis with social equity implications." *Transportation Research Record: Journal of the Transportation Research Board* 1895: 1–7.

Ness, Immanuel and Stuart Eimer (2001). *Central Labor Councils and the Revival of American Unionism: Organizing for Justice in our Communities.* Armonk, NY: M. E. Sharpe.

Nowak, Martin A., Karen M. Page and Karl Sigmund (2000). "Fairness versus reason in the ultimatum game." *Science* 289(5485): 1773–1775.

Orfield, Myron (1997). *Metropolitics: A Regional Agenda for Community and Stability.* Washington, DC: Brookings Institution Press.

Orfield, Myron and Thomas Luce (2010). *Region: Planning the Future of the Twin Cities.* Minneapolis: University of Minnesota Press.

Orfield, Myron, Thomas Luce and AMEREGIS (2008). "Northeast Ohio Economic Revenue Study." Minneapolis: AMERERGIS.

Osterman, Paul (1999). *Securing Prosperity: The American Labor Market: How It Has Changed and What To Do About It.* Princeton, NJ: Princeton University Press.

Otiso, Kefa M. and Bruce W. Smith (2005). "Immigration and economic restructuring in Ohio's cities, 1940–2000." *Ohio Journal of Science* 105(5): 133–137.

Panizza, Ugo (2002). "Income inequality and economic growth: evidence from American data." *Journal of Economic Growth* 7(1): 25–41.

Parks, Virginia and Dorian Warren (2009). "The politics and practice of economic justice: community benefits agreements as tactic of the new accountable development movement." *Journal of Community Practice* 17(1): 88–106.

Partridge, Mark (1997). "Is inequality harmful for growth? Comments." *American Economic Review* 87: 1019–1032.

Pastor, M, (2006). "Cohesion and competitiveness: business leadership for regional growth and social equity." In OECD (ed.) OECD Territorial Reviews: Competitive Cities in the Global Economy. Paris: OECD, pp. 288–298.

Pastor, Manuel and Justin Scoggins (2007). "Working Poor in the Golden State: A Multi-Measure Comparison Using the 2000 and 1990 Public Use Microdata Samples." Santa Cruz, CA: Center for Justice, Tolerance and Community, UC Santa Cruz.

Pastor, Manuel and Chris Benner (2008). "Been down so long: week market cities and regional equity." In Rick McGahey and Jennifer Vey (eds.), *Restoring Prosperity in Older Industrial Areas.* Washington, DC: Brookings Institution Press, pp. xx–xx.

Pastor, Manuel and Chris Benner (2011). "Planning for equity, fighting for justice: planners, organizers and the struggle for metropolitan inclusion." In Ethan Seltzer and Armando

Carbonell (eds.), *Regional Planning in America: Practice and Prospect.* Cambridge, MA: Lincoln Institute for Land Policy, pp. 83–115.

Pastor, Manuel, Peter Dreier, Eugene Grigsby and Marta Lopez-Garza (2000). *Regions That Work: How Cities and Suburbs Can Grow Together.* Minneapolis: University of Minnesota Press.

Pastor, Manuel, Rachel Rosner, Chris Benner, Martha Matsuoka and Miranda Smith (2008). "Coming Together: Lessons on Collaboration from California Works for Better Health." San Francisco, CA: The California Endowment.

Pastor, Manuel, Bill Lester and Justin Scoggins (2009a). "Why regions? Why now? Who cares?" *Journal of Urban Affairs* 31(3): 269–296.

Pastor, Manuel, Chris Benner and Martha Matsuoka (2009b). *This Could Be the Start of Something Big: How Social Movements for Regional Equity are Reshaping Metropolitan America.* Ithaca, NY: Cornell University Press.

Pastor, Manuel, Chris Benner, Rachel Rosner and Martha Matsuoka (2009c). "Looking Forward: Lessons for Philanthropy from CWBH." Report to the California Endowment. Los Angeles: Program on Environmental and Regional Equity, USC.

Pastor, Manuel, Chris Benner, Rachel Rosner and Martha Matsuoka (2009d). "Scaling Up: Regions, Communities and CWBH." Report to the California Endowment. Los Angeles: Program on Environmental and Regional Equity, USC.

Pastor, Manuel, Justin Scoggins, T. William Lester and Karen Chapple (forthcoming). "Building Resilient Regions Database" [machine-readable database]. Los Angeles, CA: USC Program for Environmental and Regional Equity (PERE).

PEERS (2003). "Workforce Intermediaries: Generating Benefits for Employers and Workers." New York: Partnership for Employer-Employee Responsive Systems, funded by the Ford Foundation.

Persky, J and Wim Wiewel (1994). "The growing localness of the global city." *Economic Geography* 70(2): 129–143.

Persson, T. and G. Tabellini (1994). "Is inequality harmful for growth?" *The American Economic Review* 84(3): 600–621.

Peters, B. Guy and John Pierre (1998). "Governance without government? Rethinking public administration." *Journal of Public Administration Research and Theory* 8(2): 223–243.

Phares, Donald (2004). *Metropolitan Governance without Metropolitan Government?* Aldershot, UK: Ashgate.

Pickett, Kate and Richard Wilkinson (2009). *The Spirit Level: Why Greater Equality Makes Societies Stronger.* New York: Bloomsbury Press.

Plain Dealer Editorial Board (2009). "Cleveland Foundation's retreat from Fund for Our Economic Future is troubling – editorial." *The Plain Dealer*, December 22. Retrieved August 25, 2011, from http://www.cleveland.com/opinion/index.ssf/2009/12/cleveland_foundations_retreat.html.

PolicyLink (2002). "Building a Healthier Sacramento Region: An Analysis of AB 680." Oakland: PolicyLink.

Powell, John A. (2004). "Civil Rights, Sprawl and Regional Equity." A presentation for the Columbus Metropolitan Club Forum, Kirwan Institute of Race and Ethnicity, June 9, 2004. Retrieved March 20, 2011, from http://kirwaninstitute.org/publicationspresentations/presentations/2004.php.

Puentes, Robert (2009). "Joining Up Transportation, Housing, and Environmental Policy." Washington, DC: Brookings Institution. Retrieved August 25, 2011, from http://www.brookings.edu/opinions/2009/0617_transportation_puentes.aspx.

Puentes, Robert and Myron Orfield (2002). "Valuing America's First Suburbs: A Policy

Agenda for Older Suburbs in the Midwest." Washington, DC: Brookings Institution Metropolitan Policy Program.

Putnam, Robert D. (2007). "E Pluribus Unum: diversity and community in the twenty first century – the 2006 Johan Skytte Prize Lecture." *Scandinavian Political Studies* 30(2): 137–174.

Rajan, Raghuram (2010). *Fault Lines: How Hidden Fractures Still Threaten the World Economy*. Princeton: Princeton University Press.

Read, Tory (2006). "The Gates Cherokee Redevelopment Project: A Huge Step Forward for Low-Income People in Denver." Baltimore, MD: Annie E. Casey Foundation.

Ream, J. W., B. G. Wagner and R. C. Knorr (2001). "Welfare to work: solutions or snake oil?" *New Directions for Community Colleges* 2001(116): 61.

Reich, Robert B. (2010). *Aftershock: The Next Economy and America's Future*. New York: Knopf.

Riley, Marilyn Griggs and Thomas J. Noel (2006). *High Altitude Attitudes: Six Savvy Colorado Women*. Boulder, CO: Johnson Books.

Robinson, Sherman (1976). "A note on the U hypothesis relating income inequality and economic development." *The American Economic Review* 66(3): 437–440.

Rodrik, D. (1999). "Where did all the growth go? External shocks, social conflict, and growth collapses." *Journal of Economic Growth* 4(4): 385–412.

Rubin, Victor (2009). "All Aboard! Making Equity and Inclusion Central to Federal Transportation Policy." Oakland, CA: PolicyLink.

Ruggles, Steven, Matthew Sobek, Trent Alexander, Catherine A. Fitch, Ronald Goeken, Patricia Kelly Hall, Miriam King and Chad Ronnander (2010). "Integrated Public Use Microdata Series: Version 5.0" [machine-readable database]. Minneapolis, MN: Minnesota Population Center (producer and distributor).

Rusk, David (1993). *Cities without Suburbs*. Washington, DC: Woodrow Wilson Center Press.

Rusk, David (1999). *Inside Game Outside Game: Winning Strategies for Saving Urban America*. Washington, DC: Brookings Institution Press.

Saito, Leland T. (2007). "Economic Redevelopment and the Community Benefits Program: A Case Study of the LA Live Project, a Los Angeles Sports and Entertainment District." Los Angeles: USC Lusk Center for Real Estate.

Sanchez, Thomas (2005). "Patterns of MPO Representation and Board Structure in Relation to Transportation Planning and Decision Making." Washington, DC: Brookings Institution.

Savitch, Hank V. and Paul Kantor (2004). *Cities in the International Marketplace: The Political Economy of Urban Development in North America and Western Europe*. Princeton, NJ: Princeton University Press.

Savitch, H. V. and Ronald K. Vogel (2004). "Suburbs without a city: power and city-county consolidation." *Urban Affairs Review* 396: 758–790.

Savitch, H. V., David Collins, Daniel Sander and John Markham (1993). "Ties that bind: central cities, suburbs, and the new metropolitan region." *Economic Development Quarterly* 7(4): 341–357.

Schoenberger, Erica (1997). *The Cultural Crisis of the Firm*. Cambridge, MA: Blackwell.

Scott, Allen John (1998). *Regions and the World Economy: The Coming Shape of Global Production, Competition, and Political Order*. Oxford: Oxford University Press.

Seltzer, Ethan (2008). "Regional planning and local governance: the Portland Story." In Tetsuo Kidokoro, Noboru Harata, Leksono Probo Subanu, Johann Jessen, Alain Motte and Ethan Paul Seltzer (eds.), *Sustainable City Regions: Space, Place and Governance*. New York, Springer-Verlag, pp. 277–298.

Silverstein, Patty (2008). "A Look at the National Housing Downturn and its Effect on the Region." Denver: Metro Denver Economic Development Corporation.

Sparrow, Glen W. (2004). "Consolidation, west-coast style: Sacramento County, California." In Suzanne M. Leland and Kurt Thurmaier (ed.), *Case Studies of City–County Consolidation: Reshaping the Local Government Landscape.* Armonk, NY: M. E. Sharpe, pp. 79–100.

Spivak, Jeffrey (2005). "Foundations touch area in big way: generosity lifts KC, even in hard times." *The Kansas City Star*, January 9, A1.

Starzyk, Edith (2009). "Cleveland ninth-graders at MC2 STEM high school to remain at GE's Nela Park campus." *The Plain Dealer*, May 12. Retrieved August 25, 2011, from http://blog.cleveland.com/metro/2009/05/cleveland_ninthgraders_at_mc_s.html.

Stiglitz, Joseph E. (2010). *Freefall: America, Free Markets, and the Sinking of the World Economy.* New York: W. W. Norton.

Stodghill, Ron and Amanda Bower (2002). "Welcome to America's most diverse city." *Time Magazine*, August 25. Retrieved August 25, 2011, from http://www.time.com/time/nation/article/0,8599,340694,00.html.

Storper, Michael (1997). *The Regional World: Territorial Development in a Global Economy.* New York: Guilford Press.

Thomas, Craig W. (1997). "Public management as interagency cooperation: testing epistemic community theory at the domestic level." *Journal of Public Administration Research and Theory* 7(2): 221.

Thorbecke, E. and C. Charumilind (2002). "Economic inequality and its socioeconomic impact." *World Development* 30(9): 1477–1495.

Tobar, Hector and Robin Fields (2001). "Columbus blazes a trail for '21st century cities'." *Los Angeles Times*, May 1. Retrieved August 25, 2011, from http://articles.latimes.com/2001/may/01/news/mn-57874.

Trendle, Bernard (2006). "Regional economic instability: the role of industrial diversification and spatial spillovers." *Annals of Regional Science* 40(4): 767–778.

Van Tine, Warren, C. J. Slanicka, Sandra Jordan and Michael Pierce (1998). *In the Workers' Interest: A History of the Ohio AFL-CIO, 1958–1998.* Columbus: Ohio State University Center for Labor Research.

Ventry Jr, Dennis J. (2010). "The accidental deduction: a history and critique of the tax subsidy for mortgage interest." *Law & Contemporary Problems* 73(1): 233–284.

Voith, Richard (1998). "Do suburbs need cities?" *Journal of Regional Science* 38(3): 445–465.

Wagner, John E. (2000). "Regional economic diversity: action, concept, or state of confusion." *Journal of Regional Analysis and Policy* 30(2): 1–22.

Walker, Richard (2010). "The golden state adrift." *New Left Review* 66: 5–30.

Warf, Barney and Brian Holly (1997). "The rise and fall and rise of Cleveland." *Annals of the American Academy of Political and Social Sciences* 551: 208–221.

Weir, Margaret and Jane Rongerude (2007). "Multi-Level Power and Progressive Regionalism." Berkeley, CA: Institute of Urban and Regional Development, UC Berkeley.

Wial, Howard and Richard Shearer (2011). "MetroMonitor: Tracking Economic Recession and Recovery in America's 100 Largest Metropolitan Areas." Washington, D.C: Brookings Institution Metropolitan Policy Program.

Wilkerson, Isabel (2010). *The Warmth of Other Suns: The Epic Story of America's Great Migration.* New York: Random House.

Williams, Dana (2004). "Cleveland's Living Wage Law: A Three-Year Review." Cleveland, OH: Policy Matters Ohio.

Williamson, Richard (1999). "Oil shale collapse preserved scenic vistas." *Denver Rocky Mountain News*.

Witkowski, Rachel (2008). "JEDC approves $884 incentive for Deutsche Bank." *Jacksonville Business Journal*, May 8. Retrieved August 25, 2011, from http://www. bizjournals.com/jacksonville/stories/2008/05/05/daily27.html?ana=from_rss.

Wolf-Powers, Laura (2003). "The Role of Labor Market Intermediaries in Promoting Employment Access and Mobility: A Supply- and Demand-Side Approach." Ph.D. Dissertation, Rutger's University.

Wolman, Harold, Coit Cook Ford and Edward Hill (1994). "Evaluating the success of urban success stories." *Urban Studies* 31(6): 835–850.

Wood, Curtis (2005). "The Nature of Metropolitan Governance in Urban America: A Study of Cooperation, Conflict, and Avoidance in the Kansas City Region." Working Group on Interlocal Services Cooperation, Paper 9. Retrieved August 25, 2001, from http:// digitalcommons.wayne.edu/interlocal_coop/9.

Wood, Curtis (2008). "The nature of metropolitan governance in urban America: a study of cooperation and conflict in the Kansas City region." *Administration & Society* 40(5): 483–501.

WSC (2002). "Building a Career Pathways System: Promising Practices in Community College-Centered Workforce Development." New York: Workforce Strategy Center.

Yin, Jordan S. (1998). "The community development industry system: a case study of politics and institutions in Cleveland, 1967–1997." *Journal of Urban Affairs* 20(2): 137–157.

Zuberi, D. (2006). *Differences that Matter: Social Policy and the Working Poor in the United States and Canada*. Ithaca, NY: Cornell University Press.

Index

CPSIA information can be obtained
at www.ICGtesting.com
Printed in the USA
LVOW01s1232181215

467084LV00005B/20/P